THE BIG CHANGE

Books by FREDERICK LEWIS ALLEN

The Big Change

The Great Pierpont Morgan

Since Yesterday

The Lords of Creation

Only Yesterday

WITH AGNES ROGERS

I Remember Distinctly

Metropolis

The American Procession

THE BIG CHANGE

America Transforms Itself 1900-1950

By

FREDERICK LEWIS ALLEN

GREENWOOD PRESS, PUBLISHERS
WESTPORT, CONNECTICUT

Library of Congress Cataloging in Publication Data

Allen, Frederick Lewis, 1890-1954.
  The big change.

    Reprint. Originally published: New York : Harper,
c1952.
    Bibliography: p.
    Includes index.
    1. United States--Civilization--20th century.
2. United States--Economic conditions--1918-1945.
3. United States--Social conditions. I. Title.
E169.1.A4717 1983   973.91   82-18395
 ISBN 0-313-23791-3 (lib. bdg.)

Reprinted with the permission of Harper and Row Publishers, Inc.

Reprinted in 1983 by Greenwood Press
A division of Congressional Information Service, Inc.
88 Post Road West, Westport, Connecticut 06881

Printed in the United States of America

10 9 8 7 6 5 4 3 2 1

Contents

FOREWORD BY RICHARD HOFSTADTER   vii

INTRODUCTORY NOTE   ix

PART ONE: THE OLD ORDER

1. A New Century Begins   3

2. Grandeur, Limited   27

3. The Other Side of the Tracks   49

4. Capitalism Indeed   63

5. Government on the Sidelines   81

PART TWO: THE MOMENTUM OF CHANGE

6. The Revolt of the American Conscience   95

7. The Dynamic Logic of Mass Production   109

8. The Automobile Revolution   121

9. Indian Summer of the Old Order   131

10. The Great Depression   145

11. The Reluctant World Power   158

12. Ole Ark A'Moverin'   177

13. Faster, Faster   187

14. More Americans, Living Longer   199

PART THREE: THE NEW AMERICA

15. The All-American Standard   209

16. Corporations, New Style   234

17. The Spirit of the Times   259

18. What Have We Got Here?   284

APPENDIX: Sources and Obligations   295

INDEX   299

Foreword

FOR over twenty years the writings of Frederick Lewis Allen have been among the most popular books assigned for reading in American colleges. These books have been at once a challenge and a boon to teachers: a challenge because they inspire us to ask why more books of comparable value in teaching cannot be found in a great many phases of our history; a boon because they have made the teaching of recent history so much more pleasant.

Many students come to college a bit jaded by their previous history courses and somewhat suspicious of "pure" history, which often smacks to them of pure antiquarianism. At their best they are alertly interested in the problems of their own time—problems of war and peace, of the distribution and uses of wealth, of race relations. They are curious about things that have an obvious personal bearing—matters connected with manners and morals, sex and marriage, careers and leisure. What they look for in their studies is a sense of relevance. Whatever they study, they want clues to life. Sometimes their interest is so thoroughly practical and urgent that it is all too easily satisfied with factitious answers. Often it is insufficiently diluted with that precious thing that Thorstein Veblen called idle curiosity, the pleasure of inquiring and knowing for its own sake.

But for those students whose impatience with antiquarianism has been qualified by a genuine curiosity about human affairs Mr. Allen's books, with their feeling for the concrete and vivid and their firm sense for the relevance of the past, have had an almost unfailing appeal. I believe that in this respect *The Big Change* will actually outdo in popularity and usefulness *The Lords of Creation, Only Yesterday,* and *Since Yesterday,* for its chronological scope is broader and its drive toward an elucidation of fundamental trends in modern American life is far more ambitious.

Chronologically *The Big Change* begins with the turn of the century, but psychologically it begins with those aspects of our national life that the student can observe everywhere and must be concerned with. It is as important that students be aware of changes in the size and significance of the national budget, of changes in styles of living from the age of the big mansion to the age of the big expense account, of the significance of modern mass production, mass communications, and advertising, as it is that they learn about the administration of Calvin Coolidge or the attack on Pearl Harbor. Above all, it is important that they acquire the beginnings of a sense of perspective and that questions be aroused in them about the ways in which their own problems have been shaped by the great developments of the past fifty years. I would hope for more than this, however, from the use of *The Big Change* in our history courses. I hope that its seductive facility with the immediate and the interesting will lure the minds of many students still further backward from the modern period with which it deals into a stronger feeling for the ultimate relevance of remoter places and times as well—and outward from the classroom and the chalky air of pedagogy toward a broader interest in the study of man.

RICHARD HOFSTADTER

Introductory Note

THIS book is an attempt to sketch some of the major changes which took place in the United States during the first half of the twentieth century.

Anybody who chooses such a subject has an immense canvas before him, on which any number of pictures may be painted. He may concentrate, after the manner of the old-fashioned history textbooks, upon American politics from McKinley to Truman. He may illuminate the contrast between the American position in foreign affairs in 1900 and our uncomfortably massive role half a century later. He may focus on American art, music, literature, or culture, or all of them together; or on the almost incredible advance in medicine and public health; or on the progress of science and technology. He may concentrate upon the waning of puritanism, the loosening of family ties, the reduced authority of parents, the increasing divorce rate, the economic and social and political emancipation of women. He may deal primarily with the changes in American thought about the nature of man and of God, the long decline in the prestige of organized religion, the mood of apprehension in which wars and rumors of wars have caused us to live, and the anxious search for spiritual security in a world full of desperate uncertainties.

Or else he may fix his chief attention upon the changes which have taken place in the character and quality of American life by reason of what might be called the democratization of our economic system, or the adjustment of capitalism to democratic ends; the way in which an incredible expansion of industrial and business activity, combined with a varied series of political, social and economic forces, has altered the American standard of living and with it the average American's way of thinking and his status as a citizen.

I choose this latter theme for the central one of this book because it seems to me to be of central importance. This, after all, is *the* American story of the first half of the twentieth century. And I choose it for another reason: that I do not believe that the changes which I shall try to describe are as yet very widely understood.

That they are not understood abroad is demonstrated again and again. When Vishinsky or Gromyko or Malik berates the United States, talking, for instance, about "lackeys of Wall Street," what he is doing is berating, exaggeratedly, the United States of 1900 rather than of today. If what he says makes an impression among many non-Communists in Europe, this is at least partly because a very large number of Europeans have been brought up on concepts of the United States long since outdated; and also because they and other Europeans, aware of the importance of business and of businessmen in the American scene, imagine that these, today, closely resemble their counterparts of a generation or two ago, and also behave like the business and businessmen of Europe. The mental picture of the United States that the average European carries about with him is lamentably irrelevant to the real United States of today.

Not only that: the changes that have taken place in the American business system and American life are not fully grasped even by most of us here at home. Our own concepts tend to date sharply, particularly when we get into arguments. The chairman of the board of a great corporation decides to say a few words on behalf of "free enterprise" and against "socialism," and one is suddenly aware that the image of "free enterprise" in his mind looks more like an old-time country store than like the vast, co-ordinated, decentralized institution which he actually manages; and that the "socialism" which he excoriates is a textbook socialism quite different in direction and meaning from anything that has found a significant place in the American scene. The labor leader, in order to encourage the van and to harass the foe from the rear, decides to denounce management and the stockholders for their "lust for profits" and to arouse the "embattled workers," and he too pulls out of a drawer a well-worn stencil, cut perhaps about the year 1920. And all of us, when we hear a phrase such as "the American way of life," are likely to see in our minds' eyes some pleasant aspect of the America we grew up in as boys and girls; and the older we are, the more anachronistic this mental picture is. It may be useful, therefore, to try to chart some of the changes that have taken place since those images were formed.

The story that I propose to tell has deep shadows in it. Some of those shadows are dark today. It is emphatically not a story of paradise gained. There is no certainty that we have yet learned how to avert economic catastrophe, to say nothing of military catastrophe. Yet in the main it is, I think, a heartening story. In these anxious times we can at least take satisfaction in recalling that the good old days for which some have always yearned were not so good; that we live, despite the wails of the pessimists, in an age of progress; and that it is also—despite the stormy international skies—an age of promise.

F. L. A.

February 24, 1952

PART ONE

THE OLD ORDER

Chapter 1

A New Century Begins

On THE morning of January 1, 1900, there was skating for New Yorkers in Van Cortlandt Park, and presently it began to snow. But the sharp cold had not chilled the enthusiasm of the crowds who, the night before, had assembled in Lower Broadway to celebrate either the beginning of the twentieth century or the beginning of the last year of the nineteenth: there was some disagreement as to the proper interpretation of the event, but none as to the size and liveliness of the gathering. The cable cars were jammed with people, Broadway in front of Trinity Church was well-nigh impassable, the crowds were dense in Wall Street as far down as the Subtreasury steps, and there was a great din of tin horns, punctuated from time to time by firecrackers. It had been a good year, and another one was coming.

In its leading editorial of January 1, the *New York Times* sounded an optimistic keynote. "The year 1899 was a year of wonders, a veritable annus mirabilis, in business and production. . . ." it proclaimed. "It would be easy to speak of the twelve months just passed as the banner year were we not already confident that the distinction of highest records must presently pass to the year 1900. . . . The outlook on the threshold of the new year is extremely bright."

Uptown, in the mahogany-paneled library of his big brownstone house at the corner of Madison Avenue and Thirty-sixth Street, John Pierpont Morgan, head of the mightiest banking house in the world and the most powerful man in all American business, sat playing solitaire as the old year drew to an end. During the next twelve months Morgan would buy paintings and rare books and manuscripts in immense profusion on a European trip; would have a temporary ballroom built beside his house to accommodate twenty-four hundred guests at his daughter's wedding, and would begin negotiations with Andrew Carnegie—the twinkling little steelmaster whose personal income in 1900 would be over twenty-three million dollars, with no income tax to pay—for the formation of the United States Steel Corporation, the biggest corporation that the world had ever seen. Morgan could not foresee all this now as he ranged the cards before him, but he was content. In the words of his future son-in-law and affectionate biographer, describing that very evening of December 31, 1899,

Mr. Morgan's house was just where he wanted it to be and it suited his mode of life. Mrs. Morgan was well and they had their unmarried daughters, Louisa and Anne, living at home. His married children and grandchildren were all well and happy, and he himself was in good health. His friends were near by. The people in his social world were of his own kind, and the bankers and business men with whom he came into contact had, for the most part, the same standard of ethics and point of view that he himself had. New York was still a friendly, neighborly city and was a pleasant place in which to live. . . . At midnight, when the bells and horns proclaimed the beginning of the New Year, he was looking forward with the eagerness of a much younger man to the great possibilities of the century that was about to begin.

There were, to be sure, hundreds of thousands of New Yorkers for whom the city was hardly "a pleasant place in which to live." On the Lower East Side there were poverty, filth, wretchedness on a scale which to us today would seem incredible. And in many other cities and industrial towns of America the immigrant families were living under comparable conditions, or worse; for at a time when the average wage earner in the United States got hardly five hundred dollars in a year—roughly the equivalent of fifteen hundred at present prices —most of the newcomers to the country scrabbled for far less. Let Van Wyck Brooks summarize what Upton Sinclair incontrovertibly disclosed a few years later about the state of the Poles and Lithuanians and Slovaks in the Chicago stockyard area:

Ignorant and stunted by European tyranny only to be utterly destroyed by American indifference, they were swindled by house-agents, political bosses . . . and judges who refused to recognize their rights. No one either knew or cared when their babies were drowned in the stinking green water that lay about their wretched shacks, when their daughters were forced into prostitution, when their sons fell into boiling vats because the employers had provided no safety devices.

"No one either knew or cared"—why not? Because it was a time of complacency. Since the end of the depression of the mid-nineties the voices of protest at the disparities of fortune in the United States had weakened. Populism was dead; the free-silver agitation had petered out; the once angry farmers of the Plains States were making out so well that in 1899 a traveler commented that "every barn in Kansas and Nebraska has had a new coat of paint." Not yet had the oncoming group of journalists whom Theodore Roosevelt, in a burst of irritation, labeled "muckrakers" begun to publish their remorseless studies of the seamy sides of American life. American fiction, like American journalism, was going through what old Ambrose Bierce called a "weak and fluffy period"; Dreiser's *Sister Carrie*, published in 1900, went almost unnoticed and then was withdrawn from circulation as too sordid or pornographic. The best journals and the best people concerned themselves very little with the fortunes of the average man, and very much with the fortunes of ladies and gentlemen, with the pomp and circumstance of Society, and with the furthering of a polite and very proper culture for the elect. If in the language of Morgan's biographer, as he described the great banker's contentment, there was discernible a faint tone of smugness, this was characteristic of the general attitude of the well born and well endowed as they contemplated the bright future.

Morgan looked confidently forward to an era of stability and common sense, in which political leaders like Mark Hanna would see that no foolish equalitarian ideas got anywhere in government, and in which the regulation of American business would be undertaken, not by politicians, but by bankers like himself, honorable men of wealth and judgment such as he liked to see in his favorite clubs.

Out in Terre Haute, in an upstairs bedroom of a high-ceilinged, eight-room house, a tall, gaunt, bald-headed Hoosier looked out over the railroad tracks and dreamed a quite different dream of the future. Eugene V. Debs was a one-time locomotive fireman. He had led the Pullman strike of 1894, had served a term in prison, had consumed Marxist literature in his cell, and had become an ardent Socialist. His exalted hopes were to take shape in the 1900 platform of the Social Democratic party, as whose candidate Debs would poll a meager 96,000 votes. But this was to be merely a beginning; had Debs but known it then, he was destined to have nearly a million followers by 1912. A friendly and merciful man with an insecure grasp of logic, Debs was hotly aware of the desperate plight of the immigrant workers, and he was sure he knew the one and only answer to their miseries. His platform called for public ownership of railroads, telegraphs, public utilities, and mines, and—somewhat more distantly— public ownership of the means of production and distribution generally. Nothing but this, thought Debs, would end the industrial horrors and inequities of the day.

Both Morgan and Debs would have been bewildered had they been able to foresee what the next half century would bring to the nation: how a combination of varied and often warring forces would produce an America which would not only be utterly unlike the America of 1900, but also would be utterly unlike the picture in either man's mind; yet an America in which an astonishing productive capacity would be combined with the widest distribution of prosperity ever witnessed in the world.

To understand the extent and nature of the big change that was to take place, we must first go back to 1900 and look about us—at the scene, the conditions of life, the people.

First, the scene.

II

If a neatly adjusted time machine could take you back to the Main Street of an American town in 1900, to look about you with your present-day eyes, your first exclamation would probably be, "But look at all those horses!"

For in that year 1900 there were registered in the whole United States only 13,824 automobiles (as compared with over 44 million in 1950). And they were really few and far between except in the larger cities and the well-to-do resorts. For in 1900 everybody thought of automobiles as playthings of the rich—and not merely of the rich, but of the somewhat adventurous and sporting rich: people who enjoyed taking their chances with an unpredictable machine that might at any moment wreck them. There were almost no paved highways outside the cities, and of course there were no roadside garages or filling stations; every automobilist must be his own desperate mechanic. Probably half the men and women of America had never seen a car. When William Allen White organized a street fair in Emporia, Kansas, in 1899, the automobile which was brought there for the occasion—and proved to be the most exciting exhibit of the fair—came from Chicago by rail; it was the first automobile ever to have crossed the Missouri River.

But horses were everywhere, pulling surreys, democrats, buggies, cabs, delivery wagons of every sort on Main Street, and pulling harvesters on the tractorless farms out in the countryside.

The sights and sounds and sensations of horse-and-carriage life were part of the universal American experience: the clop-clop of horses' hoofs; the stiff jolting of an iron-tired carriage on a stony road; the grinding noise of the brake being applied to ease the horse on a downhill stretch; the necessity of holding one's breath when the horse sneezed; the sight of sand, carried up on the tires and wooden spokes of a carriage wheel, spilling off in little cascades as the wheel revolved; the look of a country road overgrown by grass, with three tracks in it instead of two, the middle one made by horses' hoofs; the special male ordeal of getting out of the carriage and walking up the steeper hills to lighten the load; and the more severe ordeal, for the unpracticed, of harnessing a horse which could recognize inexperience at one scornful glance. During a Northern winter the jingle of sleigh bells was everywhere. On summer evenings, along the tree-lined streets of innumerable American towns, families sitting on their front porches would watch the fine carriages of the town as they drove past for a proud evening's jaunt, and the cognoscenti would wait eagerly for a glimpse of the banker's trotting pair or the sporting lawyer's 2:40 pacer. And one of the magnificent sights of urban life was that of a fire engine, pulled by three galloping horses, careening down a city street with its bell clanging.

It is hard for us today to realize how very widely communities were separated from one another when they depended for transportation wholly on the railroad and the horse and wagon—and when telephones were still scarce, and radios non-existent. A town which was not situated on a railroad was really remote. A farmer who lived five miles outside the county seat made something of an event of hitching up and taking the family to town for a Saturday afternoon's shopping. (His grandchildren make the run in a casual ten minutes, and think nothing of it.) A trip to see friends ten miles away was likely to be an all-day expedition, for the horse had to be given a chance to rest and be fed. No wonder that each region, each town, each farm was far more dependent upon its own resources—its own produce, social contacts, amusements—than in later years. For in terms of travel and communication the United States was a very big country indeed.

No wonder, furthermore, that the majority of Americans were less likely than their descendants to be dogged by that frightening sense of insecurity which comes from being jostled by forces—economic, political, international—beyond one's personal ken. Their horizons were close to them. They lived among familiar people and familiar things—individuals and families and fellow townsmen much of their own sort, with ideas intelligible to them. A man's success or failure seemed more likely than in later years to depend upon forces and events within his own range of vision. Less often than his sons and grandsons did he feel that his fortune, indeed his life, might hang upon some decision made in Washington or Berlin or Moscow, for reasons utterly strange to his experience. The world at which he looked over the dashboard of the family carriage might not be friendly, but at least most of it looked understandable.

III

Your second exclamation, if you found yourself on a Main Street sidewalk of 1900, would probably be, "But those *skirts!*"

For every grown woman in town would be wearing a dress that virtually swept the street; that would in fact actually sweep it from time to time, battering and begriming the hem, if its owner had not learned to hold it clear. From the high collar of her shirtwaist to the ground, the woman of 1900 was amply enveloped in material. (There were, to be sure, arbitrary limits to this envelopment. The evening dress of a woman of fashion might be as décolleté as that of the television star of the nineteen-fifties. But it also had a train, which she must hold up as best she could when dancing.) Even for country wear, in fact even for golf or tennis, the skirt must reach within two or three inches of the ground, and a hat—usually a hard sailor hat—must almost imperatively be worn. Pull out today a photograph album of the year 1900 and your first impression will be that even at the seashore or in the mountains all the women are wearing city clothes.

At any season a woman was swathed in layer upon layer of under-pinnings—chemise, drawers, corset, corset cover, and one or more petticoats. The corset of those days was a formidable personal prison which did its strenuous best, with the aid of whalebones, to distort the female form into an hour-glass shape. Dresses almost invariably came in two pieces, and the discipline begun by the corset was reinforced by the bodice part of the dress, which was stiffened to complete the hour-glass effect. The bosom was compressed as nearly as possible into a single structure, and the correct posture called for a rearward-sloping "straight-front" effect from this eminence downward; the fashion-plate artists represented the well-dressed woman as almost falling forward—despite the counterbalancing effect of an unsubdued posterior—in the effort to achieve the perfect stance.

As for the men, their clothes, too, were formal and severe by today's standards. Collars were high and stiff. The man of affairs was likely to wear, even under his everyday sack suit (of three-button coat, obligatory waistcoat, and narrowish trousers), a shirt with hard detachable cuffs and perhaps a stiff bosom too. If he were a banker or a businessman of executive stature he probably wore a frock coat to the office, and a silk hat instead of the less formal derby—except between May 15 and September 15, when custom decreed a hard straw hat (or, for the affluent, possibly a Panama). To go hatless, except in the wide open spaces, was for the well-dressed male unthinkable. If the weather were intolerably hot, he might remove his coat, and in certain informal offices—newspaper city rooms, for instance—he customarily did so. But his waistcoat *must not come off* (a rule which, considering the sort of shirt he was wearing, was not without aesthetic merit). The term "shirt sleeves" remains in our language as a survival of that custom.

In the country he might wear a blue serge coat with white flannel (or, more economically, white duck) trousers, or, under the proper circumstances, a tweed coat with riding trousers or knickerbockers. But when a man returned to the city, or a farmer put on town clothes for a visit to the county seat, he must invariably get into the severe three-piece suit, with starched collar and cuffs—even under a July sun.

These implacable costumes, male and female, reflected the prevailing credo as to the relations between the sexes. The ideal woman was the sheltered lady, swathed not only in silk and muslin but in innocence and propriety, and the ideal man, whether a pillar of rectitude or a gay dog, virtuously protected the person and reputation of such tender creatures as were entrusted to his care. If unmarried, a girl must be accompanied by a chaperone whenever she ventured out to an evening's entertainment in the city. If she were a daughter of the rich, a maid might take the place of the chaperone; it was never quite clear, under these circumstances, who was supposed to protect the maid's virtue. Eleanor Roosevelt has recorded in her autobiography her relief when, at the age of twenty or so, she found that her friend Bob Ferguson was considered close enough to the family to be permitted to escort her home from evening parties at the studio of Bay Emmett the painter. "Otherwise I always had to have a maid wait for me—that was one of the rules my grandmother had laid down." And James W. Gerard has added his testimony as to the iron code which still governed New York Society in that period. "Even when I was thirty years old," wrote Gerard in his old age, "if I had asked a girl to dine with me alone, I would have been kicked down her front steps. If I had offered her a cocktail, I would have been tossed out of Society for my boorish effrontery." Needless to add that a woman must never be seen in a bar—or even a smoking car.

The chaperone was, to be sure, chiefly an urban institution. In the smaller places, especially west of the Alleghenies, and among city people vacationing in the country, the rules were greatly relaxed. As Henry Seidel Canby has said, there was developing

a free association of boys and girls in their teens and early twenties that perhaps never has existed on the same plane elsewhere in the history of the modern world. We had confidence in each other, and we were confided in. All through the Adirondack woods we climbed together in summer, sleeping in cabins, girls on one side, boys on the other, following by couples all day lonely and difficult trails, and in the winter skated far-off ponds, or sat all night in the spring on moonlit Delaware hills, falling in and out of love with never a crude pang of sex, though in a continual amorous excitement which was sublimated from the grosser elements of love.

But throughout these companionships one might almost say that an imaginary chaperone was always present. What was operating was in effect an honor system: these boys and girls knew they were expected to behave with perfect propriety toward one another, and only rarely did they fail to do so. As Mr. Canby adds, "The boys sought elsewhere for what they did not get in friendship and the respectful amorousness of equals. They raided the amusement parks or the evening streets in search of girls that could be frankly pursued for their physical charms. 'Chippies' was the cant name. . . ." But the boys preferred to think of "nice" girls of their own class in other terms, and under the code which they followed a kiss was virtually tantamount to a proposal of marriage.

The idea of the sheltered lady was of course difficult to maintain in a country in which 20.4 per cent of the female population were engaged in working for a living. This unhappy fact of life caused the moralists of the day deep concern. If there was a steadily increasing number of women working in offices, it was understood that they were victims of unfortunate financial circumstance; their fathers, poor fellows, were unable to support them properly; and it was hoped that their inevitable contacts with rude men of business would not sully their purity. If women who had not had "advantages" worked by the millions in shops and factories—at wages as low as six or eight dollars a week, roughly equivalent to eighteen to twenty-five a week in 1950—this was understood to subject them to appalling temptations; one of O. Henry's most touching stories deals with a poor shopgirl who, though she kept a picture of Kitchener of Khartoum in her room as the embodiment of male knightliness, was pursued by a low character named Piggy who would one day have his way with her because she was starving on her meager wages.

There were also servant girls innumerable; but in the cities they were mostly of immigrant stock, or colored, and therefore, it was thought, could hardly hope for a better lot. And anyhow they were protected from temptation by being given very few hours off. In the country towns the servant girls were likely to be farmers' daughters who would presently marry a clerk or a man in the railroad office and set up housekeeping—with, one hoped, their innocence still unimpaired. (Incidentally, only among a minority of the wealthy were servants referred to as such, except in the South; however mean their status, an American deference to the democratic idea compelled them to be spoken of as "the girls," or, in less sophisticated circles, as "the help.")

If unhappy circumstances forced a "nicely brought up" young woman to work for a living, a career as schoolteacher, or music teacher, or trained nurse was considered acceptable for her. If she had the appropriate gift she might become a writer or artist or singer, even an opera singer. Some went on the stage; but at the grave risk of declassing themselves, for actresses were known to be mostly "fast." (Always, in discussions of the economic status and opportunities of women, the effect of a woman's occupation upon her sexual virtue was recurrent.) There were pioneers who, with flaming intensity, took up other careers—as doctors, for instance—against every sort of opposition; but it was an unusual community in which they were not considered unfeminine cranks for doing so, and one of the most telling arguments marshaled against their decision was that a girl who set out to earn money was selfishly causing her father needless embarrassment: somebody might think that he couldn't support her. By common consent the best—and safest—thing for a girl to do was to sit at home and help her mother about the house and wait for the "right man."

Such a code might be expected by people of this post-Freudian day to have produced a generation of inhibited neurotics. I think Mr. Canby is right when he argues, in *The Age of Confidence*, that on the whole it did not. If the rule of reticence and repression damaged many lives, it was not conspicuously harder for most people to live by than the rule of frankness and comparative sexual latitude. But it had its unhappy aspects. So inexorable were the silences that surrounded the sexual functions (except in men's smoking-room conversation) that a large majority of American women entered marriage with only the vaguest—and often the most terrified—notions of what it would involve. And it is possible, if not probable, that to an equally large majority of married women the sexual life remained, year after year, a distasteful necessity, to be submitted to only because men had beastly instincts which must be appeased (lest they be driven into adventures with bad women), and because it was one's right and duty to have children.

It is true that already the divorce rate was rising; in the year 1900 there was one divorce for every 12.7 weddings, as compared with one for every 2.6 weddings in the abnormal postwar year 1946 and for every 4.1 weddings in the more normal year 1949. But even the 1900 figures give no idea of the black disfavor in which divorce was held in the average American community. A marriage might be a nightmare to both partners, but it must go on and on: that was the decree of public opinion.

As a result, there was hardly an American town of any size in which one could not point to a middle-aged or elderly couple who had not spoken to one another in years, so deep was their mutual enmity, but who continued to share the same house, eat at the same table, bring up a family of children, and even, perhaps, share the same bed—in the stubborn conviction that they were treading the only path of virtue.

IV

You could not travel far, on your return to the America of 1900, without noticing how much smaller the cities and towns were. For in that year the population of the continental United States was just about half what it would be fifty years later—a little less than 76 millions as against a little more than 150 millions in 1950. And although you would find open fields where there are now villages, and villages which have since grown into towns, it would be in the cities and their suburbs that the contrast would be most striking. Especially in the cities of the West Coast and Texas. For example, you would find Los Angeles a fast-growing little city of only 102,489 people—about one-nineteenth of its 1950 population; Baedeker's guide said in 1899 that within the preceding decade "its adobe houses have given place almost entirely to stone and brick business blocks and tasteful wooden residences." You would find Houston a pigmy city of 44,633 inhabitants, as against over thirteen times as many in 1950; Dallas, another pigmy with 42,638 people, as against over ten times as many in 1950.

Not only would the thinness of the Western population remind you how much farther east, in those days, was the center of gravity of American industry and American cultural institutions; even in the Eastern cities you would miss many of the commonplace features of modern city life. Skyscrapers, for instance: the tallest building in the country was the Ivins Syndicate Building on Park Row in New York, which rose 29 stories, with towers which brought its utmost altitude to 382 feet. Not yet did visitors to New York remark upon the "famous skyline." And in other cities a ten- or twelve-story building was a thing of wonder.

There was little electric street-lighting; a commonplace sight at dusk in almost any American city was the appearance of the city lamplighter with his ladder, which he would set against a lamppost and climb to turn on the gas street-light. Nor was there, as yet, much illuminated advertising. New Yorkers could marvel at the great Heinz sign on the site of the future Flatiron Building at Fifth Avenue and Broadway and Twenty-third Street, a fifty-foot sign, with a huge pickle represented by green light bulbs, and HEINZ written across it in white bulbs, and slogans such as "57 Varieties" flashing on and off below; but this was a pioneer spectacle: not yet had Broadway truly become the Great White Way.

As for public transportation in the cities, there was only one completed subway, a short one in Boston, though in New York ground was broken for another during 1900; and if New York and Chicago had their thundering elevated railroads (New York was just electrifying its line, which had previously run by steam), most urban Americans got about town in trolley cars, the screaming of whose wheels, as they rounded a corner, seemed to the countryman the authentic note of modern civilization. Electric trolley lines were booming; the financial journals were full of advertisements of the securities of new trolley enterprises; to put one's money into street-railroad development was to bet on the great American future.

Each city had its outlying residential areas, within walking distance of the railroad or trolley lines: long blocks of single-family or two-family houses, rising bleakly among the vacant lots and fields; comfortable lawn-surrounded houses for the more prosperous. And there were many commuters who made a cindery railroad journey to work from suburban towns. But those outlying towns were quite different from what they were to become in the automobile age. For only if one could be met at the station by a horse and carriage—which was inconvenient unless one could afford a coachman—or was an exceptionally hardy pedestrian, was it practicable to live more than a mile or so from the railroad or trolley. So the suburbs were small, and backed by open country. Nothing would have been more incredible to the commuter of 1900 than the notion that within a generation the fields and woods in which he went walking of a Sunday would be studded with hundreds of suburban cottages, all easily accessible in a motorized age.

As you traveled away from the cities into the countryside, one of the things that would have puzzled you, if you had been able to look about you with the eyes of the mid-century, would have been the comparative shortage of city people's summer cottages. The rich, to be sure, had their holiday resorts: Bar Harbor, Islesboro, and North Haven on the islands off the Maine coast; Nahant, Beverly, and Manchester on the shoreline north of Boston; Newport and Narragansett Pier in Rhode Island; Lenox in the Berkshires; in the New York area, Tuxedo Park, Lakewood, Cedarhurst, and the newly-fashionable north shore of Long Island; Atlantic City and Cape May; the Springs of Virginia and West Virginia; Saratoga Springs for the racing season; Palm Beach for the winter season; Santa Barbara on the West Coast. If the overwhelming majority of the places in this list seem to be in the northeast part of the country, the reason is obvious; most Southerners went north if they could, and most Westerners went east, for a prosperous holiday. And many places whose warm winter climate subsequently made them popular pleasure resorts were then chiefly known as health resorts. Said Baedeker's guide, 1899 edition:

The best known winter-stations are in Florida, California, the Carolinas, Georgia, and Virginia. A large proportion of the invalids visiting these regions are the victims of consumption, but sufferers from gout, rheumatism, neurasthenia, chlorosis, anaemia, diseases of the kidneys, affections of the heart, insomnia, chronic bronchitis, asthma, and overwork are often signally benefited. . . .

Baedeker especially recommended for invalids such places as Los Angeles, Santa Barbara, San Diego, and San Bernardino in California; Colorado Springs in the Rockies; and Thomasville, Georgia, and Aiken, South Carolina, for "weak-chested persons."

In most of the leading resorts there were fine country houses; in some of them, opulent ones. There were also many prosperous families whose special taste for the wilds would lead them to buy large tracts of Adirondack woodland and build luxurious "camps"; or

whose liking for the simplicities of Cape Cod, or the White Mountains, or the Lake Michigan shoreline, or the rugged Monterey coast,
would lead them to build more modest cottages for a two or three
months' stay. But their choice of places was limited by two things—
accessibility to a railroad, and the limited holiday time available to
all but a few. The boom in summer-cottage building was only just
beginning; probably there were only something like a tenth as many
cottages as in 1950. It was still the heyday of the big summer-resort
hotel, to which well-to-do vacationists would come for a short stay,
ranging usually from a week to a month: the shingled hotel with
towers and turrets and whipping flags, with wide piazzas and interminable carpeted corridors, and with a vast dining room in which
were served huge meals on the American plan, with a menu which
took one from celery and olives through soup and fish and a roast to
ice cream, cake, and nuts and almonds, with sherbet as a cooling encouragement in mid-meal.

For those who could not afford such grandeur, there were boardinghouses innumerable, with schoolteachers rocking on the porch and
a group of croquet players on the lawn; and, here and there along
the seashore or the lakeside, crowded colonies of tiny shingled shacks,
each labeled clearly with its sentimental or jocose name—"Bide-a-
Wee Cottage," "Doocum Inn," or the like. But the overwhelming
majority of Americans outside the upper income brackets stayed at
home, through the full heat of summer. And being carriageless, they
had to satisfy their holiday dreams by taking a special reduced-rate
railroad tour by day-coach to Niagara Falls or Atlantic City; or, more
likely, an occasional trip out of town in an open trolley car to the
Trolley Park, an amusement park at the end of the line.

So there was still lots of room to play in America—thousands of
miles of shoreline, hundreds of lakes and rivers, hundreds of mountains, which you could explore to your heart's content, camping and
bathing and hunting and fishing without asking anybody's permission, if you could only somehow reach them. Already there were far-
sighted conservationists pointing out that for generations Americans
had been despoiling the land while subduing it; that forests were

being hacked to pieces, farm land misused and overused, natural resources plundered right and left; and that national parks would be
needed, both to conserve these resources and to give the people room
to play. But to most people such warnings just didn't make sense. If
lumbermen destroyed one forest, there were others to enjoy; if cottagers bought up one beach, there were others open to any bathers.
The bounties of nature seemed inexhaustible. As Stuart Chase was to
remark long years later, the prevailing attitude was that of the Mad
Hatter, who if he soiled one teacup simply moved on to the next one.

For the small minority who were lucky enough to have a summer
cottage to go to, the ritual of departure was complex. First, the city
house would be put through a thorough cleaning and dismantling, a
process that lasted for days. On Departure-Day-Minus-One the ex-
pressman called for the trunks, which were many; it would have
astonished a family of the 1900 era to be told that in later years vacationists would manage for weeks with nothing but suitcases. On the
fateful morning the family would grasp bags, overcoats, umbrellas,
and such other possible incumbrances as fishing tackle, golf clubs,
dog, cat, and caged canary, and proceed to the station in one or more
horse-drawn cabs. Then came the long journey—either by Pullman
car, incredibly grand with its elaborate paneling of the Chester A.
Arthur vintage, or by open-platform daycoach, very cindery. Arrived
in the neighborhood of Elysium, the family would dismount on a sun-
baked board platform, assemble its belongings, and proceed in a big
three-seater wagon (for the family and personal equipment) followed by an even larger wagon (for the trunks). A six-mile drive
would take an hour, for there was that sandy stretch by the cemetery
where the horses moved at a straining walk, and there were a couple
of long hills (now taken by all automobiles in high). It was a dirty
and sticky family that finally watched the trunk wagon being backed
up to the side porch of the cottage; whether they were more exhausted
than their grandchildren, who now make the 300-mile journey packed
tightly into the family Buick, is less certain.

To the city-bred children of that time, the farmers they met in the country seemed a race apart, foreign in everything but language. And why shouldn't they have been? With no automobiles, no radio, no rural free delivery, no big mass-circulation magazines; with, in many places, no access to any schooling but the most elementary; and with rare chances, if any, to travel to a city, they were imprisoned in rural isolation. If, as we have already noted, the world they saw about them was moved by more understandable and therefore less terrifying forces than those which impinged upon their descendants, it was also unbelievably more limited.

V

As you continued your investigation of the United States of 1900 you would find yourself, again and again, struck by the lack, or the shortage, of things which today you regard as commonplace necessities.

Electrical services and devices, for instance. Most of the city houses of the really prosperous were now electrified; but the man who was building a new house was only just beginning to install electric lights without adding gas, too, lest the current fail suddenly. And the houses of the great majority were still lighted by gas (in the cities and towns) or oil lamps (in the country). Millions of Americans of the older generation still remember what it was like to go upstairs of an evening and then be consumed with worry as to whether they had really turned off completely the downstairs gas jets. A regular chore for the rural housewife was filling the lamps; and a frequent source of family pride was the possession of a Welsbach burner that would furnish adequate light for a whole family to read by as they gathered about the living-room table.

Of course there were no electric refrigerators—to say nothing of washing machines and deep-freeze units. Farmers—and summer cottagers—had icehouses in which big cubes of ice, cut during the winter at a neighboring pond or river, or imported by ship from north to south, lay buried deep in sawdust. When you needed ice, you climbed into the icehouse, scraped the sawdust away from a fine hunk of ice, and carried it in your ice tongs to the kitchen icebox. If

you lived in the city, the ice company's wagon showed up at the door
and the iceman stowed a huge cube in your icebox.

For a good many years there had been refrigerator cars on the railroads, but the great national long-distance traffic in fresh fruits and
vegetables was still in its infancy; and accordingly the prevailing
American diet would have shocked deeply a visitor from 1950. In
most parts of the United States people were virtually without fresh
fruit and green vegetables from late autumn to late spring. During
this time they consumed quantities of starches, in the form of pies,
doughnuts, potatoes, and hot bread, which few would venture to absorb today. The result was that innumerable Americans were in slug-
gish health during the months of late winter and early spring, when
their diet was short of vitamins. If as a visitor from 1950 you found
yourself staying in an average American house in the winter season
at the turn of the century, you would soon find yourself yearning for
orange juice, tomato juice, fresh lettuce, or grapefruit—every one of
them unobtainable then.

By the turn of the century running water, bathtubs, and water
closets were to be found in virtually all the town houses of the prosperous, though many a fine house on a fashionable street still held
only one bathroom. But not only did factory workers and farmers
(except perhaps a few owners of big farms) still not dream of enjoying such luxuries, but even in the gracious houses of well-to-do
people beyond the reach of city water lines and sewer lines, there was
likely to be no bathroom at all. They washed with pitcher and basin
in their bedrooms, each of them pouring his dirty water from the
basin into a slop jar, to be emptied later in the day; and after breakfast they visited the privy behind the house. In his lively book, *The
Age of Indiscretion,* Clyde Brion Davis tells how, if you lived in
Chillicothe, Missouri, you might on occasion extend your political
education by beholding the Governor of Missouri, a resident of
Chillicothe, "without his silk hat or frock coat and with his fawn-
colored vest unbuttoned and the tab of his stiff-bosomed shirt unbut-

toned and hanging outside his trousers . . . looking very thoughtful as he sauntered to the privy."

At a luxurious hotel you might, if you paid extra, get a room with private bath, but not until 1907 did Ellsworth M. Statler build in Buffalo the first hotel which offered every guest a room and private bath at a moderate price. And not until 1916 did the double-shell enameled bathtub go into mass production, replacing the painted cast-iron bathtub, with roll rim and claw feet, which was the standard article of the 1900 period.

As a visitor from the nineteen-fifties to the era of that cast-iron bathtub it might or might not occur to you that personal cleanliness was not so readily achieved then as in your own time, and that if the Saturday-night bath offered to millions of Americans their only weekly immersion in warm water, this was chiefly because bathrooms were few and far between. But pretty certainly there was one custom of those days which would strike you as filthy. In the Eastern cities well-bred people disapproved of spitting in mixed company, though the cuspidor was likely to be a standard office fixture beside the executive's desk; but in the West and South, and in the small cities and towns especially, spitting was a standard prerogative of the sturdy male; there were cuspidors everywhere, not only in offices, hotels, and public buildings, but in the leading citizen's parlor; and when it took too much of an effort to reach a cuspidor—which many men prided themselves on being able to hit with a stream of spittle at a considerable distance—many otherwise cleanly people considered it their privilege to spit in the fireplace or on the floor.

Perhaps the dwindling of this ancient American custom during the years since 1900 has been affected by the changing use of tobacco. In 1900, when the population of the United States was half what it was in 1950, Americans smoked a slightly larger number of cigars, consumed a much larger amount of pipe tobacco and a very much larger amount of chewing tobacco—and smoked only about one-hundredth of the number of cigarettes that they did fifty years later. (In 1900 about four billion cigarettes were manufactured in the United States; in 1949, 384 billions.)

Telephones, in 1900, were clumsy things and comparatively scarce; they were to be found chiefly in business offices and in the houses of such well-to-do people as enjoyed experimenting with new mechanical devices. In the whole country there were only 1,335,911 of them—as compared with over 43,000,000 at the end of 1950. In Muncie, Indiana, the local press warned people that, when using the telephone, they "should not ask for a name but refer to the number list." And so strange, to most people, was still the idea of such an impersonal instrument of personal communication, that many a housewife would cry out politely as the telephone began ringing, "I'm coming, I'm coming!"

As for the instruments of mass communication which, in the years to come, were to do so much to provide Americans of all classes and conditions with similar information, ideas, and interests, these too were almost wholly lacking. There would be no radio for another twenty years; no television, except for a very limited audience, for over forty-five years. Crude motion pictures were occasionally to be seen at vaudeville theaters, or in peep-show parlors, but the first movie which told a story, *The Great Train Robbery*, was still three years in the future. There was as yet no magazine with a circulation of over a million. Already the days were ending when a group of splendid and sedate periodicals designed for polite readers with intellectual tastes—such as *The Century, Harper's,* and *Scribner's*—had dominated the magazine field. Munsey and Curtis and McClure had begun to show that many readers could be attracted by magazines which offered less literary but more human and popular fare, and that such magazines could as a result attract lucrative advertising. But although Cyrus Curtis had pushed the circulation of his *Ladies' Home Journal* to 850,000, he had only just begun his extraordinary demonstration of the way in which popular magazines could serve as a medium for national advertising on a huge scale. His *Saturday Evening Post* had only 182,000 readers in 1900, and an advertising revenue of only $6,933.

Accordingly there were sharp limits to the fund of information and ideas which people of all regions and all walks of life held in common. To some extent a Maine fisherman, an Ohio farmer, and a Chicago businessman would be able to discuss politics with one another, but in the absence of syndicated newspaper columns appearing from coast to coast their information would be based mostly upon what they had read in very divergent local newspapers, and in the absence both of the radio and of newsreels it is doubtful if any of them—except perhaps the Chicago businessman—had ever heard with his own ears the silver voice of William Jennings Bryan. There was no such common denominator of acquaintance as there would be in 1950 between people who could instantly recognize not only Harry Truman, but Bob Hope, Van Johnson, and Betty Hutton, who had laughed simultaneously at Jack Benny's colloquies with Rochester, and who knew Bing Crosby's voice the moment they heard it on the air.

And if the instruments of mass communication were lacking, so also were many social institutions which today Americans take for granted. A nation of individualists, accustomed to the idea that each person must fend for himself as an independent unit, was moving into an age of interdependence but was still slow to recognize the fact and slow to organize the institutions which such an age required. Consider, for example, what a small Midwestern town had to offer a boy by way of recreation and educational opportunity. Tradition said that boys must find their own chances for recreation—swimming at the old swimming hole of hallowed legend, playing baseball in the open fields, hunting and fishing in the neighboring woods and streams. But already industrialism was contaminating the rivers, the open country was being built up and cultivated, the natural playgrounds were being despoiled—and few substitute diversions had been provided.

I know of no better demonstration of the plight of a boy in such a town than is given in Clyde Brion Davis's *The Age of Indiscretion*. In Chillicothe, Missouri, says Mr. Davis, there was no place "where a youngster could enter the water except the really filthy ponds and the equally dirty and dangerous river where drownings occurred every season. . . . We, in our district, had no place to play baseball except a wholly inadequate and rutty lot down by the Milwaukee tracks. . . . There was no tennis or golf or badminton or basketball. There was not a gymnasium in town or anything approaching physical education even in high school." There was no public library (unless you counted a small semipublic library in the high school). There was no Y.M.C.A., no Boy Scout organization, no 4-H organization, no school band, school orchestra, or school glee club.

It seems to be a continuing characteristic of American life that communities perpetually fail to catch up institutionally with their own growth; at any rate, it was glaringly true that the American town of 1900 had failed to adapt itself to the necessities of the onrushing industrial age.

VI

In the development of organized sports there was the same sort of lag. The frontier tradition and the old American individualism died hard. Most American boys and men were still expected to get their active amusement on a catch-as-catch-can basis out in the open countryside—hunting, fishing, camping, swimming, riding—or to get it out of contests (such as target-shooting) which grew directly out of the conditions of the open countryside. Baseball had long been the national game and millions of boys had learned to play it, but mostly on local sandlots, from which, if proficient, they might graduate to play on the town team against a neighboring town. As for girls, the traditional idea was that they were too weak, or at any rate too proper, to engage in such rough goings-on. Organized games which required special costumes and equipment were mostly considered affectations of the rich, and to the average small-town American any such notion as that of offering "supervised play" for boys and girls would have been quite bewildering.

Already this old-time tradition was breaking down. Organized games were growing rapidly in the schools and colleges: football, baseball (which was a college sport with much more prestige then than later), rowing, track, and on a minor scale soccer and lacrosse.

(Basketball was still known only to a comparative few. It had not even been invented until 1892.) Among the games which older people, too, could enjoy, golf and tennis were spreading fast in popularity; a considerable number of people bowled; and men and women by the hundreds of thousands bicycled for recreation. But as we look back on the sports of those days, the most striking thing is the extent to which they centered in the East—and also were still regarded as the prerogative of the well-to-do.

Tennis, for example, was overwhelmingly Eastern, and the annual championships were held as a matter of course at Newport, the center of summertime fashion. Golf had reached Chicago at the time of the World's Fair of 1893, and already there were no less than twenty golf clubs in California, but the best amateur players were mostly well-to-do Easterners, and the best professionals were nearly all Scotch. Red-blooded Americans outside the influence of urban wealth and fashion tended to regard golf as downright silly; any business-man could get a laugh by remarking that he couldn't see any sense in chasing a little white ball up and down a field.

And as for football—which in 1900 was a bone-breaking contest in which no forward passing was allowed and the teams crashed into one another and piled up in sweating heaps in the effort to gain five yards in three downs—it is instructive to look at the *New York Times* for Sunday, November 25, 1900. There, on the front page, right-hand column, you will learn that the Yale football team, the preceding afternoon, had become the undisputed "football champions" of the year—because, after having beaten Princeton, they had beaten Harvard, which had already beaten Pennsylvania. It was as simple as that. The Yale-Harvard game had been played at Yale Field, with 20,000 people in the bleachers, and speculators offering seats at prices from $10 to $20. Following the *Times*'s account of the game itself you will find a headline reading SOCIETY AT THE GAME, informing you that "the society and club worlds of this city exhibited an intense interest in yesterday's game," and that "to give a list of the well-known men and women present would be to reprint whole pages of the Social Register."

It is only fair to add that in 1900 there were college football teams from coast to coast and that some of the Midwestern ones displayed considerable prowess. *Outing* magazine, reviewing the season, devoted separate sections of its survey to Midwestern, Southern, and Pacific Coast football. Yet, like the *New York Times,* it had no doubt as to where pre-eminence lay. It selected an All-America team consisting of four players from Yale, two from Harvard, and one each from Cornell, Columbia, Lafayette, Pennsylvania, and West Point. (Incidentally, when Frank Hering went to Notre Dame to coach football in the fall of 1896, he "had a hard time working up enough enthusiasm to get a squad on the field," according to Arthur J. Hope's history of the university.)

Even if one makes allowance for a certain degree of condescension on the part of Eastern chroniclers, the evidence is overwhelming that at the turn of the century athletic sports centered in the East and that the public thought of them as surrounded by an aura of fashion. Far ahead were the days of tennis champions from municipal courts, golf champions from the public links, expert college teams playing in huge stadiums so numerously that no one selecting an All-American eleven could see more than a few of the best ones play; Californians moving into the top ranks in sport after sport; high-school basketball teams organized by the thousands from one end of the country to the other; and Americans of both sexes, to the estimated number of well over ten millions, enjoying at least an occasional evening of bowling.

Chapter 2

Grandeur, Limited

O<small>F</small> ALL the contrasts between American life in 1900 and half a century or more later, perhaps the most significant is in the distance between rich and poor—in income, the way of living, and status in the community. At the turn of the century the gulf between wealth and poverty was immense.

One illustration may help to point the contrast. I have already mentioned Andrew Carnegie's income. During the year 1900 Carnegie owned 58½ per cent of the stock of his great steel company. That year it made a profit of 40 million dollars. Carnegie's personal gain that year, whether or not he took it in dividends, was therefore well over 23 million dollars—*with no income taxes to pay*. During the five years 1896-1900 his *average* annual income, computed on the same basis, was about 10 millions. And these figures include no other income which he may have had from any other property.

At the time that Carnegie was enjoying this princely income, tax free, the average annual wage of *all* American workers was somewhere in the neighborhood of four or five hundred dollars; one economic calculator has arrived at a figure of $417 a year, another makes it $503. Remember that these figures are averages, not minimum incomes.*

* To translate these figures into the terms of 1950 one must make allowance for the dwindling value of the dollar. This it is difficult to compute; for though statisticians may arrive at precise index figures for the rise in prices, money was spent in such different ways then, and nominally identical goods were in fact so

In short, Andrew Carnegie's annual income was at least twenty thousand times greater than that of the average American workman.

There you have the basic contrast. Andrew Carnegie was one of the very wealthiest men of his day, but many others had incomes in the millions. And their way of life showed it. Let us take a look at this way of life.

To begin with, they built themselves palatial houses.

During the last twenty years of the nineteenth century, when a great many American millionaires had decided that the thing for a rich man to do was to build himself a princely mansion, it had been the Vanderbilt family who had set the pace for the rest to follow. By the middle eighties there were no less than seven great Vanderbilt houses within the space of seven blocks on the west side of Fifth Avenue. One should perhaps question the published reports of the cost of these palaces—three millions for William H.'s, three millions for William K.'s, and so forth—but it would seem safe to say that the seven, between them, must have represented a family outlay of well over twelve millions (which, one must remind oneself, was roughly equivalent to over thirty-six millions today).

The first three of these buildings—William H. Vanderbilt's and the pair of houses he built for his daughters Mrs. Shepard and Mrs. Sloane—conformed outwardly, in everything but scale, to the New York brownstone tradition; but William H.'s contained a bewildering variety of statues, paintings, tapestries, and urns from all over— English, French, German, Japanese. For a pattern was forming: the American millionaire wanted to live like a prince; and since princes were foreign, and princely culture was likewise foreign, he must show

---

different, that any index figure is suspect. For convenience I shall assume in this book that the 1900 dollar bought three times as much as the 1950 one, which is at least close to the reality. Translate the wages of 1900 into these terms and we find that the average 1900 wage, in terms of what it would buy in 1950, was somewhere in the neighborhood of $1,200 to $1,500—which looks considerably less appalling than $400 to $500.

But if we multiply the worker's wage in this way we should likewise multiply Andrew Carnegie's. And we find that in terms of 1950 purchasing power his income came to more than 60 millions, tax free, in 1900, and to more than 30 millions per year for the five years 1896-1900.

his princeliness by living among foreign furnishings and foreign works of art, in as great variety and profusion as could be managed.

The William K. Vanderbilt house and the Cornelius Vanderbilt house carried the idea a step further. They abandoned the New York brownstone and New York exterior aspect. For William K., Richard Morris Hunt designed a limestone castle that was reminiscent of the Château of Blois and even more so of the fifteenth-century French mansion of Jacques Cœur at Bourges; for Cornelius, George B. Post provided a brick-and-stone château that likewise carried people's minds back to Blois. Both were splendid buildings, ornaments to Fifth Avenue, but their foreignness amused the architect Louis Sullivan, who felt that houses should harmonize with the lives of the people who lived in them. "Must I show you this *French château*, this little Château de Blois, on this street corner, here, in New York, and still you do not laugh?" wrote Sullivan in his *Kindergarten Chats*. "Must you wait till you see a *gentleman* in a silk hat come out of it before you laugh? Have you no sense of humor, no sense of pathos? Must I tell you that while the man may live in the house physically . . . he cannot possibly live in it morally, mentally, or spiritually, that he and his house are a paradox, a contradiction, an absurdity . . . ?"

No such misgivings as these troubled the Vanderbilts, nor did they let anything stint their zeal for grandeur. Subsequently, the family fortune went also into the building of several massive Newport houses, of which the most immense was Cornelius Vanderbilt's The Breakers, which resembled an oversized Italian villa, and the most dazzling was William K.'s Marble House, the construction, decoration, and furnishing of which was alleged to have cost some eleven millions. There was also Frederick W. Vanderbilt's great house at Hyde Park, in which the dining room was approximately fifty feet long. There was William K. Vanderbilt's Idle Hour, at Oakdale, Long Island—with 110 rooms, 45 bathrooms, and a garage ready to hold 100 automobiles. But the champion of all the turn-of-the-century châteaux was George W. Vanderbilt's ducal palace at Asheville, North Carolina, which he called Biltmore.

Biltmore, too, was French, designed by Hunt after the manner of the great castles of the Loire. It had forty master bedrooms, a Court of Palms, an Oak Drawing Room, a Banqueting Hall, a Print Room, a Tapestry Gallery, and a Library with 250,000 volumes. It was surrounded by an estate which gradually grew until it covered some 203 square miles, giving Vanderbilt ample scope to exercise his interest in scientific farming and forestry. To serve as his director of forestry, Vanderbilt hired a young man named Gifford Pinchot, who was enabled to offer what a standard work on American forestry calls "the first practical demonstration of forest management on a large scale in America."

J. Sterling Morton, who was U. S. Secretary of Agriculture in the middle nineties, regarded Vanderbilt's experimental work in agriculture and forestry with admiration not unmixed with envy. "He employs more men than I have in my charge," said Secretary Morton. "He is also spending more money than Congress appropriates for this Department."

No wonder a chronicler of the time reflected that "what with the six or seven great New York houses of the Vanderbilt family, and their still larger numbers of country estates, it could plausibly be argued that among them they have invested as much money in the erection of dwellings as any of the royal families of Europe, the Bourbons alone excepted."

And the Vanderbilts were far from alone in the building of vast villas and châteaux. The Goelet, Belmont, and Berwind houses at Newport; the Flagler house at Palm Beach; the Gould house at Lakewood, New Jersey; the Widener house near Philadelphia; the Phipps house at Pittsburgh—these were only a few of the mightier constructions in which the multimillionaires of the 1900 period sought to lead the princely life.

As one compares photographs of one palatial interior after another, with their marble floors, curving marble staircases, tapestries, urns, velvet hangings, carved and painted ceilings, brocaded chairs, mural paintings, pipe organs, potted palms, and classical statues holding electric light fixtures, one wonders if life in such surroundings must not have seemed a little unhomelike. One is reminded of Anna Robeson Burr's description of Henry C. Frick, the steel millionaire, "in his palace, seated on a Renaissance throne under a baldacchino, and holding in his little hand a copy of the *Saturday Evening Post*." And not only was there nothing cozy about these marble halls; Paul Bourget, the French novelist, found in their furnishings an absence of moderation, of restraint. "On the floors of halls which are too high there are too many precious Persian and Oriental rugs," commented Bourget after a Newport visit. "There are too many tapestries, too many paintings on the walls of the drawing rooms. The guest-chambers have too many *bibelots*, too much rare furniture, and on the lunch or dinner table there are too many flowers, too many plants, too much crystal, too much silver."

One is reminded, too, of the apt comment of Harry W. Desmond and Herbert Croly in their book, *Stately Homes in America*, to the effect that the European palaces and châteaux which the millionaires' architects had copied had not been private houses only but public buildings also, crowded with tenants and retainers of the noble family which controlled the destinies of the region, and that as public buildings they "could with propriety be magnificent." In a land without a peasantry such palaces as these were anomalous. No wonder a Newport or New York or Pittsburgh château with no such neighborhood traffic surging through it made an oddly illogical frame for a magnate who had made his millions by merging steel companies, or for a magnate's wife to whom a rocking chair by a Franklin stove had once seemed the last word in luxury—even if the architect had provided for them not only Italian Renaissance paintings and Greek statuary and Flemish tapestries but also bathrooms, electric lights, automatic elevators, a lavish heating system, and a complete internal telephone system.

Some of the millionaires eschewed palatial magnificence. For example, J. Pierpont Morgan, though he lived a truly regal life, preferred masculine comfort to marble splendor (except in the Library which he built after the turn of the century to hold part of his

extraordinary collection of rare books and masterpieces). Morgan's
town house at 291 Madison Avenue, New York, was commodious
rather than grand: one could run it with a staff of a dozen servants
or so. His country house at Highland Falls was ample but unpretentious; many American country clubs of today are bigger. His
double house in London did not suggest a palace, though it contained a collection of paintings at which connoisseurs of Dutch,
French, Spanish, and English art gasped. But he had also a sizable
country house outside London; a thousand-acre place in the Adiron-
dacks; a private apartment at the Jekyll Island Club on the Georgia
Coast; a "fishing box" at Newport; special suites at the Hotel Bristol
in Paris and the Grand Hotel in Rome which were set aside for his
use whenever he wanted them; and, in addition to all these, the
302-foot steam yacht, *Corsair III,* which served him as an additional
residence either on the Atlantic coast or in the Mediterranean. (He
also had a private Nile steamer built to order for his pleasure whenever he should be in Egypt.) And Morgan could hardly have been
accused of penny-pinching when, wanting carpets for *Corsair III*
exactly like those on *Corsair II,* and finding that such were no longer
made, he ordered the old patterns set up on the looms so that his
new carpets, made to order, should be identical in design.

Andrew Carnegie's preferences, too, were in many respects simpler
than those of the millionaires who frequented Newport. The house
which he built for himself on Fifth Avenue at Ninety-first Street,
though very large, didn't try to look like a palace; it had a subdued
neo-Georgian aspect. His yacht, the *Seabreeze,* was not in a class
with the *Corsair.* But during the nineties he acquired an estate in his
native Scotland, Skibo, on which he really let himself go. Eventually
the estate reached 32,000 acres in size. Carnegie had two or three
hundred tenants; he poured out money on the construction of roads;
and though he preferred informal dress and informal entertainment,
and at Skibo Castle almost invariably wore a light gray Norfolk
jacket and knickerbockers, he and his guests were awakened at eight
o'clock each morning by the Carnegie bagpiper approaching the castle
from a distance and then circling it and skirling beneath the bedroom

windows, and a little later they ate breakfast to the music of an organ played by the Carnegie organist.

Nor was there anything especially palatial about the house in which John D. Rockefeller lived much of the year at Pocantico Hills, close to Tarrytown, New York. Rockefeller did not care for pomp and circumstance; his tastes were Baptist rather than Medicean, and after his retirement from active business in the mid-nineties he was further handicapped by ill-health, so that in the years immediately following the turn of the century he was living on a diet of graham crackers and milk, and was utilizing for his daily golf game a bicycle, on which he rode from shot to shot. Rockefeller was moved less by a lust for splendor than by a concern for personal protection, since he knew that the ruthless methods of his Standard Oil Company had made him violent enemies. What he did at Pocantico Hills was to build up, gradually, a vast personal enclosure within which he might live a prudently well-ordered life unmolested.

The estate was not completed until long after the turn of the century, when the discovery of oil in Texas and Oklahoma and the increasing popularity of the automobile were between them multiplying his millions faster than he could give them away; but the pattern was more nearly that of 1900 than of his declining years. If Rockefeller's own house was not a palace, it was one of more than seventy-five buildings on his estate; if he himself used one car for fifteen years, the garage on the estate was built to hold a fleet of fifty. Within his estate there were seventy miles of private roads on which he could take his afternoon drive; a private golf links on which he could play his morning game; and anywhere from a thousand to fifteen hundred employees, depending on the season.

All this, by the way, was for Pocantico Hills only; Rockefeller also owned an estate at Lakewood, which he occupied in the spring; an estate at Ormond Beach in Florida, for winter use; a town house on Fifty-fourth Street in New York; an estate at Forest Hill, Cleveland, which he did not visit; and a house on Euclid Avenue in Cleveland, likewise unused by him. Never, perhaps, did any man live a more frugal life on a more colossal scale.

II

But if Rockefeller lived frugally, there were those that did not. When one is trying to measure the lavish scale of life among the very rich of those days, it is a little unfair to dwell unduly upon such extreme extravagances as the Bradley Martin ball given early in 1897 —when the country was just pulling out of a grievous depression— at a reported cost of $369,200 (roughly the equivalent of a million dollars today); or the James Hazen Hyde ball of a few years later, for which Stanford White transformed Sherry's restaurant in New York into the semblance of the interior of the Grand Trianon, with marble statues brought from France, waiters tricked out in eighteenth-century livery and perukes, and entertainment provided by the great French actress, Réjane, and members of her company, likewise imported for the occasion. Both the Martins and Mr. Hyde found they had misjudged the public attitude toward such expenditures, and the fact that they both thereafter went abroad to live was not wholly unrelated to this discovery. Let us look at a less publicized and more representative part of the record. Let us visit Newport at the height of the 1902 season, the tennis week at the end of August, during which the Dohertys of England were able to defeat many of the best American tennis players in the matches at the Casino, and only a successful defense of the American title by William A. Larned in the "challenge round" turned back R. F. Doherty's assault.

On Monday evening of that week, August 25, Mr. and Mrs. Cornelius Vanderbilt were "at home" at Beaulieu, the William Waldorf Astor villa which they had taken for the summer. If you had been invited, and the words "at home" had suggested to you a quiet chat in the drawing room, you would have been surprised to find yourself entering the estate through a specially-built arched entrance, 25 feet wide and 18 feet high; proceeding up a brilliantly illuminated midway along which there were shooting galleries, Negro dancers, singing girls, a Punch and Judy show, and other exhibits characteristic of an amusement park; and in due course continuing to a temporary theater, on the construction of which two gangs of carpenters had worked night and day for five days. And in this theater you would have witnessed the first act of a successful Broadway musical comedy, *The Wild Rose,* featuring Marie Cahill, Eddie Foy, and Irene Bentley. The Knickerbocker Theater in New York had been closed for the evening in order that the entire cast of the show, with the first-act scenery, might be transported to Newport to delight Mrs. Vanderbilt's guests. When the show was over, these guests adjourned to the house for supper, while the theater was cleared for dancing; after supper there was a ball with, according to the *New York Times,* "two cotillion leaders and elaborate figures with beautiful and costly favors."

Two evenings later Mrs. Ogden Goelet gave a dinner dance at Ochre Court, with two orchestras and another cotillion; one figure of the cotillion required 700 gardenias, the provision of which offered something of a problem to Newport florists; according to newspaper reports, the gardenias were distributed "from a Russian sleigh." And the very next evening Mrs. William Astor gave a ball at "Beechwood" to open her new Louis XV ballroom, with another cotillion, led by Harry Lehr.

In the nineties Paul Bourget had commented favorably on several aspects of Newport life. He had remarked that there were no courtesans, because virtually all the men came only for week ends and holidays and the life of the place did not lend itself to secluded intimacies; that there were no adventurers, because nobody was admitted to society whose earnings and investments could not be at least roughly ascertained; and that most of the people looked healthy rather than dissipated. His points were well taken. This was not a depraved or debauched community; it had standards of conduct and decorum.

To explain the Newporters' look of health, M. Bourget described an average day in the life of a young girl there. She would be out riding before nine; she would return from her ride and change in time to watch a tennis tournament match at the Casino; then her carriage would take her to a yacht landing and she would be ferried out for lunch on a yacht; at half past four or thereabouts she would

leave the yacht to watch a polo match; then she would go home,
bathe, and change for a dinner party, which would probably break
up by ten-thirty because many of those who had been out in the
open air would have difficulty keeping their eyes open any longer;
after that she might go on to a ball. Paul Bourget, however, apparently did not attend any ball. If he had, it is safe to guess that this
acute observer would have found in a grand Newport entertainment
the same lack of restraint which he had found in the decoration of
the houses. For these people had more money than they knew what
to do with, and they were engaged in a competition to see who could
toss it about most superbly.

The visitor from France might have wondered at the expenditure
of thousands upon thousands of dollars in order that during one
evening a couple of hundred people might see part of a musical show
that could be seen in its entirety, and to better advantage, on Broadway, or might frolic in a midway that was in essence a small imitation of Coney Island. But it was characteristic of Newport entertaining that no expense was spared to bring to the place things that
didn't belong there at all. For instance, according to Lloyd Morris,

Mrs. Belmont imported Chinese artisans to construct a red and gold
lacquer tea house on the cliffs at Marble House. The structure was gorgeous
and authentic, but contained no provision for making tea. A miniature
railroad was therefore laid from the pantry of the mansion to the cliffs, its
course masked by elaborate planting, and footmen with trays were thereby
whisked down to the lacquered toy.

At several houses in New York and Newport the hostesses prided
themselves on being able to serve dinner for a hundred or more
people on a few hours' notice—a feat which required, of course, a
profusion of servants. But servants were not lacking: in some country
houses they might number fifty or sixty in all, including the gar-
deners, chauffeurs, and grooms, and they were organized in a hierarchy of their own, English fashion. A few years after the turn of
the century a young man fresh out of Harvard found himself installed
for the summer in one of the marble mansions of Newport as tutor

to the son of the family. The young man was an earnest athlete, and it dismayed him that the boy in his charge was getting no chance to learn about teamwork in sports. One afternoon he found the butler and the other chief menservants playing soccer in a secluded part of the grounds. The very thing, he said to himself, and proposed that he and his young charge take part in the game. But it didn't work at all. For the moment the boy got possession of the ball, opposition melted away; these men, born and bred in a tradition of subservience, simply could not bring themselves to get in the way of the young master.

If my mention of people's being able to serve dinner to a hundred guests on short notice suggests some sort of casserole operation, be assured that there was nothing casual about a fashionable dinner at the turn of the century. The internal capacity of the prosperous of those days was prodigious. Seven or eight courses were likely to be served, with a variety of wines. In my life of Pierpont Morgan I printed the menu of a dinner enjoyed by the members of the Zodiac Club, a private dining club in New York. It is a little hard today to be sure, from that menu, which dishes were served as alternate choices and which constituted separate courses for all, but it appears to have been a ten-course feast: oysters, soup, hors d'oeuvres, soft clams, saddle and rack of lamb, terrapin, canvasback ducks, a sweet, cheese, and fruit—the dinner being preceded by sherry (instead of cocktails), accompanied successively by Rhine wine, Château-Latour, champagne, and Clos-Vougeot, and washed down with cognac (along with the coffee). It is difficult to imagine hunger being any more thoroughly assuaged; in fact, from the perspective of the nineteen-fifties it is difficult to understand how the diners could have faced the canvasback ducks with anything but dogged resolution.

If the members of the Zodiac Club dined heavily and well, they at least made no special attempt to enhance the grandeur of the surroundings in which they ate. A more all-round effort was made by Randolph Guggenheimer when he gave a dinner for forty ladies and gentlemen at the old Waldorf-Astoria on February 11, 1899.

His guests found the Myrtle Room of the Waldorf transformed into a garden, with roses, hyacinths, and tulips in bloom, and with hedges of fir. Nightingales, blackbirds, and canaries sang in the greenery. (It had been something of a trick to induce the zoo authorities to loan some nightingales for the affair.) The table was set in an arbor with a vine-covered trellis overhead and with green turf underfoot. The menus were painted in gold on scraped and polished cocoanuts; there were fans for the ladies on which the wine list had been painted. As favors there were beautifully engrossed vinaigrettes for the ladies, and jeweled matchboxes for the gentlemen. To provide music, six Neapolitans in native garb played guitars. And the dinner, which was served on gold plates, went as follows:

> Buffet Russe
> Cocktails
> Small Blue Point Oysters
> Lemardelais à la Princesse
> Amontillado Pasado
> Green Turtle Soup
> Bolivar
> Basket of Lobster
> Columbine of Chicken, California Style
> Roast Mountain Sheep, with Purée of Chestnuts (the sheep
>   having been brought to New York by fast express in small,
>   portable refrigerators)
> Jelly
> Brussels Sprouts Sauté
> New Asparagus, Cream Sauce and Vinaigrette
> Mumm's Extra Dry and Moët & Chandon Brut
> Diamond Back Terrapin
> Ruddy Duck (likewise rushed by express in small refrigerators)
> Orange and Grapefruit Salad
> Fresh Strawberries
> Blue Raspberries
> Vanilla Mousse
> Bonbons, Coffee, Fruit

What did the evening's pleasure cost? Ten thousand dollars—$250 a head. (Again, these were 1899 dollars; the cost in today's terms was $750 a head.) So said Oscar of the Waldorf, who should have known because he planned and staged the party for Mr. Guggenheimer.

One further word may not be wholly superfluous to some readers in the nineteen-fifties: these great feasts and elaborate balls did not go on anybody's corporate expense account. They were paid for by individuals, out of their own vast incomes.

III

In those days the word Society (with a capital S) carried much more definite connotations than it would today. In every community, probably, and in any generation, there is social emulation: there are certain families, or certain individuals, association with whom will seem to other people to number them among the elect. You will find this emulation in its most acute form today in the fraternity systems of some colleges; in adult communities the lines are less inexorably drawn. The smaller and less fluid the community, the clearer this phenomenon is likely to be; in larger cities, and in suburban communities where there is a constantly changing population, it is usually confused and obscured. One may find a great variety of groups, such as the old, tradition-bound leading families; the fashionable group; the newly prosperous who are not yet admitted to fashionable standing; the well-bred professional people and intellectuals who touch these other groups but do not quite belong to them; the earnest business people who are pillars of the churches and charities; the second rank of business people who live comfortably but have little traffic with these other groups; and so on through the whole vaguely defined spectrum—the pattern being sharply modified in each community by factors of national origin and of religious, professional, and business association. What was striking about the social pattern of 1900, as we look back upon it today, was that in most communities it was much clearer and simpler, the stratifications more generally recognized; and especially that they were generally taken much more seriously than they are today.

Visitors from England or France would explain to their countrymen that Society in the United States was not centered in any one metropolis such as London or Paris, but that each big city here had a Society of its own; yet that of New York was pre-eminent. When Ward McAllister, in 1892, made his famous remark to the effect that even if Mrs. Astor's ballroom held only four hundred people it was big enough, since there were only about four hundred people in Society, there was much scornful laughter; but there were also great numbers of people to whom McAllister seemed to be defining the limits of the most select and enviable company in the land.

A few years earlier, Henry Clews had written fulsomely about the attractions of Manhattan life, asserting that "New York . . . is really the great social center of the Republic. . . . Here is the glitter of peerless fashion, the ceaseless roll of splendid equipages, and the Bois de Boulogne of America, the Central Park." Clews had insisted that "it does not take much of this kind of life to make enthusiastic New Yorkers of the wives of Western millionaires, and then nothing remains but to purchase a brownstone mansion, and swing into the tide of fashion with receptions, balls, and kettle-drums, elegant equipages with coachmen in bright-buttoned livery, footmen in top boots, maid-servants and man-servants, including a butler and all the other adjuncts of life in a great metropolis." Clews's enthusiasm may have been comic, but he was describing a recognized phenomenon. While the socially established were striving to hold the ranks of Society intact against the inroads of the new rich, the new rich in their turn were striving even more furiously to gain recognition by irresistibly lavish but carefully correct entertaining; and there were uncounted women to whom an invitation to one of Mrs. Astor's massive dinners would have seemed a ticket of admission to paradise.

For sidelights on the drama of social climbing and social exclusion at the turn of the century there is no better source than the satirical drawings of Charles Dana Gibson. Here one will find, over and over again, the beautiful girl of socially secure but financially insecure family trying to decide between the bald-headed, aging millionaire and the handsome young man who is a penniless nobody; the ungainly little middle-aged man whose wife and daughters drag him to entertainments where they hope to meet the right people; the foreigner whose sole attraction is his title, but whom the millionaire's wife wants her daughter to marry; and the misery of the social climber to whose sumptuous party nobody will come. In one graphic picture Gibson shows a fat, coarse-looking woman sitting all alone at the edge of a great empty ballroom. The picture is captioned "Mrs. Steele Poole's Housewarming," in obvious reference to the combinations of steel manufacturing companies that were making new millionaires right and left as the nineteenth century closed. What is most impressive about these Gibson sketches as a social commentary is that hundreds of thousands of Gibson admirers were impressed with the significance of what he was satirizing. It is difficult to imagine *The New Yorker*, let us say, finding in our own time any such eager audience for a series of cartoons of the drama of social aspiration; not enough readers would care.

The same sort of drama was going on in other cities the country over: there was the same eagerness for admission to the gatherings of the socially elect, whether these were assemblies, cotillions, sewing circles, the gatherings of some local association, or a leading family's annual ball. It continues today, of course, in somewhat altered forms; the difference is that today comparatively few people take the drama seriously as involving social ranking, and that the whole phenomenon is complicated by the preferences of news photographers, gossip columnists, television audiences, and publicity-hungry restaurateurs and entertainers. In 1900 Society was Society indeed. It was scornful of public entertainers. It was scornful of the attentions of the press; indeed, there were fathers who told their sons that "a gentleman's name appeared in the papers only three times: when he was born, when he was married, and when he died." And it was confident that it represented what was most patrician, most brilliant, and most important in American life.

That is one of the explanations for the international marriages between American heiresses and foreign noblemen that were so frequent in those days. The first important one had taken place in the

eighteen-seventies between Jennie Jerome of New York and Lord
Randolph Churchill (it had produced one of the great men of a
future day, Winston Churchill). By the nineties they were becoming
epidemic. In *McCall's* magazine for November, 1903, there was a
list of fifty-seven of them to date, including the matches between
Miss Mary Leiter and Lord Curzon, Miss Anna Gould and Count
Boni de Castellane, and Miss Louise Corbin and the Earl of Oxford;
in that very month of November, 1903, Miss May Goelet married
the Duke of Roxburghe, and outside St. Thomas's Church on Fifth
Avenue great crowds gathered in the hope of getting a glimpse of
the Duke and his new Duchess.

For this spate of international marriages there were two reasons.
One of them was that to a Prince or Duke or Count it was very
agreeable to get both a charming girl and a lot of money. And sometimes there was nothing conjectural about the money. Read, for
example, these sentences from a contract signed November 6, 1895,
the day when Consuelo Vanderbilt married the Most Noble Charles
Richard John, Duke of Marlborough:

Whereas, a marriage is intended between the said Duke of Marlborough
and the said Consuelo Vanderbilt . . . the sum of two million five hundred
thousand dollars in fifty thousand shares of the Beech Creek Railway Company, on which an annual payment of four per cent is guaranteed by the
New York Central Railroad Company, is transferred this day to the trustees. And shall, during the joint lives of the said Duke of Marlborough,
Consuelo Vanderbilt, pay the income of the said sum of two million five
hundred thousand dollars, unto the Duke of Marlborough for his life, and
after the death of the said Duke of Marlborough, shall pay the income of
the said trust fund unto the said Consuelo Vanderbilt for life. . . .

Yet there was another reason for such alliances. The American
girl's parents felt that a noble wedding set upon them the authentic
stamp of aristocracy. What if the country was traditionally a democracy and its Constitution decreed that "no title of nobility shall be
granted by the United States"? There were, of course, wealthy and
socially impeccable Americans who took these traditions seriously
and regarded the collecting of ducal sons-in-law with amused con-
tempt; but there were others who felt that in truth the people of the

United States constituted a social pyramid, with Society at its apex, a peerage in all but name; and that if the families of this peerage intermarried with the lords of other lands, the alliances gave fitting recognition of their true patrician worth. Just as some Americans of wealth, for all their patriotism, felt that the best art and culture were European, so they recognized that the insignia of aristocracy, too, were European—and equally worth embracing. It was good to feel sure one belonged to the American nobility.

IV

Somewhat below these Himalayan heights of affluence there were hundreds of thousands of Americans who might have been classified as rich, prosperous, or well-to-do—ranging from the families of the less glitteringly successful manufacturers, merchants, and businessmen, and the top-of-the-heap professional men, down the income scale to the families of, let us say, minor business executives, shopkeepers, run-of-the-mill lawyers and doctors, and the better-paid professors and ministers. Naturally any group so inclusive and ill-defined as this represents at any time such a great diversity of occupations, incomes, and modes of life that to generalize about it is risky. What, one might ask, did a family with a 1900 income of $20,000 (equivalent to something like $60,000 net today, or $100,-000 before taxes) have in common with a family with a 1900 income of only $2,500 (equivalent to something like $8,500 today before taxes)? Or what did an ill-educated but canny speculator in street-railway stocks, who delightedly leaped into sudden wealth and bought the best trotting horse in town, but still was free with the toothpick, have in common with the members of old families who were trying to maintain a polite mode of life of which he had no inkling? Yet for all their variety, most of the members of this group—which we might very loosely identify as the upper middle class—did have one thing in common, as we look back at them today. Though many of them suffered intermittently from acute financial worry, their general position seems to people of similar status today to have been amply comfortable.

One reason for this becomes apparent the moment one begins to translate 1900 income into 1950 income. Assuming that the cost of living tripled in the interval, one figures at first that, let us say, the holder of a professorship which paid $3,000 a year in 1900 would have to receive $9,000 a year in 1950 to be as well off; but this calculation takes no account of income taxes: actually, the 1950 professor would have to receive $9,000 *after taxes,* or probably between $10,000 and $11,000 before taxes, to be as well heeled as his predecessor was. The chances are slim that the salary of his professorship has jumped at that rate. The same thing holds for a great many salaried jobs in businesses and other professions; and for the income from any but the most cannily chosen and carefully watched securities. By and large, salaried people and those living on inherited means or on savings have lost financial ground as a result of our progressive inflation.

A further advantage these people undoubtedly had over their comparably circumstanced grandchildren. They had more room to turn round in.

Because wages in the building trades—and the costs of building materials—were much lower than today, they could live in much larger quarters. Because servants' wages were much lower and candidates for servants' jobs were in abundance, they could staff these larger quarters amply. Furthermore they were spared many of the expenses which most of their descendants take as a matter of course: the cost of an automobile (much greater than that of a horse and carriage); the cost of such extra gadgets as electric refrigerators, washing machines, radios, television sets, or what not; the cost of a college education for children of both sexes; and very likely the cost of an extra home for week-end or summer use. (As we have seen, fewer reasonably well-to-do Americans had "summer places" then than now.) So the man whose salary now would command a rather cramped apartment might then have occupied a house which today would seem grandly large.

Wherever you may live today, you probably know some street which at the turn of the century was the abode of the prosperous and which has not been wholly rebuilt since then. As you walk along it, you may wonder how anybody with an income of less than princely size could have afforded to live in one of those big houses (most of which have probably been broken up into apartments within the past generation).

Take, for example, Commonwealth Avenue in Boston, from Arlington Street to Massachusetts Avenue, which in the main looks today very much as it did in 1900. Consider that although its residents in those days included many of the very rich, there could not have been enough very rich Bostonians to occupy all those hundreds of brick four-story-and-basement houses. Look at the hulking corner mansions, three windows or more wide on the Avenue side and five or six windows wide on the side street. Look at some of the extra-width houses in mid-block, with broad steps leading up to a front door flanked on either side by two amply-spaced windows. Or glance at the much more numerous houses of comparatively modest dimensions—a frontage on the Avenue of something like twenty-five feet, with only a single bay window beside the front door; even these lesser buildings have four stories above the basement, and must have contained some fifteen to twenty rooms, plus several bathrooms and many ample-sized closets and storage rooms. You may be sure that some of these houses were occupied in 1900 by families with incomes of well under ten thousand dollars a year—the equivalent of forty thousand or less before taxes today. That is a handsome income, but it won't command in the nineteen-fifties anything like so much space on the finest street of a big city. How did these families manage?

Here are some of the answers. They employed a cook at perhaps $5 a week, a waitress at $3.50 a week, a laundress at $3.50 a week; the waitress and laundress shared the upstairs work. They could add the once-a-week services of a cleaning woman to come in at $1.50 a day, and also the very part-time muscle of a choreman who served several other houses, and they would still be able to keep up the house (and get most of their laundry done at home, too) at a total annual cost of perhaps $800 a year—the equivalent of say $2,400 today. Some of the clothes for the women of the family were bought ready-made in the stores, or were made by professional dressmakers who had their own establishments, but the chances are that most of them were run up at home by dressmakers and seamstresses who came in at $3.50 to $1.50 a day. (One room would be set aside for this work; the floor would be covered with a sheet, which by the end of the day would be littered with pins and snippets of cloth; and here the dressmaker, with the aid of French fashion books and patterns, would improvise and fit the dresses.) Even when one added the cost of materials bought by the yard, clothes thus made were not expensive. This family probably owned no carriage, but got about on foot and by trolley—or, in bad weather or on festive occasions, by hired cab.

The head of the house would probably have been outraged if his daughter had even thought of taking a job: wasn't he able to support her? But on the other hand he saved money on her education. She would go to a private school, but in all probability not to college, though her brother would be sent to college as a matter of course, and perhaps would go to boarding school as well.

With these various savings such a family would be able to live a life of spacious and well-served comfort. And because the house was so large, they would accumulate more possessions—furniture, rugs, ornaments, pictures, books, china, silver, linen, and keepsakes of every sort—than their grandchildren would ever dream of burdening themselves with.

The pattern varied endlessly, of course, by communities and according to individual tastes. Even in a row of almost identical houses, the scale and manner of living were anything but standardized; in order to underline the contrast with present conditions, I have been describing the living scheme of the sort of people who preferred space and service to other comforts. Wages and prices tended to be lower in the smaller communities, and wages in particular were still lower in the South. Well-to-do families in the West were less likely to send their children to private schools than their counterparts in the East. But this was the general nature of life among the comfortably prosperous.

One should add, too, by way of a footnote, that such a way of living could be approximated by people who had much smaller incomes with which to gratify their genteel tastes. A college professor on a salary of $2,000 to $3,000, for example—roughly equivalent to $6,500 to $10,500 today before taxes—had to watch every penny and forego many satisfactions which he felt were the natural right of well-educated people, but he could afford a fair-sized house and at least one maid. In 1896, when Professor Woodrow Wilson of Princeton was trying to persuade Professor Frederick Jackson Turner to join the Princeton faculty, Mrs. Wilson set down a reasonable budget for a professor on a $3,500 salary. It included food and lights, $75 a month; rent, $42 a month; coal, $12 a month; water, $4 a month; and servants, $29 a month. This was for two servants, and was presumably figured at a rate of $3.50 a week per servant.

By dint of the most scrupulous economy it was even possible for a family with an income of only $1,500 (read perhaps $4,800 today) to play a part as a "member of society" in a town of 20,000 people, living in a modest two-story house on the best street in town, employing a full-time colored maid who came in for the day at $4 a week, entertaining graciously though modestly, and being invited to the most enviable functions of the local elite. Such a family could afford no travel at all; for us in the automobile age it is difficult to realize how circumscribed geographically was their life. But within limits they could follow, without great discomfort, the pattern of the prosperous.

Elderly people who look back today upon childhoods lived under any of the circumstances which I have just been describing sometimes regard them with nostalgia. Life seems to have been much simpler in its demands then, and certain of the amenities seem to have been much more accessible. It was easier then than now, these people feel, to maintain a sense of the identity of the family. People who live in ample houses are better able to take care of old or invalid or ineffective relatives than families with less space at their command. Indeed it is quite possible that part of the social security problem of our time—the widely expressed need for pensions, medical insurance,

unemployment insurance, etc.—arises out of the fact that many
families no longer can shelter those whom they used to consider their
dependents—grandma, who used to have a third-floor room, or
eccentric Cousin Tom, who was tucked away in the ell. (Part of the
problem today, of course, results from what inflation has done to
savings, and still more of it is a product of the revolution in social
concepts which this book is attempting to outline.) Even when one
makes every allowance for the many good things of today which the
prosperous of 1900 (and those who approximated their way of life)
had to go without, one must admit that there is a basis for the nostalgia. Space and service add up to a good deal.

Yet we must remember that the Commonwealth Avenue family's
ample life in their big house was made possible by the meager wages
of the maids who lived in narrow rooms at the very top of the house,
four flights above the level on which they did most of their interminable work; by the meager wages of dressmakers and seamstresses,
of the carpenters and masons who had built the house, of the workers
in factories and stores who produced and sold the goods they used;
and that the space and service which were at the disposal of even the
$1,500 family were likewise made possible by low wages. There is
another side of the shield to be looked at.

Let us travel clear to the other end of the economic and social
spectrum—by-passing on the way the majority of the Americans
of 1900—and take a glance at life as it was lived on the other side
of the tracks.

Chapter 3

The Other Side of the Tracks

IN THE early days of the factory system in England, David Ricardo enunciated the grim principle which he called the Iron Law of Wages; the principle that all wages tend to fall to the level which the most unskillful or most desperate man will accept. In pre-industrial times this law had not often operated unchecked. The prince, or the baron, or the squire, or the neighbors had tended to look after those who by reason of incompetence or illness or adversity were in want. And in the United States of pre-industrial days, men and women who were in cruel straits—whose crops had failed, or whose trade was dwindling, or whose family store had gone broke—had at least been able to go on working, for whatever pittance they could command, or could move on elsewhere to try again. But the coming of industrialism had brought a change, in America as well as in Europe.

For when a man built a mill or factory, around which there grew up a mill village or factory town, those who came to work for him were in great degree imprisoned by their choice. They did not own the tools with which they worked, and therefore were dependent upon what employment the mill offered; and anyhow there was not enough work in such a community for all who would be looking for it if the mill shut down. And if their wages were really low they could not afford to look elsewhere for jobs. So they ceased to be free agents. They were at their employer's mercy. The code of conduct of the day did not require him to feel any responsibility for what happened to them. And the Iron Law really went into action.

Likewise in a city slum into which there flowed a steady stream of newcomers from abroad—almost penniless people, ignorant, inexpert, often friendless, and unable to speak the language of the country—men and women were likewise imprisoned by circumstance. Theoretically there were all manner of occupations open to them; theoretically they were dependent upon no single employer. But in practice poverty, limited skills, and ignorance kept them—the great majority of them—where they were, year after year, to battle fiercely for chances to earn a living, and to accept whatever miserable wage was offered to them. Here too the Iron Law ruled.

Nowhere in the United States, in the middle years of the nineteenth century, had the Iron Law brought quite such abominations as it had produced in England, where the wages, hours of work, and sanitary conditions in the new industrial towns and the mining areas had been a stench in the nostrils of decency; but in all conscience they had been bad enough. For in the second quarter of the nineteenth century wages had fallen in the mill towns of New England until by 1850 whole families were laboring at the machines for three or four dollars a week per worker; a twelve-hour day was average, and a fourteen-hour day was not unusual; there were even children of what we would consider junior high school age who had to spend the hours from five o'clock in the morning till eight o'clock at night—with half an hour off for breakfast and half an hour for dinner—six days a week, in an ill-lighted, ill-ventilated factory, foregoing sunshine, recreation, education, and health itself to keep the family alive; and all this even if the employer was raking in high profits. It had been conditions such as these, appearing wherever the new industrial capitalism seemed to be making its most active forward progress, that had prompted Karl Marx to see if he could not invent a different system.

During the latter half of the nineteenth century, industrialism had advanced with mighty strides in the United States. A remarkable series of inventions and technological improvements had sparked its progress. By 1900 what had formerly been a land mostly of farmers and villagers had become a land increasingly of cities and roaring industrial towns; and comforts, conveniences, and wealth had so piled up that it almost seemed as if a whole new world had been invented for people to work and play in. But the wealth still tended to flow into a few people's pockets.

During most of this incredible half century, to be sure, the general standard of living in the United States had happily shown considerable improvement. Prosperity had tended to sift down through the ranks of society and to improve the conditions of life for the great majority of Americans. For instance, economists calculated that between 1860 and 1891, wages in twenty-two industries had increased on the average over 68 per cent, while wholesale prices had declined over 5 per cent. Those figures represented a real gain. But during the hideous depression of the mid-nineties wages had been widely slashed; and, although there had been some improvement in the lot of the workers afterward, as good times returned toward the turn of the century (an improvement, at least, in their chances of regular employment) there was no further gain in the trend of what the economists call "real wages," which is to say wages as measured against prices. What was happening to prevent the new wealth which the millionaires were so happily raking in, and from which millions of Americans in the middle economic ranks were directly or indirectly benefiting, from percolating all the way down to the lower levels of American society?

One thing that was happening was that the good American land was filling up. Traditionally, when the American workingman's position had become intolerable, he could always go west—if he could raise the cash to go. The West had been the land of new hope, not only for men of adventurous ambition, but also for the discards of industrialism. But now the frontier was closed, and though there were still chances for a man to arrive in the West with nothing and then to achieve comfort, these chances seemed to be dwindling. And a second thing that was happening was that the United States was continually importing a proletariat of such size, and such limited employability for the time being, that the labor market in the large cities and industrial towns was glutted and the wage level was held down.

Throughout most of the nineteenth century this proletariat had been coming across the Atlantic. For a time it had been mostly Irish: in the eighteen-forties and -fifties it had been the Irish who were the diggers of ditches, the builders of levees, the mill workers who labored twelve or thirteen or fourteen hours a day for a microscopic wage. Then, as the Irish began to better themselves, the Italians had begun to pour in. And then, increasingly, the Jews and Slavs of Eastern Europe. As each group arrived, it tended to form a proletarian level under the previous one. (Always at or near the bottom, in menial and ill-paid jobs, remained our Negro population, slaves no longer, but condemned nevertheless to a servitude of ignorance and exclusion from opportunity.)

Little by little, most of the members of these foreign groups caught the contagion of freedom and ambition in the American air and began to lift themselves out of poverty. But as they did so, their places on the lowest economic level were taken by still newer immigrants, lured from Europe by the glowing reports (sometimes fictitious) of relatives and fellow townsmen who had preceded them, or by the bright promises held out by industrial agents. So fast did they come that they filled up the slums of New York and Boston and Philadelphia and Chicago, and the factory towns of New England and Pennsylvania and Ohio, more rapidly than American opportunity could drain them off. During the single year 1900, the number of immigrants who arrived was 448,572; during 1901 it was 487,918; the figure kept on rising until in 1907 it reached a peak of 1,285,349. Here was irony indeed: so brightly did the Goddess of Liberty's lamp glow, with its promise of hope to the dispossessed of many lands, that the very numbers in which they answered its invitation tended to keep the wage level down, not only for these new arrivals but for native-born Americans as well, and delayed the modification of the Iron Law.

(Incidentally, a certain tendency among many Americans, then and later, to be arrogant or condescending toward Europeans may be partly due to the fact that for generations almost the only Europeans that the average native-born American saw were poor, ignorant, ill-dressed, and often dirty members of this imported proletariat, jabbering in incomprehensible tongues while they did menial jobs. They were scornfully known as Dagoes, Polacks, Hunkies, Kikes. As they bettered themselves, they became in most cases less Italian or Polish or Serbian or Czech or Russian, more American; and so the unfavorable image of Europeans in the American mind persisted.)

But, one may ask, what about those traditional foes of the Iron Law, the labor unions? The answer is that they were few and—except in a few favored crafts—weak; that they existed in peril of the law, which in general upheld the notion that what an employer chose to pay a man, and what that man chose to accept, were those two men's business and nobody else's; and that they were generally viewed by the rest of the public with fear and dislike.

In 1900 the total trade union membership came to 868,500; of these, the unions in the American Federation of Labor claimed 548,321. In a few successfully organized trades, such as the cigar makers', their pressures had pushed wages up. Robert A. Woods of the South End House in Boston, a scrupulously careful observer, reported in 1902 that unskilled laborers in Boston were making from $9 to $12 a week—when work was available; skilled labor artisans in general were making $13.50 to $19.50—again with "some lost time"; but cigar makers, by contrast, were making $15 to $25, with "little lost time." The head man of the AF of L was a cigar maker himself, Samuel Gompers, a thickset, strong-jawed, wide-mouthed man with unruly hair and rimless pince-nez glasses who took a strictly limited view of the aims which the unions under his influence should pursue. In his youth Gompers had learned German in order to read the works of Marx; but since then he had seen American unionism so often weakened by the impracticality of revolutionary theorists, and by the hatred that their imported revolutionary theories aroused among the public at large, that he stuck rigidly to the principles of craft—as opposed to industrial—unionism, opposed any attempt to put his unions into politics (as by forming a labor party), and bade them bargain only for improvements in wages, hours, and conditions of work.

But to cite the modest aims which Gompers pursued is to give an utterly misleading picture of unionism in general at the turn of the century. Most big industries were not unionized at all; and where unions did exist, or where attempts were made to organize the men, there were likely to be violent, headlong, and bloody conflicts, with ferocious battles between rebellious workmen on the one hand, and their implacable employers and the employers' scabs and perhaps the militia on the other hand.

In 1898, when the United Mine Workers won their first important strike, a group of them at Virden, Illinois, "armed with shotguns, revolvers, and rifles, vanquished a trainload of similarly accoutered strikebreakers and company guards, with great loss of life on both sides," according to Herbert Harris's history of *American Labor*; Mr. Harris adds aptly, "By means of superior marksmanship, the union was granted all its demands." That was the sort of spirit in which labor and capital were more than likely to be opposed.

Such was the temper of the times that when Oliver Wendell Holmes, in 1896, dissented from an antipicketing decision of the Massachusetts Supreme Court, he was convinced that his dissent had shut him off from all chances of future judicial promotion. The decision granted an injunction to a shopkeeper, named Vegelahn, to prevent two men from picketing outside his shop. There had been no suggestion of violence, no threat to physical property; nevertheless when Holmes suggested that the men were within their rights in thus advertising that they thought their employer was unfair, he was propounding what public opinion considered gross heresy.

Under such circumstances it is not remarkable that labor unions had, on the whole, only a minor influence in 1900. And anyhow they could not reach down to the very bottom ranks of labor to protect the men and women on whom poverty bore down most cruelly of all.

There were other reasons than the closing of the frontier, the flood of immigrants, and the weakness of organized labor for the fact that the Iron Law still held much of its old force; we shall come to these in due course. But it is time for us now to look at a few of the hard facts of life on the other side of the tracks at the turn of the century.

II

Here are a few cold figures:

1. WAGES. The *average* annual earnings of American workers, as I have already said, were something like $400 or $500 a year. For unskilled workers they were somewhat less—under $460 in the North, under $300 in the South. A standard wage for an unskilled man was a dollar and a half a day—when he could get work. That qualification is important: one must bear in mind that according to the census of 1900, nearly 6½ million workers were idle (and therefore, in most cases, quite without income) during some part of the year; that of these, nearly 2 million were idle four to six months out of the twelve.

In Boston, Robert A. Woods reported in 1902 that the average wage of shopgirls in the North and West Ends was from $5 to $6 a week. In the South, in 1900, nearly a third of the male employees over sixteen years of age in the cotton mills were getting less than $6 a week. Nor was this anywhere near the bottom of the scale. Investigating the condition of Italian workers in Chicago at about this time, the federal Bureau of Labor found one class of unskilled laborers who averaged as little as $4.37 a week. Woods reported further that in the garment shops of Boston, women were earning from $5 a week down to $3 a week, and added that "women sewing at home cannot earn more than 30 cents or 40 cents in a long day"; and he was echoed by Jacob A. Riis in New York, who reported in 1900 that he had seen women finishing "pants" for 30 cents a day. Try translating *that* into the terms of today: even after you have multiplied it by three to take account of the tripled cost of living, you arrive at the noble sum of 90 cents a day, which is $5.40 a week, which is $280.80 for a full working year!

2. HOURS. The average working day was in the neighborhood of 10 hours, 6 days a week: total, 60 a week. In business offices there was a growing trend toward a Saturday half holiday, but if anybody had suggested a five-day week he would have been considered de-

mented. At the time when the International Ladies' Garment Workers
Union was established in 1900, the hours in this trade, in New York,
were 70 a week.

3. CHILD LABOR. Among boys between the ages of ten and fifteen, no less than 26 per cent—over a quarter—were "gainfully employed"; among girls in the same age groups, 10 per cent were. Most
of these children were doing farm work, but 284,000 of them were in
mills, factories, etc., during years in which, in any satisfactorily arranged society, they would have been at school.

4. ACCIDENTS. The standards of safety were curiously low from
our present-day point of view. Consider this set of facts: in the single
year 1901, one out of every 399 railroad employees was killed, and
one out of every 26 was injured. Among engineers, conductors, brake-
men, trainmen, etc., the figures were even worse than this: in that
single year, one out of every 137 was killed.

The accident hazard could be particularly acute for children working in industrial plants. "In the large stamping works and canning
factories in a city like Chicago," Professor William O. Krohn had
told the National Conference of Charities and Correction in 1897,
"not a day passes but some child is made a helpless cripple. These
accidents occur after three o'clock in the afternoon. The child that has
begun his work in the morning with a reasonable degree of vigor,
after working under constant pressure for several hours, at about three
o'clock becomes so wearied, beyond the point of recovery, that he can
no longer direct the tired fingers and aching arms with any degree of
accuracy. He thus becomes the prey of the great cutting knives, or of
the jaws of the tin-stamping machine."

5. THE HUMAN RESULT. Robert Hunter's book, *Poverty,* published in 1904, was a conscientious attempt to define the extent and
nature of the group of people in America who were "underfed, under-
clothed, and poorly housed."* Hunter defined poverty very strictly,
as a condition in which people, "though using their best efforts, are

* Were these words of Hunter's in Franklin D. Roosevelt's mind in 1937, when
in his second inaugural address he said, "I see one-third of a nation ill-housed, ill-
clad, ill-nourished"?

failing to obtain sufficient necessaries for maintaining physical efficiency." His best guess, after studying all available statistics, was that there were at least 10 million of them in the United States, of whom 4 million were public paupers—people dependent upon public or private charity—while the rest gained no such relief from their pitiable state. Hunter admitted that his figure of 10 million might be far short of the truth; there might be 15 million, or 20 million. He was dismayed that a nation devoted to the use of statistics had not shown real interest in getting an answer to what seemed to him a vital question. *"But ought we not to know?"* he asked.

III

And what did those cold figures mean in human terms? To read the reports of qualified observers of poverty at its worst in the big city slums and the grim industrial towns at the beginning of the century is to hear variation after variation upon the theme of human misery, in which the same words occur monotonously again and again: wretchedness, overcrowding, filth, hunger, malnutrition, insecurity, want.

"It is impossible to describe the mud, the dirt, the filth, the stinking humidity, the nuisances, the disorder of the streets," wrote G. Giacosa, an Italian dramatist who visited his fellow countrymen's quarter in New York in 1898.

In March, 1899, the consulting architects of the City of Boston made a report on certain tenements they had found in the North and West Ends of the city. They had found, they said, "dirty and battered walls and ceilings, dark cellars with water standing in them, alleys littered with garbage and filth, broken and leaking drain-pipes, . . . dark and filthy water-closets, closets long frozen or otherwise out of order . . . and houses so dilapidated and so much settled that they are dangerous."

Even in far more hygienic quarters the overcrowding could be acute. M. E. Ravage, arriving as an immigrant from Rumania, became a tenant, at 50 cents a week, of Mrs. Segal's apartment on Rivington Street in New York's Lower East Side. During the day, he reported later in his book, *An American in the Making*, Mrs. Segal "kept up the interesting fiction of an apartment with specialized subdivisions"—a parlor, a dining room, a kitchen, a young ladies' room, Mrs. Segal's own room, a children's room. But at night, between nine and ten o'clock, the place "suddenly became a camp." Sofas opened up, carved dining-room chairs were arranged in rows; the sofa in the parlor alone held four sleepers, broadside, with rocking chairs arranged to support their feet. One night the parlor alone was occupied by nine men, some of them on the floor. "The pretended children's room was occupied by a man and his family of four." The windows had been puttied tight shut, and the air was "heavy with the reek of food and perspiration."

Far more filthy and insanitary habitations than this were equally overcrowded. A few years earlier, Paul Bourget had found in the Italian part of the Bowery two rooms on the street level, "small as a boat's cabins," in which eight men and women were "crouched over their work, in a fetid air, which an iron stove made still more stifling, and in what dirt!" And Bourget had gone on to inspect various workshops in the Jewish quarter, where he had found "hunger-hollowed faces" and "shoulders narrowed with consumption, girls of fifteen as old as grandmothers, who had never eaten a bit of meat in their lives—a long, lamentable succession of the forms of poverty."

In 1908 a Hungarian churchman, Count Vay de Vaya und Luskod, told in a book, *Nach Amerika in einem Auswandererschiffe,* how the life of the Hungarian immigrants in the steel town of McKeesport, Pennsylvania, had looked to him when he had visited the place a few years earlier.

Fourteen thousand tall chimneys are silhouetted against the sky along the valley that extends from McKeesport to Pittsburgh, [he wrote], and these fourteen thousand chimneys discharge their burning sparks and smoke incessantly. The realms of Vulcan could not be more somber or filthy than this valley of the Monongahela. . . . Thousands of immigrants wander here from year to year . . . and here they suffer till they are swallowed up in the inferno. . . . Scarce an hour passes without an accident, and no day without a fatal disaster. But what if *one* man be crippled, if *one* life be extinguished among so many! Each place can be filled from *ten* men, all eager for it. Newcomers camp out within sight of the factory gates, while a little farther away others arrive with almost daily regularity—thousands of immigrants to don the fetters of slavery.

A surplus of labor, a desperate willingness to take any job, under whatever conditions, just to fill the stomach: the theme occurs again and again in the reports of these observers. Here is Robert Hunter, writing not about the steel districts of Pennsylvania, but about Chicago:

On cold, rainy mornings, at the dusk of dawn, I have been awakened, two hours before my rising time, by the monotonous clatter of hobnailed boots on the plank sidewalks, as the procession to the factory passed under my window. Heavy, brooding men; tired, anxious women; thinly dressed, unkempt little girls, and frail, joyless lads passed along, half awake, not one uttering a word, as they hurried to the great factory. . . . Hundreds of others, obviously a hungrier, poorer lot . . . waited in front of a closed gate until finally a great red-bearded man came out and selected twenty-three of the strongest, best looking of the men. For these the gates were opened, and the others, with downcast eyes, marched off to seek employment elsewhere or to sit at home, or in a saloon, or in a lodging house. . . .

Still another note recurs frequently in these reports: the idea that these dregs of the industrial population, being foreign, were cut off from the rest of America by their foreignness.

A few years ago [wrote Hunter], when living in Chicago in a colony of Bohemians and Hungarians who had been thrown out of work by the closing of a great industry, I went about among the groups clustered in the streets or gathered in the halls. I felt the unrest, the denunciation, the growing brutality, but I was unable to discuss with them their grievances, to sympathize with them, or to oppose them. I was an utter stranger in my own city.

That there were alleviating aspects of these miserable scenes even these very chroniclers agreed. That even the hungriest people were better dressed than one might have expected struck almost all visitors from abroad. Ravage, fresh from Rumania, noted that almost nobody wore patched garments, and added that ". . . if you went merely by their dress, you could not tell a bank president from his office boy." He was echoing what Giacosa wrote after riding on a New York elevated train: "Some elegant Wall Street bankers are marked by special clothes of English cut. But with that exception, no European would be able to pick out by eye who there represents the infinite variety of professions, trades, states, fortune, culture, education, that may be encountered among the whole people." After visiting the Chicago slaughter houses—which he found inexpressibly filthy— Giacosa was struck by the dignified and well-dressed look of the workers when they emerged from their horrible labors at the end of the day; how very like Woods's comment on the people who lived in the South End of Boston: "Among the young men and women, the young women especially, it is surprising to find what becomingly dressed persons can come out of really miserable abodes."

Nor should we forget how many of the immigrants in these very slums found things new to them which delighted them. Ravage was pleasantly surprised by finding soap used for everyday purposes; egg-plant and tomatoes in winter; beer, in a pitcher from the corner sa-loon. Mary Antin, as a child newly arrived from Russia, was entranced with canned foods, iron stoves, washboards, speaking tubes, and street lamps—"so many lamps, and they burned till morning, my father said, and so people did not need to carry lanterns." Even more wonderful, to her and her parents, was free public education—"no application made, no questions asked, no fees." Her father "brought his children to school as if it were an act of consecration."

It was quite true, too, that little by little the worst horrors of the slums were being eliminated. Investigating commissions, tenement house commissions, and other groups of the more fortunate citizens had been aroused by such reports as that of Jacob A. Riis in his memorable book, *How the Other Half Lives,* published in 1890. Ten years later Riis was able to report that in New York the worst of the rear tenements were gone, the dreadful police-station lodging rooms were gone, "Bottle Alley is gone, and Bandit's Roost, Bone Alley, Thieves' Alley, and Kerosene Row—they are all gone." And it seemed to Riis that by 1900, on the East Side, rags and dirt had become the exception rather than the rule. A beginning had been made in the job of providing parks, playgrounds, and gymnasiums for the poorer parts of New York. Not only in New York but in other cities and states, legislation was nibbling away at the worst abominations of factory employment and of housing.

Yet, as the floods of immigration continued, and wages obeyed the Iron Law even though industry was booming, and dirty and dilapidated habitations acquired new layers of grime and sagged still further, those who made it their business to wrestle with the problem of American poverty often felt helpless to bring about any real improvement. "The real trouble," wrote Woods, "is that people here are from birth to death at the mercy of great social forces which move almost like the march of destiny." Did not what was happening make a mockery of the very idea of a democratic society? "We are witnessing today, beyond question, the decay—perhaps not permanent, but at any rate the decay—of republican institutions," said the sociologist Franklin H. Giddings to the members of the Nineteenth Century Club. "No man in his right mind can deny it."

And when Edwin Markham wrote his poem, "The Man with the Hoe," which appeared in 1899, even people whose contact with American poverty had been slight felt a vague sense that a portent had been described; that in these verses, written by Markham after seeing Millet's famous painting of a brutalized toiler, they were getting a picture of what industrialism was doing to the common man and might, perhaps, do to themselves some day if the social forces which they had seen in operation were not somehow reversed. Markham saw the toiler as a man with

> The emptiness of ages in his face,
> And on his back the burden of the world.

Markham asked:

> Who loosened and let down this brutal jaw?

And commented:

> There is no shape more terrible than this—
> More tongued with censure of the world's blind greed—
> More filled with signs and portents for the soul—
> More packed with danger to the universe.

And concluded:

> O Masters, lords and rulers in all lands,
> How will the future reckon with this man?
> How answer his brute question in that hour
> When whirlwinds of rebellion shake all shores?
> How will it be with kingdoms and with kings—
> With those who shaped him to the thing he is—
> When this dumb Terror shall rise to judge the world,
> After the silence of the centuries?*

From the vantage point of the nineteen-fifties one can read those prophetic lines and declare that they proved not to be prophetic for the United States. But surely it was significant that when the century was beginning a great many Americans were far from sure that the "dumb Terror," asking his "brute question," would not cause the "whirlwinds of rebellion" to shake, not only Europe, but also an America in which such gaudy wealth was contrasted with such inhuman misery.

* Reprinted by permission.

Chapter **4**

Capitalism Indeed

I N 1899 there died in New York a man who, though he had never made much of a study of economics and had a curiously immature mind, may have had a more pervasive influence on the thinking of American businessmen at the turn of the century than all the professors of economics put together. This man's name was Horatio Alger, Jr., and what he had done was to write more than a hundred books for boys—success stories called *Bound to Rise, Luck and Pluck, Sink or Swim, Tom the Bootblack,* and so forth—the total sales of which came to at least twenty million copies.

Horatio Alger was a creature of paradox. The unfailing theme of his books was the rise of earnest, hard-working boys from rags to riches; yet he himself did not begin life in rags and did not by any means achieve riches; during his later years he lived mostly in the Newsboys' Lodging House on one of New York's drearier streets. His paper-bound guides to success were, and are, generally regarded by educated readers as trash; they were literal, prosy, unreal, and un-subtle to a degree. Yet they were the delight of millions of American boys during the years between the Civil War and World War I, and it is possible that most of these boys got from Horatio Alger their first intelligible picture of American economic life.

The standard Horatio Alger hero was a fatherless boy of fifteen or thereabouts who had to earn his own way, usually in New York City.

He was beset by all manner of villains. They tried to sell him worth-less gold watches on railroad trains, or held him up as he was buggy-riding home with his employer's funds, or chloroformed him in a Philadelphia hotel room, or slugged him in a Chicago tenement. But always he was strong and shrewd and brave, and they were foolish and cowardly. And the end of each book found our hero well on the way toward wealth, which it was clear resulted from his diligence, honesty, perseverance, and thrift.

To the farmer's son, thumbing his copy of *Andy Grant's Pluck* by lamplight on the Illinois prairie, or to the country banker's son, scanning the *Brave and Bold* series in a Vermont village, the lesson of Horatio Alger seemed clear: business was a matter of trading among individuals and small groups of men, and if you worked hard and saved your money, you succeeded. The basic principles of economic conduct were the same as those laid down by Benjamin Franklin's Poor Richard:

"God helps them that help themselves."

"Early to bed, and early to rise,
Makes a man healthy, wealthy, and wise."

"If we are industrious we shall never starve, for, as Poor Richard says, *At the working man's house, Hunger looks in; but dares not enter.*"

"A fat Kitchen makes a lean Will."

And, to sum up: "In short, the way to wealth, if you desire it, is as plain as the way to market. It depends chiefly on two words, *industry* and *frugality.*"

There was no denying that the Alger thesis had a certain magnificent validity. Look at John D. Rockefeller, who had begun as a $4-a-week clerk in a commission merchant's house in Cleveland, and by the beginning of the twentieth century was becoming the richest man in the world. Look at Andrew Carnegie, who had begun at thirteen as a $1.20-a-week bobbin boy in a Pittsburgh cotton mill, and had become the greatest of steel manufacturers. Look at Edward H. Harriman, who had begun as a broker's office boy at $5 a week, and was building a railroad empire. And as for thrift, look at the great banker, George Fisher Baker, who not only had begun his career as a clerk, but during his early married life had imposed upon himself and his wife the discipline of living on half their income and saving the other half. These were only a few of the examples which proved the formula for success: begin with nothing, apply yourself, save your pennies, trade shrewdly, and you will be rewarded with wealth, power, and acclaim. To which the natural corollary was: poor people are poor because they are the victims of their own laziness, stupidity, or profligacy.

Naturally it was pleasant for succesful businessmen to believe that these were, in fact, the first principles of economics. But, one might ask, hadn't they learned in the classroom that economics is just a little more complex than that?

To this question there are two answers. The first is that mighty few of the tycoons of 1900 had ever studied economics. Take, for instance, eight of the most successful of all: John D. Rockefeller, Carnegie, Harriman, and Baker, whom we have just mentioned; and also J. Pierpont Morgan, William Rockefeller, James Stillman, and H. H. Rogers. Of these eight, only Morgan had had anything approaching what we today would call a college education; he had spent two years at the University of Göttingen in Germany, where he had pretty certainly not studied anything that we would now classify as economics. And it is doubtful if even in the prime of life many of these men, or of their innumerable rivals and imitators, had much truck with economic science, or thought of professors of economics as anything but absurdly impractical theorists. A man who had come up in the world liked to describe himself as a graduate of the School of Hard Knocks. Education was all right in its way, and you sent your son to college if you could, if only because it was a good place to make useful contacts with the right people; but these college professors knew nothing about business, which was a battlefield for hard-shelled fighters. And anyhow the principles laid down by Ben Franklin, and somewhat foolishly simplified for boys by Horatio Alger, were fundamentally sound.

At the turn of the century there were, however, several hundred thousand Americans who *had* gone to college. Of these, a somewhat smaller number had gone to institutions so up-to-date as to include economics in the curriculum. And a still smaller number had actually studied the subject. What had they been taught about economic life?

Despite the efforts of men like Richard T. Ely, Charles S. Walker, Simon N. Patten, and John Bates Clark, during the last quarter of the nineteenth century, to modernize the science of economics and bring it into accord with the changing actualities of a new financial and industrial era, most of these college graduates had been indoctrinated with the theories of "classical" economics. These theories were supposed to explain how individual men, or groups of men, behaved when they bought and sold goods. The classical economists had been bemused with the notion that just as the physicists could expound the laws of nature which accounted for the behavior of inanimate matter, so they themselves ought to be able to expound the laws of economics which accounted for the behavior of economic man in the market place: such as the law of supply and demand, the law of diminishing returns, and the law that bad money drives out good. They assumed, for their theoretical purposes, that any man, when he did business in the market place, was animated exclusively by motives of pecuniary self-interest—in other words, by the selfish love of gain. They assumed that, under normal circumstances, men thus motivated would tend in their buying and selling to produce an equilibrium of supply and demand, thereby automatically determining how much labor would earn, how much management would earn, and what would be the return on invested capital. They might admit, when pressed, that man was in actual fact animated by a variety of motives, such as the desire to be in the swim, the desire to do the decent thing, the desire to look successfully lavish. They might also admit that the normal operations of the market place were being constantly abnormalized by the efforts of pools, trusts, and holding-company combinations to enforce monopolies; that battles between rival interests for the stock-market control of this property or that had violent indirect effects on the course of other businesses; that tariffs, and factory laws, and labor conflicts altered or interrupted the orderly workings of economic law. But such phenomena as these, they felt, were "abnormal":

it was better to focus one's attention upon the normal course of the supposedly self-regulating markets. (It was somewhat as if meteorologists should find it more logical to concentrate upon the behavior of fair weather than upon the behavior of storms.) Furthermore, such present-day concepts as those of the national economy, the national income, the national gross product, and the interdependent functioning of economic groups, had not yet entered their thinking; the principles they propounded dealt with the behavior of individual, independent units of mankind.

Fascinated by the laws they had discovered, these classical economists tended to feel that anything which upset these laws was bad. In short, they taught the economics of laissez faire. Everything worked best when you let it alone. Even the gentlest and most amiable of men, for instance, would proclaim that "legislative interference with wages and hours" was "an abomination."

Nobody expounded the folly of tampering with the laws of economics more eloquently than Yale's great teacher of political economy, the dynamic William Graham Sumner. In his book *What Social Classes Owe to Each Other,* published in 1883, he had put the reformers to rout. "The yearning after equality," he had written, "is the offspring of envy and covetousness, and there is no possible plan for satisfying that yearning which can do aught else than rob A to give to B; consequently all such plans nourish some of the meanest vices of human nature, waste capital, and overthrow civilization."

This emphatically did not mean that Sumner was opposed to a better life for everybody. On the contrary, as a man of high and generous principle—he had begun his working life as a clergyman—he was heartily in favor of it. But he believed in the wider extension of opportunity, not in changing the rules under which business was conducted. He argued that

instead of endeavoring to redistribute the acquisitions which have been made between the existing classes, our aim should be to *increase, multiply, and extend the chances.* Such is the work of civilization. Every old error or abuse which is removed opens new chances for development to all the new energy of society. Every improvement in education, science, art or government expands the chances of man on earth. Such expansion is no guarantee of equality. On the contrary, if there be liberty, some will profit by the chances eagerly and some will neglect them altogether. Therefore, the greater the chances, the more unequal will be the fortune of these two sets of men. So it ought to be, in all justice and right reason.

Sumner would not have argued that there were not some ways in which legislation could protect the economically helpless. But he thought that most reform legislation was conceived in ignorance and drafted in folly. "You need not think it necessary," he would tell his Yale classes, "to have Washington exercise a political providence over the country. God has done that a good deal better by the laws of political economy."

Sumner was in dead earnest, just as John D. Rockefeller was when he said, "God gave me my money." The laws of economics were benign. All you needed to do was to let them work unhindered. If they seemed to shower benefits upon one man while others scrabbled for crumbs outside the back door of the restaurant, that was part of God's design.

The irony of the situation lay in the fact that for generations men had been tinkering with economic law to their own advantage, and in the process had produced institutions which were emphatically not God's work—as most of Sumner's hearers presumably supposed them to be—but man's. The corporation, for instance, was not an invention of God's. It was an invention of man's. It was a creature of the state: its privileges, its limitations, were defined by legislation. As put to work for the furtherance of industry and business in general, the corporation was one of the great inventions of the nineteenth century: an instrument of incalculable value. Yet, by taking adroit advantage of the legislative acts which defined its privileges, one could play extraordinary tricks with it. Corporate devices could be used to permit A to rob B—or, let us say, more charitably, to permit A to drain off all the gravy in sight and leave none for B. And it was a little foolish to defend such devices on the ground that one must let economic nature take its course.

It was largely as a result of the discovery of tricks that could be played with corporations, and particularly with their capital stock, that the wealth produced in such a tremendous spate at the turn of the century flowed in large proportion into a few well-placed hands. While the eyes of boys in Economics A were fastened upon the benignity of the law of supply and demand, the eyes of corporation lawyers and their clients were fastened upon the benignity of the New Jersey Holding-company Act. Most of these gentlemen would have regarded an income tax, let us say, as a flat transgression by man of economic law. But few of them regarded the Holding-company Act in any such light, even though it made the theoretical rewards of capital, as defined by the classical economists, look trifling.

I once amused myself by studying a number of Horatio Alger's stories to see how the young hero ultimately became rich. Clearly, his initial steps up the ladder of success were the direct fruits of his own industrious labor. These might lift him from five dollars a week to ten dollars a week. But that was not quite wealth. And I noticed that at the end of the book he had a way of getting his hands on capital.

Sometimes this capital was inherited: the supposed orphan, ragged though he was, proved to be the son of a man whose mining stock, previously considered worthless, was good for $100,000. Sometimes the capital was a gift: the boy's pluck made such a good impression upon rich Mr. Vanderpool that the old fellow made over to him the $50,000 that the boy had helped him to save from the robbers. Or the boy befriended an invalid gentleman in a Tacoma hotel, and out of gratitude this gentleman gave him a part interest in some house lots which promptly soared in value. The method varied; but when the time came for our hero to get into the money, it was a transaction in capital which won the day for him.

Manifestly the lesson of these books was not supposed to be that hard work brings in but a pittance and that the way to succeed is to stand in with the rich. The lesson was rather that capital comes as a reward from heaven to him who labors mightily, puts his pennies in the savings bank, and shuns the fleshpots. Work, save, be a good boy, and presently the railroad stock will fall into your lap and all will be well.

Perhaps the Horatio Alger stories help to explain to us why it was that a generation of businessmen who sincerely believed that wealth was the fruit of virtue and poverty the fruit of indolence, and that one should not tinker with economic law, were simultaneously shaping economic and social institutions which often seemed to follow quite different—and much more dynamic—principles. Let us look at some of these institutions.

II

In 1900 capitalism was capitalism indeed. Businesses were run by their owners, the people who had put up or had acquired the capital with which to finance them. There was very little of what Paul Hoffman has called the "diffusion of decision-making power." It would have seemed wildly irrational that a man should manage the destinies of a corporation while owning only a minute fraction of its stock, as so frequently happens today. Only two-thirds of the manufactured products of the country were made by corporations; the other third were made by partnerships or individual proprietors. No corporation in the country had over 60,000 stockholders; American Telephone and Telegraph, which by 1951 could boast a million of them, had in 1900 only 7,535. The Pennsylvania Railroad had 51,543; the Union Pacific, 14,256; United States Steel, shortly after its formation in 1901, had 54,016. These, it must be understood, were among the big stock-market favorites of the day; in most concerns, ownership was concentrated in far fewer hands. Witness, for example, Carnegie's personal holding of 58½ per cent of the stock of his huge Carnegie Steel Company.

The head of a company was likely to be a man who had started with an idea and some money to finance it—either his own money or his friends'; or else, if the concern were older, he might be the inheritor or purchaser of most of its capital stock. If the company were a large one whose shares were listed on the Stock Exchange, he might have bought a controlling interest in the course of stock-market trading. In any case he was likely to have a sense of personal proprietorship which few heads of businesses possess today, except in small or young concerns. And his freedom to do as he personally pleased with this working property of his was only slightly restricted either by law or by custom. The very idea of a "managerial revolution" would have been unintelligible to him. The business belonged to him, didn't it?

In many cases he felt that how he ran it was nobody else's affair. Some companies made ample reports to their minority stockholders, but others made scanty ones, and some made none at all. During the years between 1897 and 1905 the Westinghouse Company apparently held no annual meeting of stockholders. The United States Express Company held no meetings and made no report, year after year. The American Sugar Refining Company—a big concern with over 10,000 stockholders—reported nothing at all to them; all one could find out about its operations was contained in a balance sheet filed with the Secretary of State of Massachusetts in order that it might hold its corporate license to do business—and this balance sheet consisted merely of four generalized items of assets and three of liabilities. When John D. Archbold, who had succeeded John D. Rockefeller as active head of the great Standard Oil Company, got hold of an advance copy of a governmental report advocating more publicity about corporate affairs, he commented to Senator Boies Penrose: "Private corporations should not be required to make public items of receipts and expenditures, profits and losses. A statement of assets and liabilities is all that can benefit the public. Items of receipts and expenditures, profits and losses can only benefit the competitors."

If even minority stockholders had no business to know what was going on, still less did the government or the courts. The records of governmental investigations and of court trials during the last years of the nineteenth century are full of instances of men saying over and over again on the witness stand, as William Rockefeller did in a railroad rate case, "I decline to answer on advice of counsel." In this particular case the lawyer who was questioning him pursued the matter, and the following colloquy took place:

"On the ground that the answer will incriminate you?"

"I decline to answer on advice of counsel."

"Or is it that the answer will subject you to some forfeiture?"

"I decline to answer on the advice of counsel."

"Do you decline on the ground that the answer will disgrace you?"

"I decline to answer on the advice of counsel."

"Did your counsel tell you to stick to that one answer?"

"I decline to answer on the advice of counsel."

There was a general laugh, in which Rockefeller himself joined. But he was not simply amusing himself. Nor was he necessarily covering up anything specifically wrong. He was preventing people from sticking their heads into what was not their business, but private business; and this should be secret.

There had long been professional stock-market operators who had bought and sold the control of businesses—of railroads especially— almost as if they were counters in a game. These operators might be quite innocent of any concern about the company's actual operations, and might interest themselves only in making a profit in buying and selling it. The greatest railroad enterpriser of the early years of the twentieth century, E. H. Harriman, had begun his career as a stockbroker, and had first got into railroading when he bought a controlling interest in the shares of a weak railroad with the idea of renovating the property and selling it at a profit to either the Pennsylvania or the New York Central—which he did a few years later. That was one way of operating; there were others of a less laudable nature. One favorite one, of which the most formidable practitioner had been Jay Gould, was to buy control of a company, then cause it to make contracts which sucked money out of its treasury into some other concern to which one had personal access; and then, after thus squeezing the juice out of it, to sell out, leaving the company a financial wreck. During the latter half of the nineteenth century many slick traders had bought, used, and thrown away railroad properties almost as casually as if they were paper cups.

If one got proper legal advice, or could bribe a judge to decide in one's favor, one could do this sort of thing time after time without running afoul of the law, and without incurring much public disfavor except among the people whose lives and fortunes had been directly brought to ruin by one's action. The attitude among other citizens was likely to be, "Well, I don't think I'd do a thing like that if I were in his place, but after all you've got to admit that he's smart."

Prominent among those who played games with capital were the stock-market speculators and manipulators—men to whom a company was not the people who managed and worked for it, or its buildings and machines, or the products which these turned out, but merely the securities which represented its ownership, and the succession of figures on the stock-market ticker which reflected the going value of these securities. Listen to Henry Clews's account of how the "Standard Oil crowd," a group of speculators headed by Archbold and Rogers of the Standard Oil Company, so cannily bought and sold the shares of other concerns—which often had nothing at all to do with the oil business—that they could manipulate prices at will. Clews was no muckracker, but a stalwart defender of Wall Street and its ways. But even he was awed by the speculative success of these men:

With them, [wrote Clews a few years after the twentieth century opened] manipulation has ceased to be speculation. Their resources are so vast that they need only to concentrate upon any given property in order to do with it what they please. . . . They are the greatest operators the world has ever seen, and the beauty of their method is the quietness and lack of ostentation with which they carry it on. There are no gallery plays, there are no scare heads in the newspapers, there is no wild scramble or excitement. With them the process is gradual, thorough, and steady, with never a waver or break. How much money this group of men have made it is impossible even to estimate. That it is a sum beside which the gain of the most daring speculator of the past was a mere bagatelle is putting the case mildly. And there is an utter absence of chance that is terrible to contemplate.

Sometimes the efforts of two competing groups of men to get control of a given property by means of buying on the Stock Exchange had convulsive effects. In the spring of 1901, for instance, the Morgan forces and the Harriman forces were both trying to acquire the

Burlington Railroad—Morgan, in order to supplement the Northern Pacific system, which his group controlled; Harriman, in order to supplement his Union Pacific system. Harriman conceived the bold idea of accomplishing this end by buying the control of the Northern Pacific itself out of his unwary rivals' hands. He bought Northern Pacific stock quietly and rapidly. The Morgan forces, taking belated alarm, in turn bought furiously. Numerous Wall Street speculators, seeing what looked to them like an unwarranted rise in the price of Northern Pacific stock, sold short (that is, sold Northern Pacific stock which they didn't own, in the hopes of buying it later at a lower price for subsequent delivery). The result was that the Morgan and Harriman forces, between them, bought more stock than existed. The price of Northern Pacific on the ticker leaped to 1,000; there was a panic as the frantic short sellers sold everything they possessed in order to save themselves.

To us today such a cause for panic would be inconceivable; the operations of the stock market are so hedged about with restrictions that nothing of the sort could happen. But in 1901 the buyers and sellers of capital could do almost as they pleased with it, no matter how much damage a collision between them might bring about.

Most businessmen believed in competition—theoretically. But in practice there was a ceaseless search for ways in which to prevent it, so that rival companies in an industry might all jack up their prices and enlarge their profits. Again and again the heads of various steel companies, let us say, would form a "pool"—make an agreement not to sell below a certain price. But often—as one industrialist put it—such agreements lasted only as long as it took the quickest man in the group to get to a telegraph office and quote a lower price in order to grab business from the others. So the search went on for a way of making agreements that would stick.

In 1879 John D. Rockefeller's lawyer, Samuel C. T. Dodd, found one. He got the owners of forty different oil companies to put their stock into the hands of a group of trustees (headed by Rockefeller), who could then operate all forty companies as a unit, charging what they pleased and forcing their competitors to the wall; hence the term "trust." During the eighteen-eighties there appeared a sugar trust, a butcher trust, a rubber trust, and many others. But so ferocious was the outcry of protest from rival businessmen against the trusts—and from the gouged public too—that the legislators went to work to outlaw such practices, the most famous of their legislative products being the Sherman Antitrust Act of 1890.

Yet even this obstacle to the consolidation of competing businesses did no more than delay the trend temporarily. For a Supreme Court sympathetic with big business interpreted the Act very narrowly for many years. And anyhow, meanwhile another lawyer had made another corporate invention.

In 1889 the Governor of New Jersey had asked a lawyer named James B. Dill to suggest a way of fattening the state's treasury. Dill had suggested that a neat way to do this would be to pass a New Jersey law permitting companies incorporated in New Jersey to buy and hold the stock of other corporations—something which up to that time had generally been held illegal. The New Jersey legislature acted; there was a rush to incorporate companies in New Jersey; the state accordingly made a lot of money out of incorporation fees. And before long a new era of American capitalism began.

For now a group of competing companies no longer needed to form a trust in order to combine themselves into a giant concern which would command the market and choke off competition. They could organize a new corporation, a holding company which would buy the stock of their various companies—or, more strictly, exchange its shares for theirs—and this holding company would thereupon control the operations of all of them.

During the last years of the nineteenth century there was a furious epidemic of holding-company incorporations, and it raged most spectacularly in the steel industry. The manufacturers of wire got together to form the American Steel & Wire Company. Another group of producers got together to form the American Tube Company; another, to form the American Tin Plate Company, and so on. At last, in the winter of 1900-1901, the combinations in turn combined. A new super-holding company was organized which exchanged its shares for those of these new consolidated concerns—and even bought, too, the control of Andrew Carnegie's hitherto independent steel company, and also some Rockefeller iron mines—thus bringing into one vast unit about three-fifths of the steel production of the entire country. This new giant was called the United States Steel Corporation. It was breathtakingly huge—the biggest business unit that the world had ever seen.

The rush to form such holding-company combinations, not only in the steel industry but elsewhere too, was enormously accelerated by the fact that you could make big money out of them, and quickly. For it was discovered that the public could be encouraged to buy the shares of the combinations at prices far exceeding the total prices of the shares of the individual component companies. Each time there was a combination, the value of shares leaped. A man who had held the controlling interest in a small steel company—perhaps a struggling one—suddenly found himself the owner of a valuable block of shares of, let us say, American Tin Plate; and then, only a couple of years later, of a far more valuable block of shares of United States Steel. Millions of dollars appeared as if from nowhere and fell into his hands. No wonder that Pittsburgh was full of new millionaires; that the city became, as Herbert N. Casson put it, "a Klondike for artists, book agents, curio dealers, and merchants who had expensive gewgaws for sale"; and that one of the beneficiaries of the consolidation boom "ordered a special brand of half-dollar cigars made in Cuba, each with his name and coat of arms on the wrapper." The bankers and promoters who launched the new issues of stock of these great combinations profited even more hugely. The total profit of the syndicate which put United States Steel on the market came to about $60,000,000, of which the share of J. P. Morgan & Company, which managed the great transaction, came to at least $12,000,000.

One could argue that the inflated value put upon the stock of these new monsters of industry was quite unjustified; that what these huge profits represented was a capitalization of the hoped-for earning capacity of the new companies for a decade or even a generation to come. One could argue that the basic aim of such consolidations was simply monopoly, and in some cases the result certainly was monopoly, though not in all. But another idea was working too; the idea of integration, of making a single efficient unit out of a multiplicity of fragments. Although the public outcry against what people still called "the trusts" continued, and although now there was a rising note of fear in it—the fear that big business would gain such a stranglehold on the country that the small enterpriser would be stifled—nevertheless there was a magnificence about these new giants of industry that provoked admiration along with fear. For by integrating operations and cutting costs, the new consolidated companies opened the way to economical mass production. In the process of playing highly remunerative games with the tokens that represented capital, the bankers and the steel men had introduced into America something new: twentieth-century industry, undisciplined still, but full of promise.

III

Two more things remain to be noted about the giant corporations. One is that in their formation, individual men of wealth, as against institutions, played a part far bigger than would be expected today. For instance, the syndicate which launched the issue of Steel Corporation stock in the spring of 1901 included approximately three hundred participants. Of the twenty-six leading ones, only four were institutions (J. P. Morgan & Co., the First National Bank of New York, the New York Security & Trust Co., and Kidder, Peabody & Co. of Boston); the remaining twenty-two were individuals. The four leading members were all individuals: the two Moore brothers, William H. and James H.; William B. Leeds; and Daniel G. Reid. American business was not as institutionalized as it is today; the rich man counted for more, the rich institution for less.

The other thing to be noted is the sort of men these combinations brought to the top. Take this new Steel Corporation, for instance. Andrew Carnegie, who had been first and foremost a steel manufacturer, was out of it. The dominant figure in it was not a steel manufacturer, but a banker—J. Pierpont Morgan. And his right-hand man was not a steel manufacturer primarily, but a corporation lawyer —Judge Elbert H. Gary.

I have said that in that age of unbridled capitalism, a company was run by the man who owned it, and he tended to be its personal proprietor. But unless he was overwhelmingly successful, and also astute enough to plow his profits back into the property—as Henry Ford did some years later—there was one group of men of whom he stood in awe: the bankers. They commanded the credit he might need to tide him over lean seasons; and if he had to reorganize his company or to sell bonds or stock to investors, they had the power and prestige in the financial world to provide—or deny—a market for his securities. To command capital was even more important than to own capital.

There was also, during the epidemic of holding-company consolidation, another species of businessman who shot into new prominence: the promoter. This man was a sort of marriage broker for corporations. He might know little about steel, for instance, but be able to bring steel companies together. He knew how to coax and threaten their owners into combining, and he knew what were the successive steps that had to be taken to get the new holding company set up. There was also the corporation lawyer, who knew the necessary legal devices. ("What looks like a stone wall to a layman," said Finley Peter Dunne's Mr. Dooley, "is a triumphal arch to a corporation lawyer.") Morgan was both a promoter and a banker; Gary was both a promoter and a corporation lawyer. The banker and his lawyer aide were becoming the presiding geniuses of big business.

Indeed as the twentieth century began Pierpont Morgan was becoming by all odds the most powerful figure in the American world of business, if not the most powerful citizen of the United States. He controlled, or at least was highly influential in, the corporations that ran a number of the most important railroads of the land; not because he was a railroad man, for he was not, but because he was a master of the art of financial reorganization, and when big railroads got into financial trouble, as many of them did during the depression of the eighteen-nineties, he was the man who could best put them on their feet again—partly by reason of the wealth that his firm directly commanded, partly by reason of his great prestige and moral force in Wall Street, and partly by reason of his reputation for insisting upon proper management of any property for which he had raised money. When Morgan reorganized a railroad company he either called the tune from then on, or else listened to the tune and intervened if he didn't like the sound of it. He was also a power among bankers; gradually he and his partners were becoming major factors in the policies of many of the leading banking houses of New York. And now, in 1901, he had become the kingpin of the great steel industry, and was looking about for more worlds to supervise. His authority was vague, but it was immense—and growing.

This gruff, thundering, awe-inspiring man with the hideous red nose and the piercing eyes—this banker, promoter, churchman, art collector, yachtsman, and philanthropist—this inwardly shy, deeply religious, narrowly patrician, and boldly enterprising gentleman was no believer in competition. Morgan seemed to feel that the business machinery of America should be honestly and decently managed by a few of the best people, people like his friends and associates. He liked combination, order, the efficiency of big business units; and he liked them to operate in a large, bold, forward-looking way. He disapproved of the speculative gangs who plunged in and out of the market, heedless of the properties they were toying with, as did the Standard Oil crowd. When he put his resources behind a company, he expected to stay with it; this, he felt, was how a gentleman behaved. His integrity was solid as a rock, and he said, "A man I do not trust could not get money from me on all the bonds in Christendom." That Morgan was a mighty force for decent finance is unquestionable. But so also is the fact that he was a mighty force working toward the concentration into a few hands of authority over more and more of American business.

When in the spring of 1901 the news broke that he had formed the Steel Corporation, there was a note of dismay in the comment even of conservative citizens. President Hadley of Yale said in a speech that unless some way could be found to regulate such trusts, there would be "an emperor in Washington within twenty-five years." John Brisben Walker, editor of the *Cosmopolitan Magazine,* which was then a journal of public affairs, wrote that between the lines of the Steel Corporation announcement could be read these words: "The old competitive system, with its ruinous methods, its countless duplications, its wastefulness of human effort, and its relentless business warfare, is hereby abolished." Others feared that if the trend toward consolidation continued, the public would rebel and embrace socialism. Said the Boston *Herald* editorially, "If a limited financial group shall come to represent the capitalistic end of industry, the perils of socialism, even if brought about by a somewhat rude, because forcible, taking of the instruments of industry, may be looked upon even by intelligent people as possibly the lesser of two evils." The Philadelphia *Evening Telegraph* likewise feared the eventual coming of "one of the greatest social and political upheavals that has been witnessed in modern history."

What irony that the revolution which these observers feared should indeed have taken place—but not in the United States! It has often been noted that when the orators of Moscow berate American capitalism and turn their invective upon Wall Street, they are a couple of generations out of date; one might say, more specifically, that a typical Communist propagandist of the nineteen-fifties sounds exactly as if he were reacting angrily to the news in the morning papers of March 3, 1901.

On that date there were true grounds for uneasiness. To a generation whose economic thinking had been running in the grooves fixed by Benjamin Franklin and Horatio Alger and the classical economists, it was disquieting enough to see the masters of capital using new instruments and devices to set at naught the traditional economics of man-to-man bargaining. It was more unsettling still to see them apparently moving, in what had been a political democracy, toward the mastery of America.

Chapter 5

Government on the Sidelines

AND what, one may ask, was the United States government doing while these portentous events were afoot?

It is hard for us, today, to realize how small the government was in 1900, and how limited in its functions and powers. It spent roughly half a billion dollars a year, about one-eightieth of what it was destined to spend half a century later (even before the Korean war stepped up the budget). In fact, the federal government in 1900 spent considerably less money than New York State did in 1950. The national debt amounted to only a little over a billion and a quarter dollars—about one two-hundredth of the 1950 debt of 257 billions. Even when one makes allowance for the diminished value of the dollar and for the way in which federal expenses and particularly the federal debt have been swollen since 1900 by wars and defense expenditures, those are incredibly small figures by today's standards.

The government had no Department of Commerce, no Department of Labor, no Federal Trade Commission, no Federal Reserve System. The reason was simple: business was supposed to be no affair of the government's. It had an Interstate Commerce Commission, which was supposed to regulate the railroad companies, but the powers of the Commission were small and uncertain. Even the Sherman Antitrust Act had been whittled down by Supreme Court decisions into a feeble instrument for the maintenance of competition in business; and during the year 1900 the Attorney General brought not one single suit under that law.

As for the White House, we have it on the authority of "Ike" Hoover, who was long the Chief Usher, that when he began work there in the early nineties "the whole Executive office staff, which was then domiciled in the White House proper, consisted of but ten people, and four of these were doorkeepers and messengers." There could not have been many more in 1900. What a contrast to 1950, when the employees of the White House office numbered 295, and those who worked for what was technically known as the "Executive Office of the President"—including not only the White House office but the Bureau of the Budget, the Council of Economic Advisers, the National Security Council, the National Security Resources Board, and so forth—totaled no less than 1,335, and occupied most of the architecturally profuse building which in McKinley's time had comfortably housed the State, War, and Navy Departments!

Two or three examples may illustrate how incidental was the role of the government in business affairs. In 1895 its gold reserve was slipping away and it desperately needed a loan of money to enable it to buy more gold with which to buttress its endangered currency. It turned, in this emergency, to the strongest private banker in the country, who was of course Pierpont Morgan; only he had the financial prestige to assure the bankers and the men of means that they might safely lend to the government. Washington without Wall Street's aid was helpless.

Twelve years later, in 1907, there was a bank panic which centered in New York. A series of conspicuous bank failures had undermined public confidence, depositors were drawing out their money right and left, and once again strong measures were needed to restore confidence and order. Again it was Pierpont Morgan who came to the rescue, bringing the bank presidents together in meeting after meeting, and through the sheer strength of his reputation and the force of his will bulldozing them into making loans which tided the weakened banks through the crisis. During that emergency the President of the United States was powerless to do anything. The Secretary of the Treasury was hardly more than one of Morgan's minor aides. There were no Federal Reserve funds to be drawn upon, nor any other federal machinery adequate to help. In effect the strong man of Wall Street served as the organizer of a private, voluntary, national reserve system.

Or take the action of President Theodore Roosevelt in ending the anthracite coal strike of 1902 by mediating between the coal operators and the United Mine Workers. For decades now we have been so accustomed to seeing management and labor going to Washington— or being dragged to Washington—to settle their major disputes that it is hard for us to realize that in 1902 the settlement of a strike by the President of the United States was absolutely without precedent. When Roosevelt invited the operators and union leaders to Washington, some observers were favorably impressed; the strike had already been going on for months, the price of anthracite coal had climbed sky high, and as winter approached there was already intense suffering. What a fine thing for the President to try to end the crisis, thought these citizens, even if it wasn't really any of his business! Not so the conservative press. The New York *Sun* called Roosevelt's proposal "extraordinary" and "dangerous." And said the New York *Journal of Commerce*:

> The President's course . . . magnifies before the public the importance and power of the unions, casts an unwarranted stigma upon the position and rights of the operators, and adds a trades-union issue to the many unwelcome politico-economic questions of the hour. . . . Worse by far than any possible strike is Mr. Roosevelt's seemingly uncontrollable penchant for impulsive self-intrusion.

It was during this strike that the leading representative of the coal operators, George F. Baer, sent his famous lines of assurance to a worried resident of Wilkes-Barre. "The rights and interests of the laboring man," wrote Baer, "will be protected and cared for—not by the labor agitators, but by the Christian men to whom God in his infinite wisdom has given control of the property interests of the country."

When the coal operators faced the President in conference in Washington, their attitude toward him was one of "studied inso-

lence," to borrow Mark Sullivan's phrase. They took the position that
the strikers were outlaws, criminal conspirators against the rights
of property. As Baer himself put it, "The duty of the hour is not
to waste time negotiating with the fomentors of this anarchy." Roosevelt succeeded in establishing a basis for the settlement of the strike,
but throughout the negotiations he was profoundly aware that he had
no power at all to intervene. What he was doing was quite outside
the normal province of the United States government.

II

But that was in 1902 and Theodore Roosevelt was an adventurous
man. In 1900 his predecessor, the stately William McKinley, sat in
the White House, and McKinley was a man of discretion, who
wouldn't have dreamed of trying to settle a strike. McKinley took
a different view of the functions of the federal government. He
believed, quite sincerely, that the government oughtn't to intervene
in business affairs unless criminal activities were involved (and there
were mighty few activities which the laws then defined as criminal);
instead, the government ought to serve business to the extent of its
modest capacity.

Nobody has described McKinley better than William Allen White,
who as a young journalist interviewed him at his home in Canton,
Ohio, on a warm day in the summer of 1901. McKinley, said White,
sat

in a large cane veranda chair in a lightweight dark alpaca coat and trousers,
with a double-breasted white vest adorned only by his watch chain, with
a dark purple four-in-hand necktie meticulously arranged; a heavy man
five feet ten or eleven inches tall but never paunchy, with a barrel torso,
a large head and face, deeply cut though not finely chiseled features—but
without spot, blemish, wrinkle, or sign of care and sorrow upon the smooth,
sculptured contour of his countenance. I was sweating, for it was a hot day.
He was stainless, spotless, apparently inwardly cool and outwardly un-
ruffled.

McKinley was dignified and courtly, with such a built-in reserve that
White felt that somewhere back in his youth he had "buttoned

himself up." When a photographer arrived to take the President's picture, McKinley laid aside his cigar, saying gently, "We must not let the young men of this country see their President smoking!"

Behind this frock-coated statue of civic righteousness, as he presided over governmental affairs, stood the stalwart Republican leader, Mark Hanna, a solid, forthright, outspoken, generous, very human man who genuinely admired McKinley, somewhat as a sales manager might admire a noble though impractical bishop, and took delight in showing him what practical course he should pursue. Hanna was a prosperous manufacturer, a Senator from Ohio, and chairman of the Republican National Committee. He knew well how to raise money from the rich and privileged. Temperamentally he was in full accord with the big manufacturers, and at ease with the big bankers. He felt that whatever served them served the country. Within the limits of feasible statesmanship, he was their earnest and devoted servant.

In the presidential campaign of 1900 McKinley was opposed by William Jennings Bryan, whom he had already defeated in 1896. Bryan was no demagogue but a genuine lover of the people, a good man, an honest man, a natural defender of human rights. He had a shallow and opinionated mind, but he had also a magical gift of speech. In those days when there was no radio and no television and when oratory was a widely appreciated art, there was no one who could hold and sway an audience as Bryan could. There are men still living who recall how they came to some county-seat meeting to hear him speak, and how they stirred restlessly on the hard benches during the preliminary addresses; how when Bryan began they listened with skepticism; and how the organ tones of his glorious great voice and the rise and fall of his rhetorical cadences so captured them that when, at last, he came to the end of his peroration, they found themselves hardly able to move their cramped muscles: for two hours they had sat motionless under the spell of his silver tongue.

Bryan based his 1900 campaign chiefly on the issue of anti-imperialism, arguing that the islands which had fallen into American hands as a result of the Spanish War should be delivered to their inhabitants. He also inveighed against the trusts, recommending that corporations be subject to federal licensing, and he even proposed an income tax; but his grasp of economics was insecure, and although millions of Americans were troubled about the trusts, Bryan failed to ignite them fully. For 1900 was a year when many of them had more money in their pockets than they had had for many a season. Mark Hanna had said before the campaign, "All we need to do is to stand pat," thereby giving currency to a phrase that has reverberated through American politics ever since; and Hanna's prediction had been sound. McKinley, the victor of the war against Spain, the majestic embodiment both of America's new importance in world affairs and of the new prosperity, won without difficulty; and Mark Hanna made ready to serve big business for four more years.

Indeed as Hanna scanned the skies during the last weeks of 1900 there was only one cloud on the horizon: the man chosen by the Republican National Convention as its candidate for Vice-President, the rambunctious Rough Rider of San Juan Hill, the unpredictable young Governor of New York, Theodore Roosevelt. As Governor this Roosevelt had been as mild in his attitude toward business as another Roosevelt was destined to be in the same office a generation later; but he was independent, he wouldn't stay tethered, and Hanna distrusted him. "Don't any of you realize," Hanna had exploded to another senator at the convention, "that there's only one life between that madman and the Presidency?"

What White called "the alliance between government and business for the benefit of business" was an honest love affair to Hanna. He felt that if the path were made easy for the great corporations to do as they pleased, the riches which they accumulated would filter down to the less fortunate, and that any attempt to change the rules of the game except to give the great corporations even more opportunity to prosper would open the way to demagoguery, mob rule, and destruction. With others the alliance was not a matter of emotional affinity or of conviction, but of purchase and sale—the prostitution of government bodies for favors and cash. Big corporations advanced their interests not only by making sizable campaign contributions—

often to both parties—but also by subsidizing or bribing legislators and even judges.

Railroad companies issued free passes to lawmakers, officials, journalists, and their families. At one state capital after another, corporation lobbyists with well-filled pockets were ready to go into action whenever there was a threat of adverse legislation or a hope of favorable legislation. And as for the United States Senate—whose members were at that time elected, not by the people, but by these amenable state legislatures—it had become the chief citadel for the defense of privilege. Most of the Senators were either rich men or carefully selected allies and messenger boys of the rich; they could deliver orotund speeches about the "full dinner pail" for the workman, but their hearts were with the big stockholder.

To quote once more from William Allen White's autobiography, written long years later:

Senators elected in the days when machines and the ownership of machines were passing into the hands of a class-conscious, organized plutocracy had no obligations to the people of their state. . . . In Kansas, it was the railroads. In western Massachusetts, it was textiles. In eastern Massachusetts, it was the banks. In New York, it was amalgamated industry. In Montana, it was copper. But the power which developed and controlled any state went to New York for its borrowed capital, and New York controlled the United States Senate. . . . The grade of senators, as far as intelligence went, was higher than the grade which the people selected, but on the whole and by and large it was not a representative government. Only a minority of the people of the United States had any control over the United States Senate. And that minority was interested in its own predatory designs.

If a Senator or Congressman needed a little persuasion, there were ways of providing it. Perhaps the neatest demonstration of the art of this sort of persuasion is to be found in the political correspondence of John D. Archbold, the active head of the Standard Oil Company, which was stolen from his files and made public by Hearst in 1908.

This correspondence showed Congressman Sibley of Pennsylvania, Archbold's chief agent in Washington, writing to say, "A Republican

United States senator came to me today to make a loan of $1000. I told him I did not have it but would try to get it for him in a day or two. Do you want to make the investment?"

It showed Senator Joseph B. Foraker of Ohio getting $44,000 from Standard Oil in four successive certificates of deposit sent by Archbold (which Foraker later claimed were retainers); and it showed Archbold subsequently writing Foraker about an "objectionable bill" that needed "to be looked after."

It showed Archbold writing on several occasions to governors to urge them, if "consistent," to appoint Judge So-and-so to fill the vacancy in such-and-such a court. "It is not necessary for me to dwell upon Judge Henderson's capabilities. They are undoubtedly well known to you," wrote Archbold on one occasion. Mild words, to which nobody could take exception. Have not citizens the right to suggest appropriate candidates for high office? Yet no governor could miss the sharp point of the request. This was a post in which Standard, in return for favors past or future, must have a man whose decisions could be counted upon.

Thus, by hints, suggestions, loans, so-called loans that were in fact gifts, and on occasion by outright secret bribes, could a big corporation make legislators, elected officials, and even judges do its bidding. The Soviet propagandists of the nineteen-fifties are forever talking about "lackeys of Wall Street." Well, in 1900 the United States government included many men who might aptly, if not quite idiomatically, have been described as lackeys of Wall Street. Moving into public life in those days was like moving into the neighborhood of a million-dollar fruit tree whose fruit could readily be dislodged if one but made the slightest move in its direction. And this was easily done, for no one much seemed to be looking.

III

Why was no one much looking? There was furious interest in political elections. The 1896 campaign had been the hottest, perhaps, in the whole history of the United States, and the 1900 one did not lack for warmth. There was, as I have already said, a very widespread popular fear that the trusts might ultimately take over the control of the United States. Why, then, did very few people seem to realize that since the nature and behavior of American capitalism was a matter of transcendent importance to them, and involved great political problems, therefore the character and performance of their political representatives should come under the closest observation?

The reasons were many. In the first place, much of the opposition to the trusts which did exist took the form of advocacy of a socialism of manifestly European derivation. It seemed foreign to the nature of Americans, who were likely to be unsympathetic toward ideologies and disinclined to think of themselves as proletarians, however miserable their lot. It was associated in American minds with the strange-looking, foreign-language-speaking people of the Lower East Side of New York and other immigrant neighborhoods. Besides, it was suspect as revolutionary—in the sense of advocating a total transformation of the business system, if not in the sense of involving barricades and bloodshed. Did not Eugene V. Debs, the 1900 presidential candidate of the Social Democratic party, himself declare that it was "not a reform party but a revolutionary party"? Even with so strong a candidate as the eloquent Debs, the Social Democrats could win no more than 96,000 votes that year.

In the second place, though many earnest Americans who did not like the trend of things had become "Christian Socialists"—following a pattern of thought later inherited in part by Norman Thomas—these were an unorganized and somewhat impractical group; and the theological student or social worker who argued that all industry should be taken over by the government, which would presumably be dominated by people as benevolent as himself, became the awkward butt of japes to the effect that if you divided up all the money in the country evenly among the population, it would soon be back once more in the smart people's hands.

In the third place, the very idea of reform had been discredited by the failure of the Populist party in the nineties and by Bryan's seduction of the Populists into the advocacy of free silver. There are few things so dead as a reform movement that has fallen for a panacea and is beginning to become aware of the error of its ways.

Yet still more important, perhaps, was the fact that there were few

people outside the inner circles of big business and corporation law
who really understood how the big business combinations were set
up, how they functioned, or how they exercised their political lever-
age; and there were still fewer who had any but the dimmest notion
of how the trend of the times could be reversed without a grave
danger of disrupting the industrial and political processes of the
nation.

This general haziness of the public mind was due in large part to
the fact that not many Americans had learned to think of economic
affairs—industry, technology, trade, commerce—as matters of general
concern to them as citizens. A man worked hard at his business, did
his level best to make money at it, talked business with other men
in the Pullman smoking compartment or in the country store; but
all that was personal and immediate, and quite disconnected, in his
mind, with the general condition of American life. Nobody had told
him that all Americans were interdependent; that each business, each
social activity, each political activity, formed a part of a general
American pattern which was affected by what everybody did; that,
in the phrase of a later day, Americans were "all in the same boat."
He was used, for instance, to thinking of American business as something which had little to do with American history, except insofar
as the tariff affected it. Was not the American history which he had
studied in high school a dreary tale of political campaigns and
maneuvers which led from the Missouri Compromise to the Dred
Scott case and from the Resumption of Specie Payments to the
Dingley Tariff, enlivened only by occasional wars? What did the
operations of his business have to do with all that?

To be sure, he was excited by presidential campaigns, and could
argue with the best that McKinley was the creature of the trusts or
that Bryan was unsound; but his political affiliation was likely to
be hereditary, and the newspaper editorials and cartoons which provided him with most of his current political education were more
partisan than illuminating. As for the popular magazines, it was true
that Ida M. Tarbell was already at work on her painstaking history
of the Standard Oil Company for *McClure's,* but not a word of this

chronicle had yet appeared in print, and very few of the magazine journalists of the day, except S. S. McClure and his staff, were much interested in probing deeply into the facts of business life in its relation to political life. And as for the great magazines of the old school, those highly respectable publications which ladies and gentlemen liked to display on their library tables, these had become so intent upon serving the interests of culture—a culture daintily remote from the crass concerns of everyday life—that the idea of examining closely the nature of any such vulgar necessity as business was repugnant to them.

Here, by way of illustration, is the table of contents of the March, 1900, issue of the *Century Magazine,* rival of *Harper's* and *Scribner's* for pre-eminence in the eyes of the elect and one of the truly splendid publications of that day:

Frontispiece. Engraving by Timothy Cole of J. M. W. Turner's painting of "Dido Building Carthage."

The National Zoo at Washington. By Ernest Seton-Thompson.

To the Lapland Longspur. *Poem,* by John Burroughs.

Paris of the Faubourgs. By Richard Whiteing.

Robert Herrick, the Man and the Poet. By Thomas Bailey Aldrich.

A Transfer of Property. *Story.* By Catharine Young Glen.

The Little Child Dead. *Poem.* By Josephine Dodge Daskam.

The "Larger Hope." *Poem.* By Elizabeth Paton McGilvary.

Engraving by Timothy Cole of J. M. W. Turner's painting of the "Fighting Temeraire."

The Bamboo Flute. *Poem.* By Richard Henry Stoddard.

Eliza Hepburn's Deliverance. *Serial Novel.* By Henry B. Fuller.

Dr. North and His Friends. *Serial Novel.* By S. Weir Mitchell.

Carpaccio's Little Angel with the Lute. *Poem.* By Josephine Preston Peabody.

The Giant Indians of Tierra del Fuego. By Dr. Frederick A. Cook.

Poverty. *Poem.* By Arlo Bates.

Oliver Cromwell. By John Morley. (The fifth paper of a series.)

The Composer Meyerbeer. By Moritz Moszkowski.

To an English Setter. *Poem.* By Thomas Walsh.

Lines and Sail-plan of the "Spray." By Joshua Slocum. (Part of an account of a voyage alone around the world.)

The Eternal Feminine. *Story.* By Eva Wilder Brodhead.

A Midwinter Tramp from Santiago to Havana. By H. Phelps Whitmarsh.

In the Gloaming. *Poem.* By John Vance Cheney.

Talks with Napoleon. By his physician at St. Helena, Dr. B. E. O'Meara.

The Warfare of Railways in Asia. By Alexander Hume Ford.

Topics of the Time—a department of editorial comment, including a piece on The Date Line (discussing whether the twentieth century began in 1900 or in 1901), a piece on Benefits of Jury Duty to the Juror, and a piece on A Neglected Art (letter-writing).

In Lighter Vein—humor.

Such was the fare that the genteel thought it proper to place before the genteel in the United States of 1900. It was lavishly varied; it was produced with distinction of thought and of phrase, and illustrated with grace and charm; it ranged through the centuries and the continents, as cultivated people should be able to; it contained nothing which could bring a blush even to a cheek ready and willing to blush. And it resolutely turned its back upon the great forces which were determining the fortunes and future of the United States.

Is it any wonder that, in a day when such a magazine stood upon the pinnacle of journalism, there was a shortage of people burning to learn exactly how the ugly factories that disfigured the industrial towns of America were linked together by corporate charters into huge combinations, and how the masters of these combinations, and the bankers who stood behind them, subdued legislators to their will?

But a change was coming. And, paradoxically, the advance agent of this change was an ignorant, demented assassin. On the 6th of September, 1901, at the Pan-American exposition in Buffalo, a man named Czolgosz shot and fatally wounded President McKinley.

Not only had Mark Hanna lost a loved and revered associate, but the cloud of uncertainty that he had discerned on the horizon when Roosevelt had been nominated for the Vice-Presidency now filled half the sky. "And now look," he exclaimed to his friend Kohlsaat, "that damned cowboy is President of the United States!"

PART TWO

THE MOMENTUM
OF CHANGE

Chapter 6

The Revolt
of the American Conscience

THERE were no signs and portents in the sky to herald the beginning of a new era when Theodore Roosevelt moved into the White House in the autumn of 1901. He announced that he would carry forward the late President McKinley's policies, and in his earliest utterances as President he gave the financial and industrial powers of the day no cause for undue alarm. In his first message to Congress he made it clear, to be sure, that he did not think all was well with business; but so neatly did he balance each adverse statement with another one defending business that Finley Peter Dunne's fictional Irishman, Mr. Dooley, aptly summarized the message as follows: " 'Th' trusts,' says he, 'are heejous monsthers built up be th' inlightened intherprise iv th' men that have done so much to advance progress in our beloved counthry,' he says. 'On wan hand I wud stamp thim undher fut; on th' other hand not so fast.' "

It was not until several months had passed that the first signal flare of the new era went up: in February, 1902, Roosevelt's attorney general brought suit for the dissolution of the Northern Securities Company under the Sherman Antitrust Act.

The Northern Securities Company was a holding company set up by J. Pierpont Morgan and Edward H. Harriman for the joint control of certain railroad properties, as part of a treaty of peace between them after the Northern Pacific panic. If it had stood the test of law it might conceivably have set the pattern for the purchase of most of the major railroads of the country by a few men in Wall Street. In moving to smash it Roosevelt not only served notice that there were limits to what the government would let men do in using the mechanism of the holding company to build up economic empires; he also struck at one of the prized creations of the great Morgan himself.

Morgan was dining at home when the news of the suit came to him by telephone. He was dismayed and indignant. He told his guests that he had supposed Roosevelt to be a gentleman, but a gentleman would not have sued; rather he would have asked Morgan privately to reorganize or abolish the Northern Securities Company in order to bring it in line with the government's wishes. The great banker felt that Roosevelt was treating him, an honorable man, like a common crook. Joseph Pulitzer, publisher of the New York *World* and a foe of the "trusts," was overjoyed at Roosevelt's action and wrote in a letter of instructions to his editor, Frank I. Cobb, that the President had "subjugated Wall Street." This was considerable of an exaggeration; but at least the battle was joined.

This battle between the President and the emerging plutocracy, during the next few years, was destined to be an intermittent and often halfhearted one. The reason was not far to seek. Roosevelt was a Republican President. He could not get too far out of step with his party. Among its members were the great majority of the rich and privileged, and the party needed their lavish financial contributions at campaign time. Politically Roosevelt must appear to be their friend, who merely disciplined them a little from time to time for their own good. It has been pointed out again and again since those days that Roosevelt's bark was much worse than his bite, and that even his bark became noticeably milder in a campaign year; that the legislation which he actually put through—such as the Hepburn Act for the further regulation of the railroads, for example—did not pack much of a wallop; that never again in his seven and a half years in the White House did he do anything so bold as to attack the Northern Securities Company; that the conservative Taft administration which followed his was much more active in bringing prosecutions under the Sherman Act than he was; and furthermore that Roosevelt had a limited and uncertain knowledge of economics and was impulsive, boyishly immature, inconsistent, and unduly addicted to the delights of political showmanship. All of which is true—but overlooks Roosevelt's most vital contribution to American history.

For what this dynamic President did was to advertise and dramatize to the whole country a point of view on business, government, and the public interest that was refreshingly new, exciting, and contagious.

Up to this time most of the outcry against the trend toward plutocracy had been the bitter outcry of people who had been hurt. The opposition had been mainly an opposition of the have-nots to the haves. Furthermore it had been, in great part, a radical if not revolutionary opposition. The farmers who had flocked into the Populist party during the early nineties had been angry men who wanted to overthrow Wall Street and big business generally. The workers who had joined such belligerent unions as the Western Federation of Miners had been violent men addicted to the use of lethal weapons and the hope of revolution. The urban laborers who formed the backbone of the Socialist parties had listened appreciatively to the preachments of leaders who had drawn upon the revolutionary ideologies of Europe. And such native-born citizens of means as had opposed the power and greed of the captains of industry had tended to be gentle, tenderhearted men of good will— ministers, social-service workers, sentimental liberals of a species to which the term "pink" was later scornfully applied. But now here, in the Presidency of the United States, was an opponent of the plutocratic trend who did not belong in any of these brackets.

Roosevelt could not be called a have-not; he had never himself been hurt by Wall Street; he was indeed rich in his own right. He was an old-stock American, and a military hero to boot. He was not a spinner of ideological theories or a sentimental visionary but a man

of action, a woodsman and hunter, a Rough Rider, a man of robust
enthusiasms, who preached the "strenuous life," who liked to tell
boys, "Don't flinch, don't foul, hit the line hard!" Everything about
him commanded popular attention: the flashing eyeglasses and grin-
ning teeth that cartoonists loved to sketch, the energetic voice rising
to a falsetto of high emphasis as he drove home an oratorical point;
the pugnacious gestures, the zest for conflict; his omnivorous interest
in big-game hunting, history, ornithology, simplified spelling, military affairs, and a dozen other contrasting subjects; his delighted
interest in all manner of people. John Morley described him as "an
interesting combination of St. Vitus and St. Paul," and as a wonder
of nature comparable to Niagara Falls.

And the burden of his speeches about "malefactors of great wealth"
and "the square deal" was not economic but moral. He sought the
"moral regeneration of the business world." He believed in setting
up a "moral standard." He preached that it was just plain wrong for
some people, by tricks and wiles, to get a stranglehold on business
and politics, while others were cheated out of opportunity. This was
the kind of talk that millions of Americans of all walks of life—
people allergic to ideologies, impatient of economic theory, but
highly susceptible to moral evangelism and devoted to the idea of a
fair chance for all—could understand and respond to. The effect
of the legislation that Theodore Roosevelt backed was minor compared with the effect of his personality and his preaching upon a great
part of a whole generation of Americans. He struck a new keynote
for the times, and it resounded all over America.

The times were ripe for it. Consider a few dates. Roosevelt moved
against the Northern Securities Company in February, 1902. Already
Miss Ida Tarbell had been at work for years on her history of the
Standard Oil Company, and it began to run in *McClure's* in November, 1902. Lincoln Steffens' first article on municipal corruption,
"Tweed Days in St. Louis," written with Claude H. Wetmore,
appeared in the same magazine a month earlier, in October, 1902. It
was these two journalists who inaugurated a new trend in American

journalism, a trend toward the deliberate, unsentimental, searching, factual reporting of what was actually going on in American business and American politics. (When Roosevelt later attacked the "muck-rakers" he was hitting chiefly at their more sensational imitators.) "Golden Rule" Jones, the reform mayor of Toledo, had been elected in 1897; the elder Robert La Follette became the energetic reform governor of Wisconsin in 1900; Tom L. Johnson was chosen mayor of Cleveland in 1901; these men were the leaders and forerunners of a whole generation of reformers in state and local government. It was in 1902 that the enthusiasm of Robert C. Ogden and his friends for the raising of educational standards was seized upon by John D. Rockefeller, with the advice of his statesmanlike counselor in charitable matters, Frederick T. Gates, to organize the General Education Board, the first of the great broad-purpose foundations which set a new pattern in giving in the public interest. These are only a few scattered examples of the new trend of which Roosevelt was to serve as the chief galvanizer and spokesman; people were showing a disposition to look about them with fresh eyes, to investi-gate what was going on, and decide to do something about it, some-thing immediate and practical.

Thus began that revolt of the American conscience which was to be the dominant phenomenon in American affairs until about 1915, when it was submerged in the oncoming tides of World War I, and which finally petered out about 1920—leaving behind it, however, influences and patterns of thinking that were to continue to this day.

II

As the historians Hacker and Kendrick have pointed out, this revolt was not an organized movement, but incoherent. It had no overall program. Those who took part in it ranged all the way from rich to poor, and were in many cases fiercely at odds with one another. It was rather a general movement of very diverse people working for different specific ends who "had simultaneously hit upon the idea of taking to the road."

There were the proponents of measures to permit more direct

popular government, unfettered by bosses—such as the direct election of Senators, the initiative and referendum, the recall of judicial decisions. There were the advocates of municipal housecleaning, the experimenters with commission government of cities, the budget experts. There were the battlers for workmen's compensation laws, the people who were trying to get decent legislation on working conditions in factories. There were the conservationists, who wanted to stop the headlong destruction of the nation's natural resources, and particularly of its forests. There were the suffragists, campaigning for votes for women; the crusaders for pure food and drug laws; the investigators and chastisers of "frenzied finance"; and the men who, after the Panic of 1907, labored to devise an adequate central banking system.

The same basic feeling that the nation and its citizens must look out for the interests of all the people, not simply of a privileged few, animated a great variety of other people who were little concerned with legislation. It was during this time that more and more men and women, following in the footsteps of Jane Addams of Hull House and Lillian D. Wald of the Henry Street Settlement, were making social service a respected profession, and that clergymen were increasingly seeing in their parishes opportunities for institutional social work. Meanwhile Gates was developing the pattern for the great Rockefeller benefactions; the Rockefeller Foundation and the Carnegie Corporation were established, with huge endowments to be presided over by students of the public welfare. The epoch-making campaign against hookworm began; and Abraham Flexner prepared the report which led to the building of great new medical centers that would help to revolutionize the methods of the healing profession. Woodrow Wilson moved into the governorship of New Jersey—and thence into the Presidency of the United States—from the presidency of Princeton, where in the spirit of the times he had been waging war against the undergraduate eating clubs, which seemed to him undemocratic. Nor was it mere coincidence that during those very years Edward Bok as editor of the *Ladies' Home Journal* was trying to teach millions of American women how they might live graciously

on small incomes; and his magazine and others of leaping circulation
—notably the *Saturday Evening Post*—were offering the advertising
business a chance to present to vast audiences the delights of mass-
produced goods that had hitherto been sold chiefly to the well-heeled;
while Henry Ford was beginning to produce a car that would not be
a plaything of the rich but an inexpensive and useful vehicle for the
people. Furthermore, it was during these years that Willford I. King
first set before the economists the concept of the national income.

Little as these people had in common, they were alike in seeing
the nation, not as a place where everybody went his own way regardless of the plight of others, but as a place where people had a common
destiny, where their fortunes were interlocked, and where wise
planning, wise statesmanship could devise new instruments of satisfaction for all men.

The contagion of reform reached even into the ranks of the very
richest and most powerful: witness Harry Davison of the House of
Morgan, Paul M. Warburg, and other influential bankers trying to
concoct a scheme for a central banking system; Mrs. O. H. P. Belmont holding suffrage meetings for the lavishly dressed ladies of
Newport; and of course John D. Rockefeller, hitherto generally
regarded as the arch-villain of unregenerate capitalism, pouring his
millions into all manner of good works.

III

One must not exaggerate the impact of this revolt. One must bear
in mind, for one thing, that although there was a gradual improvement in the status of organized labor—marked by the establishment
in 1913 of the Labor Department and the passage in 1914 of the
Clayton Act, which at least theoretically gave legal standing to collective bargaining—there were still large areas of industry in which
labor was totally unorganized, and others where the struggle between
capital and the workers was a battle between tyrants with hired thugs,
on the one hand, and revolutionaries or murderers, or both, on the
other. One need only recall the contest between union structural
workers and non-union stairway makers on a building job in New

York in 1906; during this contest bolts, bars, and tools had such a way of falling from the upper levels upon the heads of stairway makers below that the company hired special watchmen, one of whom was killed by being beaten up and then dropped from the eighth floor to the fifth. Or the murder in 1905 of ex-Governor Steunenberg of Idaho, who had been a foe of the Western Federation of Miners, by a man who named as his accomplices William D. Haywood and other high officials of the union. (The verdict as to Haywood and the others was "not guilty," but in the opinion of many who attended the trial this signified "not proven" rather than "innocent.") Or the dynamiting of the Los Angeles *Times* building in 1910—twenty dead, and the building wrecked—under the direction of the McNamara brothers, one of whom was the secretary-treasurer of the militant Ironworkers International Union, and the other of whom was "handy with the sticks."

Or one might cite the formation of the I.W.W. in 1905—the International Workers of the World, the "Wobblies"—the preamble of whose constitution stated that "the working class and the employing class have nothing in common." The actual methods of the I.W.W. were by no means always lawless, but the great strikes which its leaders managed, such as the Lawrence strike of 1912 and the Paterson strike of 1913, were bitter and savage to a degree seldom even approached in recent years, and its chief leaders were undeniably revolutionists at heart.

Furthermore during these very years the Socialist party—which was committed to an eventual total change in the management of American industry—continued to gain, until in the 1912 election its candidate, Eugene Debs, piled up no less than 897,000 votes.

In short, not all those who sought for changes in the face of America were proponents of orderly step-by-step amelioration, or of minor structural·changes in the existing way of doing business.

Nor should one forget that during these years Pierpont Morgan still moved with a mighty tread in Wall Street; and as old age came upon him, the economic power which he had long exercised through the terrific force of his personality was being institutionalized into a smooth-working, though vaguely defined, pattern of influence extending from his partners at the corner of Broad and Wall Streets into the headquarters of scores of great banks and corporations. When the congressional investigating committee headed by Arsène Pujo studied what it called the "money trust" in 1912-13, it produced impressive diagrams of the Wall Street "control" of large sectors of American business. These diagrams suggested a pattern of direction much more sharply drawn than was the actual influence exercised by the House of Morgan, Baker of the First National Bank, Stillman of the National City Bank, and the other princes of finance; but the power was there, however sketchy it might be in outline, and it remained immense and far-reaching even after Morgan's death in 1913.

For years after the turn of the century, furthermore, the members of the Standard Oil crowd of speculators were raking in millions through their smoothly managed operations on the Stock Exchange. Nor was there any conspicuous sign of slackening in the activities of the more piratical traders in stocks and bonds; they continued to hornswoggle the trading public right and left. In general, the men of Wall Street viewed the progress of reform with dismay; excoriated Theodore Roosevelt and, later, Woodrow Wilson; contributed to the Roosevelt campaign chest chiefly for fear of getting something worse —and continued to build up, more discreetly than in former years but not necessarily less effectively, the structures of power and wealth that the reformers were resolutely trying to chip away.

IV

So strongly, however, did the tides of reform run that in the election of 1912 they reached an astonishing height.

Four years earlier, Theodore Roosevelt, deciding not to run for reelection, had yielded the Republican nomination with his blessing to his portly and genial Secretary of War, William H. Taft, upon whom he relied to carry out his progressive policies. But Taft, in office, proved to be a pliant conservative; as Senator Dolliver once remarked, he did indeed carry out Roosevelt's policies, but "on a shutter." When Roosevelt returned from Africa, where he had been hunting wild animals, he presently succumbed to a variety of emotions. These included disgust at what he considered Taft's betrayal of him, an inability to stay out of a good rousing battle, a genuine crusading fervor, and a very human conviction that Roosevelt followers and the forces of righteousness were necessarily one and the same. He attacked Taft savagely, ran against him for the Republican nomination in 1912, and, failing to get it, formed overnight his own Progressive party and sought the election.

Meanwhile the Democrats nominated the austere, long-jawed, brilliant, energetic ex-professor, Woodrow Wilson. Though there were minor differences between the Roosevelt position and the Wilson position, essentially they were both reformers, both belonged on the same side of the fence. And in the voting they both, incredibly, outran the staunch Republican Taft. And this despite the fact that the Socialist party had collected nearly a million votes (as against about 3½ million for Taft, over 4 million for Roosevelt, and over 6 million for Wilson). Reform was at its apogee.

But Wilson had been in the White House only a year and a half—pushing through Congress measure after measure of his New Freedom program—when, unbelievably, war broke out in Europe. And as the conflict that we now call World War I grew in fury and scope, the issues which it provoked began so to dominate the American scene that gradually the impulse toward reform was overwhelmed. Or rather, the crusading spirit was translated, by the time the United States entered the war against Germany in 1917, into making the war a crusade for freedom—or a crusade, as Woodrow Wilson put it, "to make the world safe for democracy." People whose memories do not go back to those days, but who recall vividly the dead-pan, let's-get-the-nasty-business-over-with, let's-not-have-any-parades-or-idealistic-talk spirit of World War II, may find it hard to appreciate the fact that in 1917-1918 an American people much less united in their acceptance of war than they were to be in 1941-1945 nevertheless went about their war tasks with genuine fervor. The great majority of American men and women had real faith that this war could be the last one ever, that victory could bring a new day of universal freedom, and they prosecuted the war with an almost evangelical dedication.

Yet the crusading spirit was like a bank whose funds were being overdrawn. It lasted long enough, at the close of the war, to complete the ratification of the woman suffrage amendment and—even more remarkably—of that prize curiosity of reformist ardor, the prohibition amendment, which at the time it went into effect in January, 1920, was expected by almost everybody to end once and for all the era of alcoholic drinking in America. But then, abruptly, the impulse to make over the nation and the world was discovered to have faded away. A people who had had enough of high causes and noble sacrifice to hold them for a long time decided to take things easy, to enjoy themselves; and although there remained many American idealists who would not abandon their quest, they found that they, too, were tired as well as outnumbered. The revolt of the American conscience was over.

V

Yet it had left behind it, embedded deep in the ever-changing American tradition, a way of looking at public problems, and particularly political and economic problems, of vast importance for the American future. This was the idea—an old idea, but strengthened now by having been put to the test and having survived intact—that when the ship of state was not behaving as it should, one did not need to scrap it and build another, but could, by a series of adjustments and improvements, repair it while keeping it running—provided the ship's crew were forever alert, forever inspecting it and tinkering with it. And that the economic machine, if it seemed to be producing the wrong kind of goods, need not be destroyed but could be fitted with a new carburetor here, a new belt there, and new spark plugs, and by observation and test be made to produce to better advantage without skipping a beat. The stress and destruction of revolution were unnecessary—and might destroy those skills and incentives which gave the machine its accelerating motive power. No need to send the designers to their drawing boards to concoct plans for wholly new and untried mechanisms; a few inspectors, a few specialists in the design of this part and that, and a will on the part of all concerned to make the machine do its true duty, would amply serve.

One realizes, as one looks back, how tentative and provisional, and of what minor long-range influence, were most of the reform measures of that time, taken one by one. There are few things deader, today, than the enthusiasms and angers which were engendered by, let us say, the initiative and referendum, or by the struggle to deprive Speaker Joe Cannon of his arbitrary authority over the House of Representatives. No wonder students yawn over the history books which conscientiously take them through the story of those battles, so dull and dry in retrospect. Ironically, of all the measures which went on the statute books during the reform era, the one that was destined to have the most positive and enduring effect upon the American economy was one which most history books tend to pass over with minor mention, because there was very little conflict over it and because its impact was at first so slight. This was the graduated income tax.

The income tax was made possible by a constitutional amendment proposed to Congress by Taft, a President generally regarded as conservative, and was passed by Congress and ratified by the states with little opposition; people realized that the time for it had come. And when it was first imposed—by a provision in President Wilson's tariff act of 1913—the rates were very low: only one per cent on net incomes up to $20,000, with a modest surtax on larger ones. No single person paid on a net income of less than $3,000; no married person on an income of less than $4,000. Believe it or not, on a $10,000 net income a married man paid only about $60, on a $20,000 net income he paid only about $160. (Are those sounds that I hear the moaning of readers for the dear, dead days?) Not until 1917 did the income tax yield as much money to the federal government as customs duties did. But by 1920 it was contributing ten times as much money as the customs; and that was only the beginning of the rise of the graduated income tax to a predominant place in the financing of a hugely expanded government, and to an important place among the instruments for the redistribution of wealth in America.

Yet it is not upon any individual piece of legislation during the reform era that one should focus one's chief attention, nor even upon the good works accomplished, or the sentimental follies committed, by the men and women who in a hundred different ways were laboring, as William Allen White said, to give the underdog a better kennel. It is rather at the basic idea which became dominant that one should look.

Many people argued then—and have gone on arguing—that the United States ought to have a conservative party and a liberal party (or radical party, if you wish), each with its neat, logical program, instead of two very similar parties each shopping for winning ideas for platform planks and feeling its way by experiment, persuasion, and compromise. Many people argued then—and some still argue today—that economic reform by patchwork is illogical and timid, and that what is needed is an uprising of the dissatisfied to effect a total transformation of the apparatus of business and industry. Both those ideas ran strongly for a time and then weakened. Roosevelt's third party, the Progressive party, made a strong bid in 1912 and then disintegrated, leaving the other parties to take over the more popular planks of its platform. The Socialists gained ground and then lost it again. For both ideas would have favored the division of the American people into classes, and both would have run counter to their pragmatic temper.

The idea that won out was that the existence of sharply defined economic and social classes was to be resisted as an offense to the American democratic ideal. That you got along much better when people of all sorts and conditions worked together for what seemed to them the benefit of all. That the way to deal with a proletariat was not either to suppress and bedevil it, or to help it to overthrow its masters, but to give it a chance at education, opportunity, automobiles, and vacuum cleaners, with plenty of instruction in the middle-class way of living and plenty of incentive to want more and more of these good things; and then in due course the proletariat might be a proletariat no more, but a body of upstanding, self-respecting citizens who could be counted on to help keep the nation in good running order. And that when you found something amiss with the way things functioned you examined what was happening and pragmatically made the necessary changes and no more. That the people who thought the machine would stop dead if you tinkered with it were wrong, and the people who thought you could invent out of hand a new machine that wouldn't knock somewhere were also wrong. The American citizenry saw the benefits of continual, co-operative, experimental, untheoretical change.

There would be ferocious debate over every proposed reform. There would be endless friction all along the way. There would be eras of new experiment and eras of consolidation and re-examination. But an America which had seemed to many people to be headed toward a reign of plutocracy seemed likely to be able to remake itself, by slow degrees, into something nearer the democratic dream, and to do this by something approaching the common consent of free men.

Chapter 7

The Dynamic Logic
of Mass Production

DURING the year 1903 a forty-year-old Detroiter named Henry Ford, having left the employ of the little Detroit Automobile Company with the idea of going into the manufacturing business for himself, designed and built a big and powerful racing car. Why did he do this? He had no great interest in speed; his idea was quite different: he wanted to make a small, light, serviceable vehicle. The reason he built a racing car was that he wanted capital, and to attract capital he had to have a reputation, and in those days when automobiles were thought of as expensive playthings in which the rich could tear noisily along the dusty roads, the way to get a reputation was to build a car that could win races.

Having constructed a car of terrifying power, Ford cast about for a racing driver; and since it would require both strength and reckless daring to control his monster at high speeds—strength because it steered with an unwieldy tiller instead of with a wheel—he hired a professional bicycle racer named Barney Oldfield, and spent a week teaching him to drive a car. Said Oldfield as he climbed into the car for his first race at the Grosse Point track late in 1902, "Well, this chariot may kill me, but they will say afterward that I was going like hell when she took me over the bank."

Oldfield did not go over the bank. He won the race by a wide margin. Ford won his reputation. And it got him enough capital—

$28,000 in cash—to start the Ford Motor Company, of which he became vice-president, general manager, designer, master mechanic, and superintendent.

During the next few years Ford produced, successfully, several varieties of cars and his manufacturing business expanded rapidly. In 1908 he put out what he considered the most satisfactory model to date; he called it Model T. And soon afterward he made a decision which astonished his associates. Let him record it in his own words: ". . . In 1909 I announced one morning, without any previous warning, that in the future we were going to build only one model, that the model was going to be Model T, and that the chassis would be exactly the same for all cars, and I remarked: 'Any customer can have a car painted any color that he wants so long as it is black.' "

This decision grew naturally out of Ford's experience and temperament. He was a Michigan farmer's son, a gadget-loving Yankee with utilitarian and democratic instincts, uninfected by higher education. As a boy he had been so fascinated with machinery that he had spent endless hours taking watches to pieces and putting them together, and then constructing watches of his own. At the age of sixteen he had seen a "road engine"—a steam engine that could use its steam power to propel itself in an ungainly way from job to job—and had thereupon been fascinated with dreams of horseless carriages, and also of machines that farmers could use to do their hard work for them. Six years later, in 1885, he had seen an Otto gas engine—a European forerunner of the automobile engines of today—and had gone to work on engine design. By the spring of 1893 he had built his first horseless carriage and tried it out on the road. During the next ten years, while he held money-earning jobs, he was forever experimenting in his spare hours, and gradually his ideas developed.

He wanted to build, not a showy car for the well-to-do, but a practical, effort-saving car for ordinary people like himself. He wanted it to be light: few things offended him as did the widespread notion that weight meant strength. He wanted it to be inexpensive; as he said later in his autobiography, "The public should always be wondering how it is possible to give so much for the money." He felt that many manufacturers were mistaken in fixing their attention upon profits, and that bankers had a bad influence upon manufacturers because they thought about improving profits instead of about improving the product. If the product and the price were right, he thought the profits would take care of themselves. And he believed that if he concentrated on a single model, he could cut the cost of manufacture so sharply that masses of ordinary people would flock to buy it.

As his sales of Model T increased, Ford deliberately dropped the price—and they increased still further. In 1913 he put in his first assembly line, and by the beginning of 1914 he was producing the entire car on the assembly-line principle. Each workman performed a single operation; each element of the car went on a power-driven moving conveyor platform past a series of these workmen, each of whom added or fixed in place some part of it; and these various assembly lines converged upon a main conveyor platform on which the chassis moved to completion.

In principle this method of manufacture was far from new. It depended upon Eli Whitney's great discovery of the principle of interchangeable parts. It owed much to the refinement of that principle by such men as Henry M. Leland, who had shown what close machining could do to make these interchangeable parts fit with absolute precision. Moreover, many a manufacturer had used the assembly-line principle to some extent. Cyrus McCormick, for instance, had done so in his reaper works as far back as the eighteen-fifties; and in particular the packers had used an overhead conveyor to carry slaughtered animals past a series of workers. Ford was indebted, too, to Frederick Winslow Taylor for his studies in "scientific management," the careful planning of manufacturing processes so as to save steps and motions. And Ransom Olds had already put a single type of automobile into quantity production—until his financial backers forced him back into the luxury market. Nevertheless the Ford assembly line, with its subassemblies, was unique as a remorselessly complete application of all these ideas.

When his manufacturing system was complete, in January, 1914, Ford made an announcement which echoed round the world.

At that time the going wage in the automobile industry averaged about $2.40 per nine-hour day. Ford announced that he would pay his men a minimum of $5 per eight-hour day.

The explanation was that he had been paying year-end bonuses to the men, and now, as profits expanded, he thought he should put the profit-sharing on a pay-as-you-go basis. The morale in the plant had been unsatisfactory; he thought this might improve it. And he also felt, however vaguely, that if more Americans got high wages, there would be a market for more industrial products, including of course Ford cars. Because he was afraid that the sudden jump in income might demoralize the spending habits in some families, he made the raise conditional upon their demonstrating that they didn't waste the money—a naïvely paternalistic idea which he later had to modify. But before long he was paying nearly all his workmen the astonishing new wages.

The public reaction to the announcement was terrific. Most businessmen were indignant: Ford was ruining the labor market, he was putting crazy ideas into workmen's heads, he would embarrass companies which couldn't possibly distribute such largess, he was a crude self-advertiser. There was much scoffing of the sort that a Muncie, Indiana, newspaper indulged in many years later: "Henry Ford thinks that wages ought to be higher and goods cheaper. We agree with him, and let us add that it ought to be cooler in the summer and warmer in winter." People with tenderer minds hailed Ford for his generosity and said that he was showing what a noble conscience could achieve in the hitherto unregenerate precincts of industry. Meanwhile the Ford plant was mobbed by applicants for jobs.

What Ford had actually done—in his manufacturing techniques, his deliberate price cutting, and his deliberate wage raising—was to demonstrate with unprecedented directness one of the great principles of modern industrialism: the dynamic logic of mass production. This is the principle that the more goods you produce, the less it costs to produce them; and that the more people are well off, the more they can buy, thus making this lavish and economical production possible.

Every successful manufacturer had followed this principle up to a point. But few had been able to follow it far; or, if able to, had been able to resist for very long the human temptation to cease expanding their output unduly and then to cash in by charging what the traffic would bear. Very few manufacturers, for that matter, had a single product to sell for which there proved to be an almost inexhaustible market if costs were reduced, or could go on, year after year, turning out this identical product with very little retooling. With these special advantages, Henry Ford—a cranky and self-willed man, in many respects an ignorant and opinionated man, and a merciless competitor, but in his own special way a man of stubborn democratic faith—followed the dynamic logic of mass production all the way, and the results were uncanny.

In 1909-10 his price per car had been $950. It went down to $780, to $690, to $600, to $550, to $490, to $440, to $360; then, after an increase due to the shortages and inflation of World War I, went down again until by 1924 the price of a Ford (without self-starter) was only $290. Meanwhile production had expanded by slow degrees from 18,664 cars all the way to 1,250,000 in 1920-21.

Ford followed the principle without compromise until 1927, when two facts caught up with him. One was that Americans wanted not only cheaper cars, but better ones; rival manufacturers had discovered that if you put out a new and improved model each year, the older ones would become obsolescent, and thus you could turn old customers into new ones; and these brighter and livelier new models had succeeded in making the gaunt and tinny Model T obsolescent indeed. The other fact was that the thirst for new and up-to-date vehicles was automatically producing a flourishing market in second- and third- and fourth-hand cars, at dwindling prices, so that Model T no longer had a monopoly of the bargain hunters' market.

In the meantime, however, Ford's experiment had had what Paul Hoffman has called "multiplier value." For he had advertised a principle which, though more often honored in the breach than in the observance, has a place of some sort in the thinking of every industrial manager today. The continuing discovery and demonstration of this principle has been one of the most powerful forces in the making of twentieth-century America. For it has had its corollaries: that a nation of men and women secure against exploitation and acute poverty is a nation of delighted buyers of goods, to everybody's profit; that it pays better to produce the same sort of food, clothing, and equipment for people of all income levels, than to produce luxury goods for a few; and that therefore one can make money by lowering class barriers. Thus is Marxism confounded—not by dogma, but by the logic of advanced industrialism itself; or, to put it another way, by capitalism turned to democratic ends.

II

The great Ford experiment was only one element in the lively industrial development of the United States during the first two decades of the twentieth century. For industry and business in general were expanding and changing as the nation gradually came of age.

It was the golden heyday of railroading. The great network of railroad lines which linked the country together from sea to sea was now virtually complete, and the amount of business which the railroads did swelled hugely. By 1920, for example, they were not only carrying vastly more freight, but were carrying more than twice as many passengers as in 1900, and carrying them longer distances than before, so that the figures for "passenger miles" almost tripled. Shares in the big railroad corporations—New York Central, Pennsylvania, Union Pacific, Northern Pacific, and so on—were the pride, and sometimes the undoing, of investors; rare was the man of means who did not have railroad bonds in his portfolio—while bigger and more powerful locomotives hauled longer and heavier freight and passenger trains from city to city, hooting disdainfully as they crossed dirt roads as yet unpaved for automobile traffic.

It was the heyday of the electric trolley lines, too. Who remembers, now, such bright flowers of the streetcar era as the "Berkshire Hills," the extra-fare interurban trolley car that ran between Great Barrington, Massachusetts, and Bennington, Vermont, for several years after 1908—an elegant white car with buff trim and gold-leaf lettering, with wicker seats inside, and red brocaded curtains, and a Wilton carpet, all at the traveler's disposal for an extra fare of fifty cents? And who knows whether any of its proud passengers had any notion that the trolley era was to be short-lived, and that the "Berkshire Hills," like many another relic of that era, would ultimately become a roadside diner?

It was the morning of the electrical age. In 1900 Henry Adams had stood transfixed at the sight of a dynamo at the Paris Exposition, and had seen in it a "symbol of infinity"; during the years thereafter, more and more dynamos—and turbines—were being built, and transmission lines were carrying the magic power far and wide. In 1889, less than 2 per cent of the power used in industry had been electric; by 1919, over 31 per cent of it was. The steel industry grew mightily too as the open-hearth process of steel making supplanted the Bessemer process. By 1920 the output of iron and steel per capita had almost tripled since that memorable day in 1900 when Andrew Carnegie, returning home from a game of golf with Charlie Schwab, had scribbled down on a sheet of paper his terms for the sale of Carnegie Steel to Morgan to form the United States Steel Corporation. Skyscrapers were shooting up in the cities; and although most of the people who craned their necks at the 41-story Singer Building, built in New York in 1908, or the 50-story Metropolitan Tower which closely followed it, or the 60-story Woolworth Building, completed in 1913, probably thought of them as splendid symbols of the American zest for doing bigger and bigger things, they were more especially triumphs of the steel industry that had made their strength and grace possible, and of the electric industry that had made their vital elevator service possible.

If the skyscrapers looked like cathedral towers, the new department stores looked like palaces. And another sort of rival to the old-time individually owned store was multiplying. The chain stores were on their way, paced by the Woolworth five-and-tens and by the A & P, which was operating 200 stores by 1900, 400 by 1912 (when it opened in Newark its first cash-and-carry store), and then—after a terrific spurt of expansion—as many as 11,413 stores by 1924. Here again, at the distribution end of the industrial process, the dynamic

logic of mass production was being demonstrated. For if you could
build enough red-fronted stores, with standardized methods and low
selling costs, you could attract millions of shoppers, and cut your
prices way down by placing huge bulk orders for goods—and still
make money.

Meanwhile the automobile industry was going through the first
and second phases of an evolution that seems to be standard in the
industrial world. First was the phase of numerous competition. During these first two decades of the century automobile manufacturers
were legion. Hundreds of mechanically-minded men scrabbled for
capital and set up their little factories to produce cars: bicycle makers
like Pope and Alexander Winton, electric-company employees like
Ford, plumbers' supply men like David Dunbar Buick, wagon builders like the associates of Clement Studebaker, axle manufacturers
like Harry C. Stutz. Innumerable makes were put on the market,
with names that now have nostalgic overtones for people with long
memories—Apperson, Briscoe, Stevens-Duryea, Franklin, Chandler,
Scripps-Booth, Peerless, Pierce Arrow, Locomobile, Owen Magnetic,
and so on endlessly.

And while this proliferation was still going on, the second phase
began. Promoters with capital at their disposal—or with a smooth
gift for selling stock—went shopping for promising automobile companies in order to merge them into combinations. At the very moment
in 1908 when Ford was first putting Model T into production, William C. Durant—a promoter who, unlike Ford, fixed his vaulting
mind upon properties and profits rather than upon machines—put
together the Buick company and the Olds company and a few others
under the management of a New Jersey holding company which he
called General Motors, and which—after extreme vicissitudes, during which Durant lost control of it, recaptured it, and then lost control once more, this time to the du Ponts and their allies—was to
become one of the giants of the third phase of the industry. This
third phase was that in which competition pushed to the wall, one by
one, all but a few monster concerns and a few minor rivals.

Meanwhile, too, this same motor industry was beginning to bring out two other products which were to affect the working lives of millions of people—the motor truck, which was destined to be the deadly rival of the railroads, and the tractor. The first crude tractors had been built about 1902. By 1910, production had reached 4,000 a year; by 1920 it had passed 200,000 a year. The mechanization of the American farm and the planting of the grasslands to wheat were getting under way fast.

All this growth and change, so various and so exciting, was accelerated by the development of a rising idea—that of the dignity and importance of national advertising. In the nineties Munsey and McClure had discovered that if you could sell a popular magazine to enough people, and thus attract enough advertisers, you could sell it for less than the cost of printing it, and still make money through your advertising revenue. It was during the next two decades that Cyrus H. K. Curtis and his editors George Horace Lorimer of the *Saturday Evening Post* and Edward Bok of the *Ladies' Home Journal* provided spectacular demonstrations of this journalistic version of the dynamic logic of mass production. What they did is summed up in the figures showing the growth of the *Saturday Evening Post* during those years. In 1902 it sold 314,671 copies per issue, and brought in an advertising revenue of $360,125. By 1922 it was selling 2,187,024 copies per issue—about seven times as many as in 1902—while its advertising revenue had climbed steeply to $28,278,755—over 78 times as much as in 1902!

What do those figures signify? First, that through this five-cent magazine, and others like it, millions of Americans were getting a weekly or monthly inoculation in ways of living and of thinking that were middle-class, or classless American (as opposed to plutocratic or aristocratic or proletarian); and second, that through the same media they were being introduced to the promised delights of the automobiles, spark plugs, tires, typewriters, talking machines, collars, corsets, and breakfast foods that American industry was producing, not for the few, but for the many. The magazine publisher, the copy writer, the advertising artist, and the advertising agent were all abetting the mass-production principle.

One further word about this principle. It got a tremendous lift from World War I. For during that war—as during World War II— manufacturers suddenly found themselves faced with one overwhelming demand: to make as many guns or shells or ships as possible, and as fast as possible. No need to worry about glutting the market. No need to worry unduly about price. Just concentrate on quantity and speed. The result took people's breath away: the volume of production was terrific. (And incidentally, it brought such fantastic profits, in the absence of any machinery for the renegotiation of contracts, that when the figures were paraded before the public during the nineteen-thirties, many people arrived at the interesting notion that there would be no more wars if it were not for profit-hungry munitions makers.)

Between 1914 and 1918 many a man who had only half believed that bigger production brought sharply reduced costs began to dream dreams of an exciting future when he saw what mechanization, unleashed, could accomplish.

III

During those same years the seeds of future industries were being sown.

On January 10, 1901, Spindletop blew in: Anthony F. Lucas struck oil at Spindletop near Beaumont, Texas. Thus began a new era for the Southwest—and a guarantee that the automobile business, then in its feeble infancy, would have as it grew to maturity an abundant source of power.

On December 17, 1903, on the sands of Kittyhawk on the North Carolina coast, Orville Wright made a twelve-second flight—and then his brother Wilbur made a fifty-nine-second flight—in an airplane they had painstakingly built. Several years went by before the public grasped what the Wrights were doing; people were so convinced that flying was impossible that most of those who saw them flying about Dayton in 1905 decided that what they had seen must be some trick without significance—somewhat as most people today would regard a demonstration of, let us say, telepathy. Never before or since, in all probability, have the newshawks of America taken longer to apprehend a momentous story. It was not until May, 1908—*nearly four and a half years after the Wrights'first flight*—that experienced reporters were sent to observe what they were doing, experienced editors gave full credence to these reporters' excited dispatches, and the world at last woke up to the fact that human flight had been successfully accomplished—though in the interval the Wrights had flown repeatedly and their longest flight had lasted a full thirty-eight minutes! The seed of the great aviation industry had been sown in 1903; it began to sprout, very belatedly, in 1908.

Wireless telegraphy had been discovered in 1895 by an Italian, Guglielmo Marconi—but its future possibilities were not comprehended in 1900, when Reginald A. Fessenden first transmitted speech by wireless; or in 1904, when Sir John Ambrose Fleming produced the radio detector or Fleming valve; or in 1907, when Dr. Lee De Forest produced the audion; or in 1912, when Edwin H. Armstrong discovered the electric generator circuit by means of which the feeble impulses received by radio could be "fed back" and multiplied many times. For that matter, as late as 1915, when David Sarnoff, assistant traffic manager of the Marconi Wireless Telegraph Company, proposed a "radio music box" and suggested the future possibilities of public broadcasting, he spoke to deaf ears. But the seeds of the radio and television industries had been sown.

In 1903 was produced the first moving picture which told a connected story, *The Great Train Robbery*. About 1905 the first nickelodeons appeared—crude motion-picture theaters, often improvised in vacant stores. And the movies began their slow march to importance as a vehicle of popular entertainment and as an inculcator of the assumptions of the classless American life.

In 1909 Leo H. Baekeland first put on the market a chemically-made substance which he called bakelite. It was not the first plastic—that honor had gone to celluloid, much earlier—but it may justly be called the seed from which the plastics industry grew. And along with

the material which, when first clumsily produced before 1920, was
known as "artificial silk," and which later came to be known as rayon,
it helped to beget one of the most important concepts of twentieth-
century invention: the idea that man could produce materials to
order—not simply synthetic imitations of nature, but often materials
superior to what nature could produce. Witness the subsequent miracle of nylon.

One might add that in 1911 Willis H. Carrier read a paper on
what he called "Rational Psychrometric Formulae," which presented
the theory and the practical data on which the air-conditioning industry was later based. And that at the St. Louis Exposition in 1904 there
was exhibited an oil engine built in Providence, Rhode Island, after
the plans of the great German inventor, Rudolf Diesel. Few people
at the time seemed unduly excited by the fact that they had met it at
St. Louis, but the Diesel engine, too, had a future.

To understand the America of today one must not only realize how
vital to its development was the revolt of the American conscience,
which implanted in Americans the idea that you could repair the
economic and political machinery of the country, so as to make it
work better for the majority, without stopping the machine; one must
also realize that the revolt of the American conscience might have
caused a mere redistribution of wealth rather than a multiplication of
wealth unless the machine had kept on running and a host of men
had been tinkering with it, revealing how it could follow the dynamic
logic of mass production, and also discovering and inventing new
things for it to do in the long and hopeful future.

Chapter **8**

The Automobile Revolution

IN THE year 1906 Woodrow Wilson, who was then president of Princeton University, said, "Nothing has spread socialistic feeling in this country more than the automobile," and added that it offered "a picture of the arrogance of wealth." Less than twenty years later, two women of Muncie, Indiana, both of whom were managing on small incomes, spoke their minds to investigators gathering facts for that admirable sociological study of an American community, *Middletown*. Said one, who was the mother of nine children, "We'd rather do without clothes than give up the car." Said the other, "I'll go without food before I'll see us give up the car." And elsewhere another housewife, in answer to a comment on the fact that her family owned a car but no bathtub, uttered a fitting theme song for the automobile revolution. "Why," said she, "you can't go to town in a bathtub!"

This change in the status of the automobile from a luxury for the few to a necessity for the many—a change which, as we shall see, progressively transformed American communities and daily living habits and ideas throughout the half century—did not come about abruptly. It could not. For it depended upon three things. First, a reliable, manageable, and not too expensive car. Second, good roads. And third, garages and filling stations in profusion. And all these three requirements had to come slowly, by degrees, each reinforcing the others; a man who had tried to operate a filling station beside a dusty rural road in 1906 would have speedily gone bankrupt. But it was during the nineteen-twenties that the impact of the change was felt most sharply from year to year.

When Woodrow Wilson spoke in 1906, and for years thereafter, the automobile had been a high-hung, noisy vehicle which couldn't quite make up its mind that it was not an obstreperous variety of carriage. It was so unreliable in its performance, so likely to be beset by tire blowouts, spark-plug trouble, carburetor trouble, defects in the transmission, and other assorted ailments, that a justly popular song of the time celebrated the troubles of the owner who "had to get under, get out and get under." The country doctors who in increasing numbers were coming to use the little brass-nosed Fords of the day had to be students of mechanical as well as human pathology. Each car had a toolbox on the running board, and tourists were accustomed to carrying with them blowout patches, French chalk, and a variety of tire irons against that awful moment when a tire would pop, miles from any help. One had to crank the engine by hand—a difficult and sometimes dangerous business. All cars except the limousines of the wealthy were open, with vertical windshields which gave so little protection against wind and dust to those in the back seat that dusters and even goggles were widely worn; and a gust of rain would necessitate a frantic raising of the folding top and a vexatious fitting and buttoning of the side curtains.

Roads were mostly dusty or muddy, with no through routes. Even as late as 1921 there was no such thing as an officially numbered highway. In that year the *Automobile Blue Book* warned those who proposed to drive from Richford, Vermont, to Montreal: "Chains on all four wheels absolutely essential in wet weather." And it advised tourists in general that "where mountain roads, sandy stretches, and muddy places are to be met with, a shovel with a collapsible handle" might prove very useful. At the time when Wilson spoke, panicky horses were still a hazard for the driver in remote districts, and speed limits set by farmer-minded local officials were sometimes low indeed: my personal memory tells me—unbelievably but I think reliably—

that in tranquil Holderness, New Hampshire, the original legal limit was six miles an hour.

Ford's energetic driving down of prices helped to make the automobile more popular, but equally responsible were a series of vital improvements: the invention of an effective self-starter, first designed by Charles F. Kettering and installed in the Cadillac in 1912; the coming, within the next two or three years, of the demountable rim and the cord tire; but above all, the introduction of the closed car. As late as 1916 only 2 per cent of the cars manufactured in the United States were closed; by 1926, 72 per cent of them were.

What had happened was that manufacturers had learned to build closed cars that were not hideously expensive, that did not rattle themselves to pieces, and that could be painted with a fast-drying but durable paint; and that meanwhile the car-buying public had discovered with delight that a closed car was something quite different from the old "horseless carriage." It was a power-driven room on wheels—storm-proof, lockable, parkable all day and all night in all weathers. In it you could succumb to speed fever without being battered by the wind. You could close its windows against dust or rain. You could use it to fetch home the groceries, to drive to the golf club or the railroad station, to cool off on hot evenings, to reach a job many miles distant and otherwise inaccessible, to take the family out for a day's drive or a week-end excursion, to pay an impromptu visit to friends forty or fifty miles away, or, as innumerable young couples were not slow to learn, to engage in private intimacies. One of the cornerstones of American morality had been the difficulty of finding a suitable locale for misconduct; now this cornerstone was crumbling. And if the car was also a frequent source of family friction ("No, Junior, you are *not* taking it tonight"), as well as a destroyer of pedestrianism, a weakener of the churchgoing habit, a promoter of envy, a lethal weapon when driven by heedless, drunken, or irresponsible people, and a formidable convenience for criminals seeking a safe getaway, it was nonetheless indispensable.

Furthermore, a car was now less expensive to maintain than in the days when the cost of successive repairs might mount up to a formidable sum each year. And it could be bought on easy payments. The installment selling of cars, virtually unknown before World War I, spread so rapidly that by 1925 over three-quarters of all cars, new and old, were being sold this way.

Over these same years more and more roads had been paved, as public officials discovered that appropriations for highway surfacing were no longer considered mere favors to the rich; and garages and filling stations had multiplied.

The result of all these developments was a headlong rush to buy cars on the part of innumerable people to whom the idea of becoming automobile owners would have seemed fantastic only a few years before. In 1915 there were less than 2½ million cars registered in the United States. By 1920 there were over 9 million; by 1925, nearly 20 million; by 1930, over 26½ million.

So it was that the years between 1918 and 1930 introduced to America a long series of novelties which are now such familiar features of the American scene that one might think we had always had them: automatic traffic lights, concrete roads with banked curves, six-lane boulevards, one-way streets, officially numbered highways, tourist homes, and tourist cabins; and lined the edges of the major thoroughfares with that garish jumble of roadside services and businesses that Benton Mackaye and Lewis Mumford called "road town"—roadside diners, hot-dog stands, peanut stands, fruit and vegetable stalls, filling station after filling station, and used-car lots.

Meanwhile an antidote to the increasing snarl and confusion and frustration of traffic through the built-up areas of the East was already in preparation. For a generation the officials of Westchester County, New York, had been disturbed by the polluted condition of the little Bronx River and by its tendency to flood, and had been planning to restrict and control its flow while making it the chief attraction of a long strip of parkway—which almost incidentally would contain a through automobile road. When this road was opened to the public in 1925, motorists and traffic commissions and regional planners happily saw in it the answer to their prayers: an ample highway, with traffic lanes separated at intervals, uncluttered by local traffic, winding through a landscape undefaced by commerce. On such a highway one could make time most agreeably. Other parkways, wider and straighter, were thereupon built, both in Westchester County and elsewhere; existing through highways were rebuilt to by-pass towns along their way; so that by August, 1931, Mackaye and Mumford, writing in *Harper's*, could announce that it had at last been recognized that the automobile was less like a family carriage than like a family locomotive, and also could look forward prophetically to a now-familiar scene. The time would come, they predicted, when a motorist with a long drive before him would ease into the fast traffic on a "townless highway" and presently would be spinning along "with less anxiety and more safety at 60 miles an hour than he used to have in the old road-town confusion at 25." When that day came, they said, the automobile would have become "an honor to our mechanical civilization and not a reproach to it."

In 1931 those days had not yet arrived. There was still no Merritt Parkway, no Pennsylvania Turnpike; there were no butterfly intersections; there was no such majestic combination of separate lanes of traffic as would be seen by the mid-century at Cahuenga Pass in Los Angeles, where no less than fourteen lanes were to run side by side. Already motor busses had arrived in quantity, but the progressive ripping up of trolley tracks had only begun. Already motor trucks were taking freight business away from the railroads, but there was still no such vast and humming all-night traffic of trucks, truck tractors, and semi-trailers between our great cities as later years were to bring. And that perfect symbol of our national mobility, the residential trailer, was only just appearing: the first trailer had been built in 1929 by a bacteriologist, for vacation use, but these houses on wheels were not to arrive in force until the mid-thirties. Yet already the pattern of the automobile age had been set.

II

No such startling change in the habits of a people could have taken place without having far-reaching social effects. Let us glance at a few of them.

1. It developed the motorized suburb. Where a suburb had previously been accessible by railroad, but had been limited in size because of the difficulty of reaching the station from any place more
than a mile or so away from it, it grew with startling speed, as real-
estate subdividers bought up big tracts of property and laid out
Woodmere Road and Edgemont Drive and Lakeside Terrace, suitable
for English-cottage-type or Spanish-villa-type or New-England-salt-
box-type (or, later, ranch-type) houses with attached garages; where
the children would have the benefit of light and air and play space,
and their parents would have the benefit of constant battles over the
policies of the local school board; where the wife would gulp down
her coffee at 7:52 to drive her husband to the 8:03 train before driving her children to school and doing the family errands.

In a suburb which had previously been inaccessible by railroad the
same phenomenon took place with only a slight variation: the earner
of the family drove all the way from his almost-rural cottage to his
place of work—and worried about the parking problem in the city.
The number of Americans whose heart and treasure were twenty
miles apart, as Agnes Rogers has put it, was vastly increased. And as
more and more people whose living was dependent upon work at the
center of the city fled to the leafy outskirts, urban planners began to
be concerned about the blighted areas around the center of the city,
where land values were falling and a general deterioration was manifest.

2. The coming of the automobile age brought other changes too.
It caused a widespread shift of business, and of economic and social
importance, from the railroad town to the off-the-railroad one; from
the farm that was four miles from a railroad station but had poor
soil to the fertile farm that was twenty or fifty miles from rail; and
from the center of the small city to its outskirts.

The hotel on Main Street, that had formerly been the one and only
place for the traveling salesman to stop, lost business to the tourist
camp on Highway 84. In due course this tourist camp was transformed into a new kind of roadside hotel, which offered overnight
privacy—and sometimes luxury—without having to carry the eco-

nomic load of high land value and of maintaining a restaurant and other public rooms. The shops along Main Street lost business to the new Sears Roebuck store at the edge of town, with its ample parking lot. City department stores, becoming painfully aware of their dwindling appeal to commuters, opened suburban branches to catch the out-of-town trade. And by the mid-century, shopping centers were beginning to be developed out in the open countryside, where the prime essential of parking space would be abundant.

The big summer hotel lost business, as the automobile opened up to a vast number of people the opportunity either to range from motel to motel or to have their own summer cottages, to which they could travel not only for the summer, but even for occasional week ends at other times in the year, by wedging the family into a car that bulged with people, suitcases, and assorted duffle. In resort after resort a pattern of change was repeated: the big hotel on the point, or at the beach, or on the hilltop was torn down, while the number of cottages in the neighborhood of its site doubled, tripled, quadrupled; and meanwhile the Friday afternoon traffic out of the city to various points, beaches, and hilltops became denser and denser. The trunk manufacturers lost business to the suitcase manufacturers, and the express companies languished.

During the single decade of the nineteen-twenties, railroad passenger traffic was almost cut in half; only commuter traffic held up. (In the outskirts of New York, the next two decades were to witness a decline even in railroad commuter traffic, as the new parkways, bridges, and tunnels into Manhattan swelled the number of commuters by bus and by private car.)

3. The automobile age brought a parking problem that was forever being solved and then unsolving itself again. During the early nineteen-twenties the commuters who left their cars at the suburban railroad station at first parked them at the edge of the station drive; then they needed a special parking lot, and pretty soon an extended parking lot, and in due course a still bigger one—and the larger the lot grew, the more people wanted to use it. New boulevards, widened roads, and parkways relieved the bottlenecks at the approaches to the

big cities—and invited more and more cars to enter. At the end of
the half century the question, "Where do I park?" was as annoyingly
insistent as it had been at any time since the arrival of the automobile.

4. The new dispensation brought sudden death. During the nineteen-twenties the number of people slaughtered annually by cars
in the United States climbed from a little less than 15,000 in 1922 to
over 32,000 in 1930; eighteen years later, in 1948, it stood at almost
exactly the 1930 figure. As cars had become more powerful, and
roads had become more persuasively straight and smooth, and speeds
had increased, the shocking death toll each week end had led to the
more cautious licensing of drivers and inspection of cars, to the multiplication of warning signs along the roadsides, and to the study of the
causes and cures of death on the highway by such organizations as the
National Safety Council and the Automotive Safety Council. But
meanwhile youngsters had learned to play "chicken," and hot-rod
enthusiasts had taken to the road; and many older drivers, after a few
drinks, found it easy to persuade themselves that they should over-
take and pass that damned old creeping car at the crest of a hill, and
even the most sedate motorist sometimes fell asleep at the wheel—
and now the accidents that took place, while less frequent, were more
lethal. So that at the turn of the half century one could still predict
with reasonable certainty that a holiday week end would bring several
hundred men, women, and children to an abrupt and gory end.

5. Along with the telephone, the radio, and the other agencies of
communication, the automobile revolution ended the isolation of the
farmer. In 1900 Ray Stannard Baker, describing a wave of prosperity
among the farmers of the Midwest, had said that when a farmer did
well, the first thing he did was to paint the barn; the second was to
add a porch to his house; the third was to buy a piano; and the fourth
was to send his children to college. By the mid-twenties the purchase
of a car was likely to come even before the painting of the barn—and
a new piano was a rarity. The widening use of the tractor was enlarg-
ing farms; and with the aid of the profusion of scientific information
which was made available through the publications and county agents
of the Department of Agriculture, the farmer was becoming less and

less a laborer by hand, using rule-of-thumb methods, and more and more a businessman of the soil, an operator of machines, and a technologist. No longer, now, when he visited town, was he a rube, a hayseed, whose wife and daughters looked hick in calico. By 1939 the Sears Roebuck catalogue was listing dresses "inspired by Schiaparelli," and in 1940 it solemnly announced that "The traditional lapse between the acceptance of new fashions . . . in metropolitan centers and on farms apparently no longer exists."

6. The automobile broadened geographical horizons, especially for people who had hitherto considered themselves too poor to travel. One could still find, here and there, men and women who had never ventured farther from home than the county seat, but their number was dwindling fast. For now the family who had always stayed at home on their day off could drive to the lakes or the shore, and on their vacation could range widely over the land, see new things, engage in new sports, meet new people. Even their daily radius of activity lengthened startlingly: by the nineteen-forties it might be a matter of routine for a rural family to drive ten or fifteen miles to do their shopping, twenty or thirty to see the movies, fifty to visit a doctor or dentist.

Furthermore, the automobile weakened the roots which held a family to one spot. Always a mobile people by comparison with the peoples of Europe, now Americans followed the economic tides more readily than ever before, moving by automobile—and before long by trailer—wherever there might be a call for construction workers, or fruit pickers, or airplane mechanics. Sober intellectuals were wont to deplore the growing American restlessness and to praise the man who was rooted to the land where he and his forefathers had been born and bred; but the automobile suited the American genius. For that genius was not static but venturesome; Americans felt that a rolling stone gathers experience, adventure, sophistication, and—with luck— new and possibly fruitful opportunities.

7. The automobile revolution engendered personal pride. When I say this I am not thinking of the envy-in-reverse of the man or woman who revels in having a finer model of car than the neighbors can af-

ford, but of something less readily defined but no less real. Someone has said that the Asiatic, long accustomed to humiliation at the hands of the lordly white European, will endure it no longer after he has once sat at the controls of a tractor or a bulldozer. Similarly the American who has been humbled by poverty, or by his insignificance in the business order, or by his racial status, or by any other circumstance that might demean him in his own eyes, gains a sense of authority when he slides behind the wheel of an automobile and it leaps forward at his bidding, ready to take him wherever he may personally please. If he drives a bus or a huge truck trailer his state is all the more kingly, for he feels himself responsible for the wielding of a sizable concentration of force.

This effect of the automobile revolution was especially noticeable in the South, where one began to hear whites complaining about "uppity niggers" on the highways, where there was no Jim Crow. But the new sense of pride was dispersed far more widely than that; in some degree it affected almost everyone on the road. In 1950 the civilian labor force of the United States was estimated to number a little less than 59 million men and women; in the same year the number of drivers in the United States was estimated to be a little larger: 59,300,000. More than one driver for every job-holder! Never before in human history, perhaps, had any such proportion of the nationals of any land known the lifting of the spirit that the free exercise of power can bring.

Chapter 9

Indian Summer of the Old Order

DURING the three or four years that followed the Armistice of 1918 there came a subtle change in the emotional weather. The torch of idealism that had kindled the revolt of the American conscience seemed to have pretty well burned itself out. People were tired. In particular their public spirit, their consciences, and their hopes were tired.

The returning soldiers were disillusioned about the crusade they had been sent off on. The war had proved to be a filthy business, in which noble purposes had been less visible than barbarity and cooties; and a good many American doughboys, allergic to foreign manners and ways of living, had seen quite enough of their noble British and French allies to hold them for some time. Foreigners began to seem a dubious lot anyhow; American enthusiasm for the League of Nations petered out, and we decided—disastrously perhaps, but under the circumstances almost inevitably—to play in our own backyard. People felt it was about time to relax; to look after themselves, rather than after other people and the world in general; and to have a good time. The prohibition law—that curious final product of the revolt of the American conscience—had not been long on the books before people began to flout it right and left; pretty soon a great many men and women who had always considered themselves patterns of law-abiding respectability began to patronize bootleggers, or home-brew very peculiar beer, or concoct even queerer bathtub gin, or wear hip-pocket flasks to parties. Even the reformers themselves were tired, and wondered why they now went limp at the thought of battling for great political causes.

Weary of striving onward and upward, the electorate chose for President in 1920 the handsome Warren G. Harding, a senator whose greatest assets, aside from his magnificent good looks, were his kindliness, folksiness, and humility. An amiable man of no lofty intellectual or moral stature, he had no conspicuous urge to improve anything; he preferred to talk about what he called "normalcy," meaning normality. And he was subsequently discovered to have had among his buddies in office some egregious grafters. When Harding died—some time before the full enormity of the scandals of his regime became known—he was succeeded by Calvin Coolidge, an honest, careful, prudent man but one of the most negative characters ever to attain high American office. Coolidge didn't grapple with any national problem until it was forced upon his attention, could sit through a prolonged social occasion without opening his mouth to utter more than an occasional monosyllable, and liked to take afternoon naps in the quiet of the White House—naps which according to Chief Usher "Ike" Hoover lasted from two to four hours. Coolidge's genius for inactivity seemed to be all right with the majority of the American people, who for the time being wanted to enjoy the sort of happiness that has been said to be the lot of the nation that has no history.

A friend of mine who was a very small boy in 1918 was told by his father that the Armistice had been signed, and asked, "Now that the war's over, what will they find to put in the newspapers?" His father laughed, but in retrospect the question seems to have had considerable point. For the fact is that gradually military affairs and foreign affairs and politics began to yield first place in newspaper coverage to scandals, crimes, disasters, human dramas, and sports, not simply in such sensational sheets as the new tabloids, but also in the more severe and discreet ones. Turn back today to the yellowing pages of the newspapers of the latter part of 1926, when the Hall-Mills murder case was unfolding, and you may be surprised to find that even the *New York Times*—a paper conscientiously devoted then, as later, to telling everything about everything important—gave front-page, right-hand-column treatment, day after day, to the news from Somerville, New Jersey, where Mrs. Edward Wheeler Hall and her two brothers and her cousin were on trial for the murder of the Rev. Mr. Hall and Mrs. Mills of his church choir. And when, the following spring, young Charles A. Lindbergh flew non-stop from New York to Paris, the papers, along with everybody else, behaved as if his feat had been the most earth-shaking event since the Creation. Nothing that Congress could do, no triumph of the devisers of foreign treaties, no public crisis, seemed to matter alongside the fact that a charming young man had made a bold and exceptionally long flight.

Something like a World-Series-week spirit—a contagion of delighted concern over things that were exciting but didn't matter profoundly—was dominant. People followed eagerly the sporting exploits of Jack Dempsey, Babe Ruth, Bobby Jones, Helen Wills, Gertrude Ederle, Red Grange, the Four Horsemen of Notre Dame, and other athletic heroes of the hour; agonized over the attempts to rescue from a Kentucky cave an obscure young man named Floyd Collins; hung on the day-to-day reports from the Scopes trial in Dayton, Tennessee, and from the murder trial of Leopold and Loeb; and welcomed to America, with showers of torn paper in New York, heroes and heroines of large and small renown. Why stop to ask whether Queen Marie of Rumania, for example, really rated a public welcome? She was a handsome woman and a queen, and anyhow the party itself, the crowds, the noise, and the torn-up telephone books and streams of ticker tape drifting down from upper windows made a wonderful show.

II

Along with this enjoyment of tremendous trivia there was a very general desire, in the nineteen-twenties, to shake off the restraints of puritanism, to upset the long-standing conventions of decorum.

There had been advance signals of this rebellion. One had been the dance craze which had arrived about 1912, and which had set stiff-jointed elderly couples to fox-trotting or doing the tango along with their juniors at innumerable *thé dansants,* to the music of Irving Berlin's jazz. Another had been the Armory Show of 1913, which had exhibited to an astonished public some remarkable samples of highly non-academic modern art. Still another had been an outburst of free verse among poets in rebellion against accepted poetic conventions. Furthermore, the war had pulled millions of young men' and women out of their accustomed environments, and given them a taste of freedom under circumstances in which it didn't seem to matter very much what Mrs. Grundy said! With many of these young people the postwar reaction took a special form: it was easy for them to think of themselves as a generation who nad been condemned to go through the hell of war because of the mistakes of their elders, whose admonitions on any subject must therefore be suspect. At any rate, by 1920 the rebellion against puritanism and stuffiness was widely visible, and it gained in impetus as the decade progressed.

It was the girls who spearheaded it. Did mothers think of corsets as the armor of respectability? A great many daughters decided that dancing without a corset was much more personal and satisfactory. Did mothers think young girls shouldn't drink? Daughters found that a gulp of illegal whiskey from the hip flask of a swain in a parked sedan added an excellent note of zest to the proceedings. Did mothers converse in ladylike circumlocutions? Daughters talked right out about sex and the libido, the latter being a word one got from Freud, who had said, according to report, that repressions were bad for you. Had mothers been brought up in the era of long skirts, when the exposure of an ankle to the public gaze had been regarded as a virtual invitation to masculine lust? Daughters reveled in the emancipation of the new styles, which by the middle of the decade had lifted the hemline all the way to the knee.

In a few short years American women in general changed almost unrecognizably in appearance. As late as 1919 they had worn amply cut, ankle-length dresses over such underpinnings as corset covers, envelope chemises, and petticoats; they had worn their hair long, and had needed hatpins; and their daytime stockings had been mostly made of black (or brown, or green, or blue) cotton or lisle; silk stockings were considered somewhat luxurious. By the latter nineteen-twenties young women had reduced the yardage of their garments by one-half, were increasingly wearing silk or rayon underwear, and sought desperately to look pencil slim. They wore their hair short—bobbed or boyishly shingled—and made frequent visits to that rising institution, the beauty parlor, which had come into its own following the widespread acceptance of the permanent wave. And since the early twenties they had been unanimously addicted to what proved to be the most durable fashion innovation of our times—flesh-colored stockings. (From their color came the term "cheesecake" for leggy photography.) Older women followed these changes more slowly, and in some cases with a reluctant feeling that they were succumbing to a pernicious cult of youth. But there was no resisting the trend.

For it fitted a changing pattern in the relations between the sexes: the much more general acceptance of women's taking jobs, whether they "needed to" or not; a sharp increase in feminine smoking; the advent of mixed drinking and the introduction of that standard social institution of later years, the cocktail party; police protection of the speakeasy, which in most places was simply a dive where one could get liquor, but in Manhattan might be a well-guarded but discreetly managed restaurant-with-bar; the rising vogue of the night club; a more playful attitude toward sex among young people, and a more tolerant attitude toward divorce, and indeed toward extramarital affairs, among people who considered themselves sophisticated. It was characteristic of the times that during the nineteen-twenties Mary Pickford, the motion-picture embodiment of girlish innocence, was succeeded as a movie goddess by Clara Bow, the "it" girl. What had happened was that feminism had gone into a new phase. Now that the vote had been won, the promised entry of women into politics on a large scale had not taken place; instead, women by and large were asserting the right to enjoy themselves like and with men.

To this generalization one may perhaps add some footnotes from the vantage point of the nineteen-fifties. The first is that by present-

day standards the social conduct of those days was not particularly
loose; much more astonishing to us, in retrospect, is the code of
puritanical restraint against which the youngsters of the nineteen-
twenties were rebelling. Which is another way of saying that,
although there have been considerable changes in the accepted modes
of social conduct since the nineteen-twenties, it was during that
decade that something approaching the present code was established.
Yet the atmosphere was different then: there was an air of novelty and
self-conscious experiment about the relaxing of the code which was
intensely exciting to the participants and shocking to observers who
were out of step with the change.

The second footnote is that sages such as Dr. Kinsey insist that
there is little change from generation to generation in the amount
of actual illicit intercourse; to which one can only answer that ardors
of a merely preliminary or tentative sort, when conducted in public
or boasted of in public, tend to convey to all and sundry the impression that the days of Saturnalia have arrived, whatever the
statistics of consummation may be.

The third footnote is that the prevailing mood was not one of
abandonment so much as of rowdiness. Witness the women's fashions,
which made mature females look like short-skirted, long-waisted,
flat-breasted, short-haired little girls trying to look worldly wise;
witness, too, the bright vogue of dances such as the "Charleston,"
which was a lively but unseductive romp. The final footnote is that of
course not everybody let himself or herself go; there were millions of
Americans to whom such goings-on as I have been hinting at were all
but unthinkable.

Along with this relaxation of the social code went a wave of
religious skepticism—wasn't science making mincemeat of the old-
time religion?—and of hedonism. Among young men and women
who prided themselves on their modern-mindedness there was a
disposition to regard church work or social service work or anything
else to which the word "uplift" could be applied as "poisonous" and
an unwarranted intrusion upon other people's privacy; and besides,

one had a right to enjoy oneself, and taking a ride in the sedan of a Sunday morning was much more fun than going to church. Statistics of church membership showed no conclusive evidence of loss, but it was clear that a lot of church members were at the golf links on Sunday instead of in their pews, and that the church was progressively losing its hold on the brighter members of the younger generation. People of a naturally aspiring turn of mind were likely to be channeling their idealism into a devotion for psychoanalysis, which looked to them like an agreeably uninhibited sort of salvation-through-science; or for progressive education, which was based upon a rebellion against the strictness of the old educational tradition; or for humanism, a rather vague sort of religion without theology.

• Disillusionment and rebellion characterized the writers of the time, too; disillusionment over the crusading spirit that had accompanied the United States into World War I, anger at the way in which the writers felt they had been repressed and tormented by dogma and convention in their youth, and scorn for the supposed vulgarity of the business civilization of the day. Hence the astonishing vogue of H. L. Mencken, who scoffed at religion, respectability, Victorian propriety and sentimentality in the arts, reformers, and politicians generally, and who at the same time was a tub-thumper for such tough-grained writers as Dreiser. Sinclair Lewis wrote of the American small town and the American absorption in business with photographic distaste, mingled with sympathy for their victims. Ernest Hemingway, in his sparing prose, convinced those younger intellectuals whose spiritual home was Montparnasse that they were indeed a lost generation, and that there was little left for them but drink and sex. Eugene O'Neill turned Freud and the stream-of-consciousness literary technique to the uses of intense if interminable drama on themes which an earlier generation would have considered shocking.

Some of the writers of the day exhibited such disillusionment even with disillusionment itself that they approached complete negation, but on the whole the new mood was not frustrating; indeed it was intensely stimulating. Throughout the world of the arts, there was a feeling that now at last one could shake off the traditional restraints upon candor and could tell the truth. And the result was a sort of intellectual renaissance: the blossoming time not only of Lewis and Hemingway and O'Neill and Dreiser but also of Dos Passos, Sherwood Anderson, Maxwell Anderson, Willa Cather, Edna St. Vincent Millay, Ellen Glasgow, F. Scott Fitzgerald, and a great many other able novelists, poets, and dramatists. Despite the rise of the movies to the status of a vast industry which drew millions of people into the theaters every twenty-four hours, the legitimate stage had never fared so well: during the single year 1927 there were no less than 268 openings on Broadway—a huge figure compared with those of recent years. It is true that the idols of the young American writers and artists were predominantly foreign, or transplanted: Proust, Joyce, T. S. Eliot, Gertrude Stein, the French modern painters, the Bauhaus architects; yet signs were multiplying that the United States was coming of age culturally.

III

The highbrows scorned Babbitt, a gross and vulgar fellow in their eyes. Yet Babbitt himself was riding high. More important in retrospect, perhaps, than the loosening of conventions or the enlivenment of letters and the arts was the brief triumphal march of American industry and business during the seven fat years from 1923 through 1929—or, to be more precise, until October, 1929.

These were booming years, and for this fact there was ample basis. For one thing, there was the great growth of the automobile industry —which meant expanding business not only for automobile manufacturers and parts manufacturers but also for dealers, garagemen, filling-station operators, trucking companies, bus companies, roadside businesses, and so on almost indefinitely. There was the sudden blooming of the radio industry after Dr. Frank Conrad put on the first scheduled broadcast in 1920; by the end of the decade radio sales totaled over three-quarters of a billion dollars a year, and the radio advertisers found they had struck pay dirt. There was the lively rise of the construction industry, as a confident business community called for bigger and better office buildings, and a more and more congested urban population called for new apartment houses, and the motorized suburbs and booming resorts called for new real-estate developments. There was the onset of the rayon industry and the multiplication of chain stores and chain services of many kinds. Better still, manufacturers had been learning what new machines and a careful planning of production could do to increase output. During the years between 1922 and 1929 the physical production of the agricultural, manufacturing, mining, and construction industries increased by 34 per cent—an astonishing figure—and between 1920 and 1930, output per man hour increased by 21 per cent!

So far, so good. The stuff could be produced all right. The question was whether it could be sold. The consensus was that a brisk enough salesman could sell it. And so the nineteen-twenties saw the canonization of the salesman as the brightest hope of America.

Sales quotas were imposed on young men setting out to vend their wares. Contests among salesmen—often merciless contests—were devised. Executives told their juniors that the day of the order taker was over; that instead of waiting for customers, they must go out and *find* them. "Look down there," Charles E. Mitchell, the sales-conscious head of the National City Bank, would say, leading one of his bond salesmen to a window. "There are six million people with incomes that aggregate thousands of millions of dollars. They are just waiting for someone to come and tell them what to do with their savings. Take a good look, eat a good lunch, and then go down and tell them." Advertising firms produced copy and pictures and layouts so glossily persuasive that they made the advertising pages of an earlier day look amateurish, and exploited to the limit the techniques of frightening the consumer into buying and of appealing to the most primitive forms of social ambition. ("Four out of five lose"—in other words, they get pyorrhea if they don't use the right toothpaste. "Often a bridesmaid but never a bride"—because she has unpleasant breath from not using the right mouthwash. "When your guests are gone—are you sorry you ever invited them?"—because, not having studied the *Book of Etiquette,* you have behaved boorishly.) Sales conventions became more plentiful and livelier, along with trade conventions—partly, of course, because it was fun for gregarious men to get away from the home folks to a place where their adventures with bootleg hooch would be uninhibited by any fear of meeting their neighbors; but also because the arts of salesmanship could be stimulated by a comparison of notes on methods and procedures, conducted in an atmosphere of positively revivalist fervor for bigger and better sales.

IV

What was there to hamper the furious onward march of business? Not the government, whose regulatory officials and commissions seemed mostly to be napping along with Coolidge. Not labor: after an angry wave of strikes immediately after the war, unionism languished; total trade-union membership in the United States dwindled from over five millions in 1920 to less than four millions in 1927 and three and a third millions in 1931. (One reason for this decline, possibly, was that union membership required effort and devotion and that union members, like other people, preferred to relax. Another was that wages were rising anyhow, though not, perhaps, as fast as productivity was rising. A third was that the prevailing union leadership was old-fashioned, large-waisted, and slow.)

What was destined to halt the forward progress of business was the fact that the businessmen of America had become bemused with paper values—with the piling up of speculative or artificially generated wealth which had little relation to the production of goods. At a time when the greatest economic need of the nation was for devices which would distribute as widely and fairly as possible the fruits of industrial progress, without destroying the incentives (to capital, to management, and also to workers) which sparked that progress, there developed a speculative mania which benefited immediately only those who could lay their hands on capital; and in addition, there were invented or improved a series of devices for distributing the fruits of prosperity—or what looked like them— into the pockets of the few.

These devices included company mergers at inflated prices which gave insiders a chance to line their own pockets; the piling of holding companies one upon another until—as in the Insull and Van Sweringen empires—they were sometimes five or six or seven deep, with the result that the heaviest cream of the profits of the concerns at the base of such a pyramid could be drawn off by the owners of the concern at the top; the formation by banks of "security affiliates" which in effect used the depositors' funds to make investments, in securities and in real estate, such as were denied to the banks themselves by law; the frequent practice of inflating corporate profits by selling properties back and forth among a group of companies at rising prices; and the formation of stock-market pools in which the officers of a company would join with brokers and well-heeled speculators to push up the price of the company's stock—and then unload the stock on a new lot of buyers, thus making money at the expense of those officers' own stockholders.

These were only a few of the widely employed devices of that day. Not only did they represent, collectively, an appalling breakdown of the fiduciary tradition; but—this is the primary fact to bear in mind— they tended, collectively, to knit speculative or even phony values into the economic fabric of the country at so many points that if values fell, bank after bank and company after company—and their depositors and employees—would be hard hit. The irresponsible actions of men who did not stop to think that they were constructing a caricature of the capitalist system were paving the way for disaster.

Accompanying the employment of these ingenious schemes—and intensified by them—came an immense speculative boom. Not long after the fantastic Florida real-estate boom exploded, in 1926, the Big Bull Market in common stocks began. It really got under way in 1927, went into high gear in 1928, and after a series of convulsive setbacks rose to its majestic climax in September, 1929.

Just how many people were speculating in stocks during those wild years is unknown, but probably a million or so were buying on margin—putting up only a fraction of the price of the stocks they bought—and a million or two more, though they were paying cash in full for their purchases, were following the stock-market quotations in the financial pages with almost equally rapt attention. Not only were financiers and businessmen of high and low degree speculating, but housewives, ranchers, stenographers, clergymen, elevator men—whoever could lay hands on some cash to put into General Motors or Radio common or Monty Ward or Case Threshing or Electric Bond & Share. The story is told of a young man who went to a financier for advice on how to get a business education and was told to buy such-and-such a stock and watch what happened to it; a couple of weeks later he came back to the financier agog: "How long has this been going on?" he asked in bewildered rapture. During most of 1928 and 1929 buying stocks was like betting at a race track at which, fantastically, most of the horses won. Prices climbed and climbed and climbed. The Standard Statistics index of common stock prices averaged 100 during the year 1926; by June, 1927, it had reached 114; by June, 1928, it had got to 148; by June, 1929, to 191; and by September, 1929, to the dizzy height of 216!

As prices soared, some of the current wise men said they had reached a permanent plateau; this was a New Era. Others advanced the bright idea that presently the whole nation would enrich itself by owning common stocks. Still others said that what was happening was a wild gamble, and a lot of people would surely lose their shirts, but a crash wouldn't matter much otherwise; after the smoke had cleared away, things would hum along as before. What they did not realize was that the speculative market had now become so huge that the mechanisms that were supposed to make it self-regulating —the automatic selling out of unlucky buyers, for example, which was supposed to cause a drop in prices which would invite new buyers—would become mechanisms for compounding disaster; and that such a large part of American business was geared to these inflated values that the repercussions of a crash would shake the whole economy.

Who could have halted the march to disaster? President Coolidge? He knew little of finance, and a boom looked good to him; he even innocently encouraged it on occasion. Andrew Mellon, his astute Secretary of the Treasury? Perhaps; Mellon once went so far as to make a mild statement, soon forgotten, to the effect that it was a good time to buy bonds; but Mellon was apparently too wedded to the idea that government must keep its hands off business to do anything more. The Federal Reserve System? It tried hard to halt the price inflation by means of banking regulations—and was roundly denounced for so doing—and failed to bring about more than a temporary halt. Said Roy Young, governor of the Federal Reserve Board, laughing one day as he looked at the rising prices on the ticker tape, "What I am laughing at is that I am sitting here trying to keep a hundred and twenty million people from doing what they want to do!"

Herbert Hoover succeeded Calvin Coolidge as President in March, 1929. Could he have stopped it? By the time he reached the White House it was too late to do so without causing at least a minor panic —and what President would want to have a panic follow immediately upon his accession to office on a campaign slogan of "four more years of prosperity"?

Well then, could the responsible leaders of American finance—the Morgan firm, for example—have stopped it? Hardly; for the Morgan firm was itself involved in some of the most ambitious of the holding-company schemes whose fortunes depended on high prices; and in any case, though it enjoyed such prestige that the lesser men of Wall Street hesitated even to breathe its name in casual conversation, pre-ferring to refer merely to "the Corner" (meaning the firm on the corner of Broad and Wall Streets), nevertheless it wielded no such direct authority as it had in the days of the implacable Pierpont Morgan the Elder.

No, there was no one in responsible power with both the will and the ability to check the onrush. So the gay summer of 1929 ran to its end, and the autumn began. . . .

Let us pause for a second to look at some other figures.

During that very year 1929, according to the subsequent estimates of the very careful and conservative Brookings Institution, only 2.3 per cent of American families had incomes of over $10,000 a year. Only 8 per cent had incomes of over $5,000. No less than 71 per cent had incomes of less than $2,500. Some 60 per cent had incomes of less than $2,000. More than 42 per cent had incomes of less than $1,500. And more than 21 per cent had incomes of less than $1,000 a year.

"At 1929 prices," said the Brookings economists, "a family income of $2,000 may be regarded as sufficient to supply only basic necessities." One might reasonably interpret this statement to mean that any income below that level represented poverty. *Practically 60 per cent of American families were below it—in the golden year 1929!* The Brookings economists added another cautious observation: "There has been a tendency, at least during the last decade or so, for the inequality in the distribution of income to be accentuated."

If the nineteen-twenties constituted a sort of Indian summer of the old order, when Wall Street seemed more than ever to be the axis on which America turned, and when bankers and brokers walked the earth like kings, and it looked as if prosperity could be soundly based upon making the rich richer and letting the gravy trickle down, drop by drop, to those in the lower ranks of society, it was nevertheless an Indian summer with a difference. The warmth of it was a false warmth because the values upon which it was founded were unreal and destined to be self-destroying, and because it deepened the gulf between the fortunate and the majority.

Chapter 10

The Great Depression

ON THE morning of October 24, 1929, the towering structure of American prosperity cracked wide open. For many days the prices of stocks on the New York Stock Exchange had been sliding faster and faster downhill; that morning they broke in a wild panic. The leading bankers of New York met at the House of Morgan to form a buying pool to support the market; Richard Whitney, brother of a leading Morgan partner, thereupon crossed the street to the great hall of the Stock Exchange and put in orders to buy United States Steel at 205; and for a time prices rallied. Pierpont Morgan had halted the Panic of 1907. Surely this panic, too, would yield to the organized confidence of the great men of the world of finance.

But within a few days it was clear that they could no more stop the flood of selling than Dame Partington could sweep back the Atlantic Ocean. On it went, session after session. On the worst day, October 29, over sixteen million shares of stock were thrown on the market by frantic sellers. And it was not until November 13 that order was restored.

In the course of a few brief weeks, thirty billion dollars in paper values had vanished into thin air—an amount of money larger than the national debt at that time. The whole credit structure of the American economy had been shaken more severely than anybody then dared guess. The legend of Wall Street leadership had been punctured. And the Great Depression was on its way.

At first business and industry in general did not seem to have been gravely affected. Everybody assured everybody else that nothing really important had happened, and during the spring of 1930 there was actually a Little Bull Market of considerable proportions. But in May this spurt was at an end. And then there began an almost uninterrupted two-year decline, not only in security prices, but also—an infinitely more serious matter—in the volume of American business: a vicious circle of ebbing sales, followed by declining corporate income, followed by attempts to restore that income by cutting salaries and wages and laying off men, which caused increased unemployment and further reduced sales, which led to increased business losses, which led to further wage cutting and further firing of men, and so on toward disaster.

During these bewildering years President Hoover at first tried to organize national optimism by summoning business executives to Washington to declare that conditions were fundamentally sound and that there would be no wage cutting. This didn't work. Then for a time he was inactive, trusting to the supposedly self-correcting processes of the market. These didn't work. Then, convinced that the financial panic which was simultaneously raging in Europe was the worst source of trouble, he organized an international moratorium in war debts and reparations—a fine stroke of diplomacy which alleviated matters only briefly. Then he set up the Reconstruction Finance Corporation to bring federal aid to hard-pressed banks and businesses—while steadfastly refusing, as a matter of principle, to put federal funds at the disposal of individual persons who were in trouble. Just when it seemed as if recovery were at hand, in the winter of 1932-1933, the American banking system went into a tailspin; even the RFC solution hadn't worked. The result was one of the most remarkable coincidences of American history. It was on March 4, 1933—the very day that Hoover left the White House and Franklin D. Roosevelt entered it—that the banking system of the United States ground to a complete halt. An able and highly intelligent President, committed to orthodox economic theories which were generally considered enlightened, had become one of the tragic victims of the collapse of the going system.

Whereupon Roosevelt, declaring in his cheerfully resolute Inaugural Address that "the only thing we have to fear is fear itself," swept into a tornado of action—successfully reopening the banks and initiating that lively, helter-skelter, and often self-contradictory program of reform, relief, and stimulation which was to keep the country in a dither during the middle nineteen-thirties and bring at least a measure of recovery.

Distressing failures are readily forgotten, whether they are personal or national; instinctively one tries to lock away the memory of them. It was quite natural, in later years, for Republicans to try to gloss over what had happened during Hoover's long ordeal; for believers in individualism to try to forget the tumble that private enterprise had taken; and, for that matter, for patriots generally to minimize what seemed a blot on the national record. And there were millions of Americans to whom the Great Depression was associated with such painful personal memories that they tried, unconsciously perhaps, to banish the recollection of it from their minds. Any writer who reaches it in his chronicle is aware that at this point some readers will be tempted to put his book down. Yet there are several things about the Great Depression that must be borne in mind if one is to understand the subsequent fortunes of the American people.

1. It was a collapse of terrifying proportions and duration. At the middle of the year 1932—more than two and a half years after the crash of 1929—American industry as a whole was operating at *less than half* its maximum 1929 volume. During this year 1932, the total amount of money paid out in wages was 60 *per cent less* than in 1929. The total of dividends was 57 per cent less; and these dividends represented the earnings of the more fortunate concerns —some might say the more ruthless toward their employees—while American business as a whole was running at a net loss of over five billion dollars.

As for stock prices, which were traditionally related to the amount of optimism in the business community, take a look at a few samples. General Motors common, which had been priced at $72\frac{3}{4}$ at the peak of the Bull Market in 1929, and had fallen in the Panic to 36, reached a 1932 low of $7\frac{5}{8}$. Radio Corporation common, which had been 101 at the peak, and 26 after the Panic, got as low as $2\frac{1}{2}$. And United States Steel, long considered the bellwether of the market, with a 1929 high of $261\frac{3}{4}$ and a post-Panic quotation of 150, sank to $21\frac{1}{4}$.

In that year over 12 million Americans were unemployed. In the industrial towns the proportion of jobless people was staggering. In Buffalo, for instance, a house-to-house canvass of nearly fifteen thousand people who were ready and able to work showed that 31 per cent of them could not find jobs, and less than half of them were working full time. And meanwhile the farmers were in desperate straits, with cotton bringing less than 5 cents, wheat less than 50 cents, and corn only 31 cents.

It was an oddly invisible phenomenon, this Great Depression. If one observed closely, one might note that there were fewer people on the streets than in former years, that there were many untenanted shops, that beggars and panhandlers were much in evidence; one might see breadlines here and there, and "Hoovervilles" in vacant lots at the edge of town (groups of tar-paper shacks inhabited by homeless people); railroad trains were shorter, with fewer Pullmans; and there were many factory chimneys out of which no smoke was coming. But otherwise there was little to see. Great numbers of people were sitting at home, trying to keep warm.

2. The Great Depression was part of a world-wide collapse: what Karl Polanyi has aptly characterized as the collapse of the market economy that had been established during the nineteenth century.

3. It marked millions of people—inwardly—for the rest of their lives. Not only because they or their friends lost jobs, saw their careers broken, had to change their whole way of living, were gnawed at by a constant lurking fear of worse things yet, and in all too many cases actually went hungry; but because what was happening to them seemed without rhyme or reason. Most of them had been brought

up to feel that if you worked hard and well, and otherwise behaved yourself, you would be rewarded by good fortune. Here were failure and defeat and want visiting the energetic along with the feckless, the able along with the unable, the virtuous along with the irresponsible. They found their fortunes interlocked with those of great numbers of other people in a pattern complex beyond their understanding, and apparently developing without reason or justice.

Even if they tried to hide their dismay, their children sensed it and were marked by it. The editors of *Fortune* wrote in 1936: "The present-day college generation is fatalistic . . . it will not stick its neck out. It keeps its pants buttoned, its chin up, and its mouth shut. If we take the mean average to be the truth, it is a cautious, subdued, unadventurous generation. . . ." As time went on there was a continuing disposition among Americans old and young to look with a cynical eye upon the old Horatio Alger formula for success; to be dubious about taking chances for ambition's sake; to look with a favorable eye upon a safe if unadventurous job, social insurance plans, pension plans. They had learned from bitter experience to crave security.

4. The Great Depression brought the abdication of Wall Street from the commanding position which it had achieved in the late nineteenth century, had consolidated under the personal leadership of Pierpont Morgan, and had institutionalized since his death in 1913. Not only had the big bankers of 1929 failed to stop the Panic, but as time went on the inability of financiers generally to cope with the down trend, their loss of confidence in their own economic convictions, and the downfall of the banking system itself all advertised their helplessness. If after 1933 a part of their former power passed to the big corporation executives who had formerly regarded them with deference, and a much larger part of it passed to Washington, which now became the economic as well as political capital of the nation, this was at least partly because nature abhors a vacuum.

5. The Depression sharply lowered the prestige of businessmen. The worst sufferers were the bankers and brokers, who found themselves translated from objects of veneration into objects of public

derision and distrust—the distrust being sharply increased by the evidences of financial skullduggery which came out in successive congressional investigations. But even business executives in general sank in the public regard to a point from which it would take them a long time to recover; and in this decline the conscientious and public-spirited suffered along with the predatory.

6. Yet the world-wide Depression—though it brought Hitler to power in Germany, and in many other lands seemed to have sounded the death knell of capitalism—brought to the United States nothing approaching a revolution. It brought an epidemic of proposals for economic panaceas—the cult of technocracy, Upton Sinclair's EPIC, the Townsend Old Age Revolving Pensions Plan, and suchlike; it brought the dictatorlike Huey Long to brief regional power; it brought riots at farmers' bankruptcy sales, a Communist-led "march" on Washington, and the briefly ominous Bonus Army march of 1932. It also saw a rapid growth in the intellectual influence and labor-union influence of the Communists—though not in their voting strength, which remained extremely small. But despite the dismay of uncounted Americans at their lot, there was no revolution—just a shift of power from one political party to the other, after the time-honored custom. And although Roosevelt's New Deal introduced a hodge-podge of reforms and regulations and interferences with what had been known as economic law, only a few people—some of the starry-eyed zealots of the Washington bureaucracy, on the one hand, and a few die-hard haters of the regime, on the other—thought of these reforms as introducing a total change in the political or economic structure of the United States.

To the *New York Times* of December 31, 1933—when Roosevelt had been in office less than a year—the English economist John Maynard Keynes contributed an open letter to the President. "You have made yourself," he wrote, "the trustee for those in every country who seek to mend the evils of our condition by reasoned experiment within the framework of the existing social system. If you fail, rational change will be gravely prejudiced throughout the world, leaving orthodoxy and revolution to fight it out." As things eventuated, orthodoxy and revolution were not left to fight it out. Experiment within the framework of the existing social system was the order of the day. Once more, as during the revolt of the American conscience, the American way of coping with a revealed defect in the national machinery was to make a series of experimental repairs while the machine was running—and to do this through the traditional party machinery of America.

The long-standing political coolness betwen the Oyster Bay Roosevelts and the Hyde Park Roosevelts should not blind us to the striking parallels between the approach to public affairs of Franklin Delano Roosevelt and of his wife's uncle Theodore Roosevelt. Both men had wealth. Both championed the underdog out of conviction, though they were upperdogs themselves. Both were men of abounding energy and captivating charm, though Theodore's was the more rugged, Franklin's the more gracious. Both were exuberantly interested in people, people of all sorts and conditions. Neither had a systematic economic philosophy; both, in devising their policies and programs, played by ear; and both thought of economic problems as essentially moral problems. Each, in his own time, was curiously fitted to bring change without the ideology or the violence of revolution.

II

There is no need to rehearse here in detail the familiar story of the New Deal: how the country was cheered and galvanized by Roosevelt's convincing and contagious confidence in the spring of 1933; how in his very first "fireside chat" over the radio, when the banks were still closed, he conveyed a serene assurance that they could be successfully opened—as they shortly were; how during the wild first hundred days he jammed through Congress, at record-breaking speed, a jumble of hastily improvised legislation; how the conservatives, and well-to-do people generally, began before long to foam with rage at him as he continued to push his reform program, and tinkered with the price of gold, and ran up big federal deficits as Harry Hopkins furnished relief through the WPA to millions of families; how he gathered about him two successive Brain Trusts composed of bright young idealists who furnished him with economic ideas and oratorical ammunition; how he defeated the Republican Landon in 1936, tangled with the Supreme Court in 1937, and faced and overcame—with the aid of further federal spending—the sharp "recession" of 1937-1938; and how he thereafter was distracted from his New Deal objectives by the storm clouds over Europe moving nearer and nearer. It is necessary only to note the hard fact that the New Deal did not at any time bring a full return of prosperity; that was not to come until defense spending went into high gear in 1940-41.

But in many ways the New Deal permanently altered the nature of the American economy, and we may well pause for a moment to look at some of the changes it brought about and the new forces it unleashed.

In the first place it rewrote a good many of the rules of the economic game as played in America. For instance, in order to prevent any recurrence of the financial follies of the nineteen-twenties, it divorced commercial banks from the securities business, forbade the issue of securities without exhaustive disclosure of pertinent facts, circumscribed pool operations on the stock exchanges and set up a federal agency to police these exchanges, and dismantled the more illogical holding-company structures in the utilities business. Not only was there a new rule book, but at many points the federal government moved in as umpire to interpret and enforce the rules.

In the second place, it intervened extensively in the economic game as protector of the underdog. For instance, because the operations of one of the old-time rules of the game, the law of supply and demand, appeared to be doing damage to the American farmer, it stepped in to jack up and then to guarantee the prices he got. (The anomalous result was that the farmers of the United States, as conservative a group temperamentally as were to be found in the land, became dependent for their very economic lives upon government decisions in their behalf!) Similarly, the New Deal continued to prop up ailing corporations through Hoover's RFC; made arrangements to prevent near-bankrupt firms from going broke; aided farmowners and homeowners in meeting their mortgage payments; underwrote the financing of new housing enterprises; insured bank deposits; gave a measure of aid to unemployed people and old people through Social Security; and wrote a minimum wage and hours law for labor.

All this was as if Washington were saying, "Do a lot of people seem likely to get gypped through the unhindered workings of economic law? All right, we'll make it up to them through subsidies, guarantees, or insurance." In short, while the New Deal did not abolish the market place as the determiner of values and rewards, it rigged the market plenty.

In the third place, it went into the active business of stimulating employment, by building dams, bridges, parkways, and playgrounds on the grand scale, and by putting even the recipients of relief to work at all manner of enterprises carefully concocted so as not to interfere with private business; and it set up the Tennessee Valley Authority to do a combined job of competing with the private electric utilities, preventing floods, and teaching farmers some of the principles of conservation.

In the fourth place, the New Deal gave a go-ahead signal to organized labor. Up to this time such laws as seemed to authorize collective bargaining, like the Clayton Act, had frequently been nullified by the courts. But now the Norris-LaGuardia Anti-injunction Act of 1932 was followed by Section 7a of the National Industrial Recovery Act of 1933, and—after that law had been set aside by the Supreme Court—by the Wagner Act. The authorization to organize being clear and specific, there was a rush to join unions. In 1935 John L. Lewis formed the CIO, which on being expelled from the A F of L became a rival outfit specializing in industrial unions. The CIO moved into the hitherto unorganized heavy industries, especially the automobile and steel industries, and a terrific struggle ensued: unreconstructed employers spending hundreds of thousands of dollars on hiring industrial spies and plug-uglies; angry workers organizing violent strikes. Within a few months from the fall of 1936 to the spring of 1937, almost half a million American men and women quit their jobs, mostly using the new—and illegal—sit-down technique fostered by Communist organizers and taken up by others too; there was a tension in the industrial towns almost as of civil war, with riots and bloodshed. But at the height of the tension Myron Taylor, chairman of the board of the great United States Steel Corporation, voluntarily entered into a union contract with a unit of the CIO; and although the little steel companies continued the struggle, it was presently clear that unionization was the order of the day.

By the end of the decade the number of union members in the United States had climbed from the 1933 figure of less than three millions to nearly nine millions; office workers who had never in their earlier years dreamed of joining a union found themselves organizing and threatening to strike; executives and their employees found themselves separated from one another by a wall of mutual distrust; and, partly because of union pressures, the average work week in business and industry was about five hours shorter than it had been at the beginning of the decade (one estimate gave a decline from 49.3 hours to 44 hours), and the two-day week end was becoming standard.

Through its general sympathy with labor, the New Deal had unleashed what J. Kenneth Galbraith has subsequently called a "countervailing force" in the American economy—a force which, acting in opposition to business managements, and generating for the time being a formidable amount of friction, served to bring about a redistribution of the national income downward to those in the lower income brackets.

Finally, the New Deal tried to do a job of managing the national economy as a whole. It abandoned the automatically operating gold standard and introduced something approaching a managed currency. It abandoned the idea that the first duty of a government was to balance its budget, and embraced the Keynesian idea of deficit spending, with the highly optimistic notion that deficits in bad years would be counterbalanced by surpluses in good years. Whatever the dangers inherent in such a dream, at least the idea became pretty solidly established that it was the job of the authorities at Washington so to manipulate their spending and their fiscal controls that the economy would run on a reasonably even keel.

The result of all these interventions—the reform measures, the subsidies and guarantees, the public works, the encouragement of labor, and the attempt to steer the economy as a whole—was certainly not a socialist order, at least in the old sense of the government's taking over the management of business and industry. For the management of the vast variety of concerns remained in private hands (though it was so often hedged in by regulations, bedeviled by taxes, and opposed by unions that many an executive felt himself a prisoner of government and labor). Nor was it a free economic order, at least in the old sense of an order in which everybody's economic fortunes were determined by the action of buyers and sellers in the open market, with the government standing aside as Herbert Hoover had tried to stand aside in 1930-1931. It was something between the two: one might call it a repaired and modified form of capitalism in which—to revert to our earlier figure of speech—the government umpires were forever blowing their whistles and rushing onto the field to penalize this player or that, or to pace off a fifteen-yard gain for a hard-pressed team.

Nor, for that matter, was this new order planned in any comprehensive way by Roosevelt and his Brain Trusters. It was a patchwork of measures devised almost without regard for one another; and as a result the American economy, after a few years, was less like a new and statelier mansion than like an old house extensively remodeled, with a new bit of roofing here, a new wing there, new supports under part of the flooring, and a greatly enlarged staff of servants.

Nor did the new order seem to work particularly well. Full disaster had been averted, it is true, and many people long forsaken by fortune had been given new hope. But it was not until the shadows of war began to deepen, and the United States began to arm feverishly for defense, that this new, hybrid American system began really to work.

However, the grim decade of the nineteen-thirties had left a number of legacies to the American people, of major importance to their future.

The first of these, and the most fundamental, was the idea that the fortunes of individual Americans are interlocked, that they are "all in the same boat." Never before had a national crisis so challenged the ability of economists, sociologists, students of government, and intelligent citizens generally to find out what was actually happening to their fellow countrymen, how they were variously affected by the actions of bankers in Wall Street, manufacturers in Detroit, legislators and bureaucrats in Washington, and how they lived from day to day. During the years 1930 and 1931, when I had been at work on *Only Yesterday,* an informal history of the United States in the nineteen-twenties, my best sources had been the daily papers and magazines of the period; the books of reportage or appraisal which I really needed to consult could have been ranged on a single shelf. In 1939 I wrote a similar book about the nineteen-thirties, *Since Yesterday*; this time, the books on which I might have drawn, had I had the time and energy, would have filled a large library building, so diligently had the pollsters, social analysts, economic statisticians, and authors of assorted surveys been examining the conditions of their contemporaries. And there was manifest, too, among great numbers of men and women, including not only scholars but comparatively untutored folk, the gradual expansion of a sort of half-mystical faith in the American people—a faith all the more striking because the ability of these people to order their affairs successfully was being so gravely tested. It was as if men and women of different circumstances and antecedents, having discovered that their fates were interdependent, had begun to regard one another with a fresh understanding and had found that on the whole they liked one another. Contending as this faith did with the political and social frictions of the times, it was hard to measure and its durability was uncertain. But I wonder if a good many readers of these pages, recalling, let us say, their reactions to the New York World's Fair of 1939, will not remember feeling—as they enjoyed the fountains, the illuminated trees, the fireworks, the artificial waterfalls streaming down the sides of

buildings, the imaginative General Motors Futurama, the girls swimming to waltz time at the Aquacade, and the brightly colored side-
shows—a sort of inner exhilaration which, if it had found words,
might have said something like this: "All these things, the beautiful
and the silly alike, reflect in their various ways the one hundred and
forty million people of this land, friendly, inventive, hopeful people
who have found that their lot is cast together."

Two more legacies of the nineteen-thirties were based upon the
first one and supplemented it. One was the idea that if individual
Americans are in deep trouble, it is the job of the rest of the people,
through their government, to come to their aid. The other was that it
is their job, again through their government, to see that there is never
another Great Depression. Each of these ideas, born in travail and
fiercely contested for years, was by 1940 implicitly accepted by the
vast majority. Whether they could be lived up to remained to be seen.

Chapter 11

The Reluctant World Power

D URING the early and middle nineteen-thirties there were occasional grim reminders from overseas that the world contained warlike nations bent on conquest. But at first these seemed hardly more than offstage noises during the drama of the Great Depression. When the Japanese invaded Manchuria in 1931, when Mussolini's Fascist Italy invaded Ethiopia in 1935, when Hitler entered the Rhineland in 1936 and gave manifest signs of an inclination to push farther, American disapproval was intense but the great majority of us felt that it wasn't up to us to do anything about such foreign depredations. For the country was in an overwhelmingly isolationist mood, convinced that it could live in safety and satisfaction behind a wall of neutrality, regardless of what was going on in the rest of the world.

This was a belief at which individual men and women had arrived by a great variety of routes. There were, to begin with, the natural-born distrusters of all things foreign. Their logic appealed to many people of Irish descent (who bore England no love) and of German descent (who dreaded another conflict with Germany) and likewise to numerous Midwesterners and Great Plainsmen who suspected Easterners generally of an undue suceptibility to the blandishments of European diplomats in striped pants. There were also men and women who had suffered deeply from the Depression and who, attributing their troubles to the greed of financiers and big businessmen, proceeded naturally to the belief that it was the sly maneuvers of "international bankers" and "merchants of death" that sucked nations into war. There were also the Communists and their dupes, whom the party line of the moment directed to join in the hue and cry against Wall Street and the munitions makers. There were men and women who so deeply distrusted Franklin D. Roosevelt that they suspected him of trying to drag the country into war in order to fasten his hold upon it the more securely. Still others conscientiously believed that, with a Depression on its hands, the United States had enough to cope with at home without venturing into foreign expeditions, and that the best contribution that America could make to democracy and freedom was to demonstrate that these ideals could be realized within its own borders.

Finally there were those men and women who, as members of the disenchanted younger generation after World War I, had become (to borrow Lloyd Morris's phrase) "truculently cynical" about that war. These youngsters of the previous decade were now coming into their middle years, and many of them, now solid and influential citizens, had settled into the conviction that America's entry into World War I had been the great tragic blunder of their parents' generation. When in the mid-thirties a Senate Committee headed by Gerald P. Nye of North Dakota exposed the huge profits made by some American corporations during that war, and succeeded in conveying the impression that the Morgans and du Ponts and their like had got us involved in it, many members of these various groups felt that their worst suspicions had been confirmed. The "revisionist" view of World War I was becoming the orthodox view.

Thus it happened that when in January, 1937, the Gallup pollsters asked the question, "Do you think it was a mistake for the United States to enter the World War?" no less than 70 per cent of those who expressed an opinion answered "Yes"; and that when, in the fall of 1935, they asked whether Congress should get the approval of the people in a national vote before declaring war, as many as 75 per cent said "Yes." It is doubtful, of course, whether many of those who gave this answer realized how long it would take to organize a national referendum (imagine our waiting for one after Pearl Harbor!); yet the answer was significant as revealing the prevailing view that peaceable people got inveigled into wars by villains and fools in their own land.

During the years 1935, 1936, and 1937 Congress expressed this isolationist mood by passing three successive Neutrality Acts aimed at preventing the United States from selling arms or munitions to any warring powers. President Roosevelt and the State Department didn't like these acts—felt that they were unrealistic, tied America's hands, and negated its influence and its rights abroad—but public opinion was too strong to counter. And when in October, 1937, Roosevelt made a speech in which he said that aggressors must be "quarantined," the uproar of protest was deafening.

Already, however, events were marching at an accelerating and ominous pace, and the offstage noises bore overtones of increasing menace. By 1937 Hitler and Mussolini were both actively aiding the dictator Franco in the Spanish Civil War. In that same year the Japanese attacked China. In March, 1938, Hitler occupied Austria. In the fall of that year, at the Munich conference, he browbeat England and France into consenting to his partial occupation of Czechoslovakia. The next spring he brazenly occupied the rest of Czechoslovakia, and Mussolini invaded Albania. In the late summer of 1939 Hitler made an alliance with Stalin and then attacked Poland; this time England and France could stand aside no longer, and World War II was under way. By the next summer—the summer of 1940— the horrified American people had seen Finland attacked by Russia, Denmark and Norway overrun by Hitler, and the Low Countries and even France unbelievably smashed; only Britain now stood between Hitler and the total conquest of Europe, and Britain's ability to endure hung in the balance.

This dismaying sequence of events—plus Roosevelt's increasingly persuasive efforts to awaken his countrymen to the full meaning of Hitler's onrush—shocked the American people into a gradual but decisive change of conviction as to the ability of the United States to live by itself and to itself. One by one the apparent moral certainties of the mid-thirties—such as the notion that wars are fomented by munitions makers—were engulfed by the news from abroad. With each portentous event American opinion shifted; sometimes the shift was so rapid that one could trace its progress in successive Gallup polls. For instance, in March, 1939, 52 per cent of those polled thought that if war broke out in Europe we should sell Britain and France airplanes and other war materials; the very next month—after Hitler's total occupation of Czechoslovakia—the percentage had gone up from 52 to 66. Naturally, then, when war did break out in the autumn of 1939 the Neutrality Act was amended to permit the cash sale of munitions. Yet still the majority of Americans, despite the nightmare change that they were witnessing across the seas, remained stubbornly reluctant to commit themselves; their neutralism died hard. It was not until France fell and Britain stood alone, confronting the prospect of "blood, toil, tears, and sweat," that their sense of the implacable necessities of the new situation began really to overcome their suspicion that somebody must be putting something over on them.

When France collapsed in June, 1940, the United States was beginning to step up its defense production very sharply. On the desperate need of the country to arm itself almost everybody could unite. Within a few weeks thereafter, Roosevelt was offering guns and over-age destroyers to Britain. By the early autumn of 1940, the American draft law was going into operation. Yet in that very season the two Presidential candidates—Roosevelt, breaking precedent by running for a third term, and Wendell Willkie, the last-minute choice of the Republicans—though they agreed upon aid to Europe, were both insisting that they opposed taking the United States into war. The orators of the "Committee to Defend America by Aiding the Allies," and of "Fight for Freedom," were vehemently opposed by the equally positive orators of "America First." During the following year, as Hitler desolated British cities with bombs, overran the Balkans, and invaded Russia, and as the Japanese began to threaten the subjugation of the Far East, opinion swung by degrees toward more and more direct intervention; the Lend-Lease Act went through Congress with a strong majority, American warships began convoying American supplies part way to England, and the United States found itself in a virtual state of undeclared war with Germany. Yet as the month of December, 1941, arrived, the country was still sharply divided emotionally.

At that moment a very large number of Americans, perhaps a majority, believed that Hitler must imperatively be defeated, even at the risk of complete American involvement. A small minority were in favor of plunging in with all we had. But a considerably larger minority regarded Roosevelt's warlike gestures with a vehement distrust. Only a handful of this latter group regarded Hitler or the Japanese imperialists with any favor; the prevailing feeling among them was simply that, despite our loathing for aggression, we must not go to war to stop it unless or until it immediately threatened the Western Hemisphere.

Then, on December 7, 1941, came the stroke which ended all doubts.

It came, ironically, not from Hitler's Germany, but from Japan. The attack on Pearl Harbor was a challenge that could not be denied. And it was promptly followed by the astonishingly obliging action of Hitler and Mussolini in declaring war on the United States, and thus relinquishing whatever hope they might have cherished that a lingering disagreement about Europe would keep America divided. The die was cast. Suddenly we were a people united in our intent to prosecute World War II to victory against the aggressors both in Asia and in Europe.

Reluctantly—like a man walking backward—we had been pushed by events into a recognition of the fact that we were not a lone nation secure on our own continent, but a world power which must live up to the opportunities and responsibilities inherent in that fact. We resented the idea. We felt we would much prefer to look after ourselves by ourselves; and we continued to feel so. But we had no choice.

II

During World War I there had been a lively crusading spirit—and there had also been considerable opposition to the war. This time there was no opposition. During the whole three years and eight months that the United States fought, there was no antiwar faction, no organized pacifist element, no objection to huge appropriations, no noticeable opposition to the draft. Yet there was also a minimum of crusading spirit. For the popular disillusionment over World War I and the controversy over involvement in World War II had left their marks.

A generation of men and women who had heard again and again how men could be seduced by war slogans and martial parades were inevitably skeptical in their inner minds. This new war was astonishingly like that of 1917-1918, in Europe at least; and despite the obvious differences and the hard logic of circumstance, something remained in the subconscious of millions of people to rise and accuse them whenever they heard a patriotic peroration. They didn't want to be victims of "hysteria." They felt uncomfortable about flag waving. They preferred to be matter-of-fact about the job ahead. Morale officers reported an astonishing indifference to instruction on American war aims; the chief war aim in most soldiers' minds appeared to be to get back home, by vanquishing the enemy if there was no quicker way; and the strongest force making for valor and endurance was apparently pride in one's outfit and loyalty to one's buddies. Few bands played, few trumpets blew, there were no parades, and people who became demonstrative about America's war ideals sensed a coolness in the air about them.

Furthermore, the emotional misgivings of those who had been anti-interventionist—and of some of those who had been merely reluctant—remained to condition them: to make them move skeptically, grudgingly, and with strenuous opposition to specific war policies that called for drastic government controls and sharp civilian sacrifices. These people were unstintedly loyal, and went to battle—or saw their brothers and sons go—without reservation; yet they remained emotionally on guard—distrustful of Britain, suspicious of our high command's disposition to put the war in Europe ahead of the war in the Pacific, and derisive over our civilian officials in Washington, who looked to some of them like another crop of Brain Trusters using the war as an excuse for getting former professors to interfere with American business.

And the Depression, too, had left its scars. People who for years had felt that fate was against them and that the next turn of its wheel might plunge them into full disaster felt that their whole future had become a huge and ominous question mark. Sure, they would fight —but where would they come out afterward? What positive thing was there that they could look forward to with genuine hope, once the enemy had been smashed? They didn't know. Talk about war aims sounded hollow to them. They would do their job, but without positive hope. And meanwhile some of them would nourish a shrewd distrust of anybody who looked like a big tycoon; it was a safe rule to follow that the boss was out to feather his own nest. It may have been a sign of the nearness of the Great Depression that the average GI felt more active resentment for his own general, who lived comfortably in the house on the hill with a shower and plenty of cocktails, than for the enemy that confronted him.

Yet, with isolated exceptions, the armed forces of the United States fought magnificently. It is very doubtful if they could have done so if in their inner beings they had deeply questioned the validity of the cause for which they were fighting. By and large, the civilian population of the United States likewise met adequately the major challenges of total war, and of them too the same thing can be said: they too fully believed in the justice of America's mission, however distrustful they might be of rhetoric about it. And even when things went worst, neither the military nor the civilians ever doubted the eventual coming of victory, however dubious they might be that it would insure a harmonious and comfortable peace. The American people were their nation's—and freedom's—disillusioned and deadpan defenders.

III

It is not for this chronicle to rehearse the military story of World War II, from the first agonizing days when the Japanese held most of the Pacific, and our troops were being smashed at Bataan, and German submarines were sinking ships in a smear of oil off Cape Hatteras, to the stunning success of D-Day, the sweep across France, the setback of the Bulge, the push into Germany, and—following a series of island-hopping Pacific victories—the dropping of the atomic bomb on Japan and the surrender of August, 1945. The generals, diplomats, military historians, and autobiographers have rung the changes on this great story again and again, describing and debating each strategic decision and each tactical move; correspondents and novelists and playwrights have taken us through the swamps of Guadalcanal and the hedgerows of Normandy, and onto the beaches of Tarawa and Salerno, and through the long nights of Pacific patrolling, and into the sky battles over Germany. Less adequately told—and yet of continuing significance to us today—is the staggering story of American production during those anxious years.

The miseries of the Great Depression had obscured a striking fact: that under the spur of necessity American industry had gained sharply in efficiency during the nineteen-thirties. The figures are revealing. According to the best estimates of which economists are capable, output per man hour had increased during the decade 1900-1910 by 12 per cent; during the decade 1910-1920, by only 7½ per cent; during the brash decade 1920-1930, by an impressive 21 per cent. During the Depression decade of 1930-1940—when many plants were shut down or working part time, and there was intense pressure for efficiency and economy—it had increased by an amazing 41 per cent. But always, in most industries, the brakes had been on, as it were. They must not overproduce. Now, with the coming of the war emergency, the brakes were removed.

For the military planners at Washington had conceived their plans on a truly majestic scale. By the end of the war the United States had a total of over twelve million men in service, as against less than five million in World War I. The devisers of the effort had resolved that these forces of ours would be the best armed, best equipped, best supplied, and most comfortably circumstanced in history—which they were. And we had to supply not only our own forces, but others too. The result, in terms of output and of cost, was astronomical.

By the end of 1943 we were spending money at *five times* the peak rate of World War I. During the nineteen-thirties, critics of the New Deal had become apoplectic over annual federal budgets of seven or eight or nine billions, which they felt were carrying the United States toward bankruptcy; during the fiscal year 1942 we spent, by contrast, over 34 billions; during 1943, 79 billions; during 1944, 95 billions; during 1945, 98 billions; during 1946, 60 billions. For the last four of these years, in fact, our *annual* expenditures were greater than the total national debt which had been a matter of such grave concern during the Depression. That national debt had risen from 19 billions in Hoover's last year in office to 40 billions in 1939 —and here was the government, only a few years later, spending up to 98 billions *per year*, and thus piling the national debt up to 269 billions by 1946! These colossal sums made anything in the previous history of the United States look like small change.

And how was the ambitious and expensive job of military production accomplished? By paying little attention to costs, and asking producers—as in World War I—to concentrate on volume and speed. "How many can you make, and how fast?"

The American manufacturer responded to the challenge with zest. For it appealed to that peculiar enthusiasm for record breaking which seems to blossom in the air of a land where radio listeners to ball games are informed by record-conscious broadcasters that so-and-so's triple with the bases full is the first triple made in the first game of a World Series since 1927, and where schoolboy runners dream dreams of being the first man in history to achieve a four-minute mile.

New plants were built, and built fast. The entire automobile industry was diverted from the manufacture of passenger cars into the production of tanks, trucks, weapons. All manner of new products and devices were assigned to American plants to produce in a hurry—ranging from synthetic rubber to radar, from landing ships to proximity fuses, from atabrine and penicillin and DDT to the Manhattan project for the atomic bomb. Always the call from Washington was for speed, speed, speed, and for quantity.

The result: in the year 1945 the gross product of goods and services in the United States came to $215 billions—well over twice the dollar total of 1939, which had been $91 billions. Even when one makes allowance for the wartime rise in prices, one finds that the product of 1945 was more than two-thirds bigger than that of 1939. American industry had achieved probably the most extraordinary increase in production that had ever been accomplished in five years in all economic history.

IV

What happened to the national standard of living when the federal government poured into the national economy war orders by the billions, and then by the tens of billions, and then by the scores of billions? Roaring prosperity. During the nineteen-thirties the New Dealers had been conscientiously trying to "prime the pump" by government expenditures of a few billions a year; what they had done with a teaspoon was now being done with a ladle.

By 1943 the last appreciable unemployment—except of people transferring from job to job, or waiting for a promised opening to materialize—had been soaked up. By 1944 the signs of prosperity were everywhere. It was hard to get a hotel room in any city. Restaurants in which it had always been easy to find a table for lunch were now crammed by a few minutes after twelve. Sales of fur coats and jewelry—many of them for cash across the counter—were jumping. Luxury goods for which there had long been a dwindling market were suddenly in demand: the proprietor of a music store reported that he was selling every grand piano, new or renovated, that he could lay his hands on. And visitors to New England mill towns which had been depression-ridden since long before the nineteen-thirties were noting newly painted houses, fences in fresh repair.

This gush of prosperity was a strange phenomenon to witness in a nation supposedly stripped down for the supreme effort of war—a nation in which airplane spotters sat under the stars of a cold winter's night to listen for an improbable enemy; in which air-raid wardens put on their armbands for practice blackouts, and waited endlessly for the dreadful moment when the word would go out, "Signal 50 received, post your wardens"; in which first-aiders took lessons in triangular bandages and talked sagely about pressure points; in which women went stockingless because they were running out of nylons, and cigarettes, butter, sugar, and coffee were in short supply, and beefsteak became the rarest of treats, and draft boards puzzled over the latest changes in the regulations from Washington, and the ubiquity of soldiers and sailors in uniform was a constant reminder of everybody's obligation to make sacrifices for the common safety. The government was doing what it could to reduce spending and thus slow down inflation—through price ceilings, rationing of scarce and essential goods, wage freezing, excess-profits taxes, and record-high personal income taxes—and with some success. Yet the prosperity was there, paradoxically overflowing. And after the long drought of the nineteen-thirties there was something undeniably welcome about it.

Who was getting the money?

Generally speaking, the stockholders of the biggest corporations were not getting very much of it. These corporations were in many cases getting huge war orders, and thus consolidating their important positions in the national economy; but excess-profits taxes, along with managerial caution over the uncertainties of the future, and with the recollection of the embarrassing scandals of 1918 war profits, combined to keep their dividend payments at modest rates. The stock market languished. Big capital, as such, was having no heyday.

Some smaller companies which had barely been able to keep alive during the Depression and now were receiving big war orders were making extraordinary money—subject both to taxes and to renegotiation of their contracts. There were also numerous small concerns, in the textile business for example, that got no war orders but profited hugely—again before taxes. But other businesses were in definite trouble. Tourist camps and roadside taverns and automobile dealers, for example, suffered because of gas rationing, and there were many manufacturers and dealers who were hard hit by shortages of materials, could not shift into war production, and went deep into the red. But what was more interesting than the sort of concerns which were getting the money was the sort of individual people who were getting it.

The rich were getting some of it, but those of them who were honest were keeping very little because of high income taxes. Most of the extravagant spending which was manifest in so many places was the result either of tax dodging or of the lavish use of company expense accounts. "It's all on the government" was the theme song of many a sumptuous party. Although the war was making a few legitimate millionaires—mainly among oil men who by reason of "depletion allowances" did not feel the full weight of federal taxes —in general the rich *and* honest did not gain much.

People outside the war industries whose salaries or wages were frozen by the War Labor Board were not gaining at all, though some of them were helped by "reclassification of jobs" or by "merit increases," with or without quotation marks. People who were dependent on dividends and interest likewise were seldom among the gainers; indeed in many cases inflation brought a real deterioration in their circumstances.

The principal beneficiaries, generally speaking, were farmers; engineers, technicians, and specialists of various sorts whose knowledge and ability were especially valuable to the war effort in one way or another; and skilled workers in war industries—or unskilled workers capable of learning a skilled trade and stepping into the skilled group.

The farmers were in clover; and it was about time. For they had long been faced with adversity after adversity. During the nineteen-twenties few of them had had seats on the prosperity band wagon; a boom in the price of farm land after World War I had overextended many of them, the failure of numerous rural banks had been disastrous to these and to others, and the prices they had got had seemed perpetually inadequate. During the Depression these prices had dropped to ruinous depths; and just as recovery was setting in, a series of droughts and dust storms had desolated whole areas of the Great Plains, sending miserable "Okies" on the desperate trek to California, where at least there was a faint hope of something better. But now prices were good, the demand for farm products was overwhelming, the weather was favorable, their methods were vastly improved, and by 1943 their total purchasing power was almost double what it had been at the end of the nineteen-thirties.

The engineers, technicians, and workers in the war plants benefited by an interesting circumstance. Since at the beginning of the war emergency there had still been millions of unemployed men and women, there had been no need for an official allocation of manpower; the war industries could absorb large numbers of workers from other occupations without crippling the economy. And they lured them largely by offering high pay. A young chemist would find himself sought out by a chemical concern at a salary he hadn't expected to earn for many a year. Mrs. Smith's waitress would leave for a job in an electrical plant that would bring her $50 a week with evenings free. A soda jerker would double his income by walking down the street to the factory that was going to make parts for tanks. And a salesgirl at a department-store stocking counter would fetch up in an airplane plant at two or three times her store pay.

Later, it is true, workers in essential industries were "frozen" in their jobs and the rulings of the War Labor Board tended to keep their pay within bounds; but the essential fact remained that these war workers became, as a group, the chief beneficiaries of the new prosperity. Look at the figures for workers in manufacturing industries. Between 1939 and 1945 their average weekly earnings went up by 86 per cent. Meanwhile their cost of living went up by an estimated 29 per cent—but even so they were far better off than in 1939. They had experienced a sharp and welcome gain in "real wages."

By and large, what the war boom did, then—with numerous exceptions—was to give a lift to people with low incomes.

We shall come back to that fact in a later chapter. It was a very important fact for the future of America.

V

During these war years there was an imposing growth in the size, authority, and complexity of the federal government, superimposed upon the growth that had already taken place under the New Deal.

At this point a word of amplification is necessary. This growth was nothing wholly new. Both the federal government and the state and local governments had been growing almost continuously even in earlier years (subject only to the principle that in wartime it is the federal government which swells while the others do not). During the years 1915-1930, for example, the cost of running the federal government had jumped by 352 per cent; and, although military and veterans' expenditures accounted for much of the increase, even the civil administrative costs had gone up by 237 per cent. As for the state governments, the cost of running them had leaped upward even during the time when the parsimonious Calvin Coolidge was holding federal outlays more or less in check; how could it help doing this when even the most conservative citizens wanted new state highways and bigger and better schools? This trend toward growth was the unavoidable result of the increasing interdependence of people in a society that is becoming ever more urbanized and more complex: anybody who has lived for any stretch of time in a rising suburb, and has seen its governmental budget swell as its population grows, will recognize the phenomenon.

But the New Deal did accelerate this trend, sharply; and the war of 1941-1945 gave it a much stronger push. In 1930, when Hoover was in the White House and the Depression was still young, there had been some $6/10$ of a million federal civil employees. By 1940, when the New Deal had done its utmost and the war boom was just beginning, the number had risen from $6/10$ of a million to a little over a million. By 1945, when the war was ending, it had shot up to more than $3\frac{1}{2}$ million.

And in the years following World War II, did it shrink back again to only a little over a million? It did not. It shrank back only part way—just as after World War I it had shrunk back only part way. In 1949, some four years after the war, and before the Korean crisis, there were still over 2 million federal civil employees.

For the failure of the roster to contract more sharply one may blame, if one wishes, the Fair Deal Administration, so anxious to be a modified carbon copy of the expansive New Deal Administration; or one may blame the inherent tendency of bureaucrats to hang onto office at all cost. In any case a major cause was our prolonged tension with Soviet Russia. Yet another cause, in all probability, was our still increasing interdependence.

I remember a talk I once had with a number of men who were deeply interested in conservation. They included a public-spirited but very conservative ex-banker. When he said that to achieve some end—I think it was the protection of watersheds—a new federal law was needed, I asked whether interstate compacts wouldn't serve, suggesting that I preferred to see such things managed if possible without conferring new authority on Washington. The ex-banker explained to me patiently that only federal action would do the trick. On the growth of federal power in general I am sure my friend would have been sulphurous. But in this field he recognized the inexorable principle that as our lives become more closely interlocked, we must needs depend more and more on federal legislation, federal regulation, federal funds.

Diligently as public-spirited bodies like the Hoover Commission, apprehensive over the groaning weight of taxes, may work for efficiency and economy in administration, and earnestly as others may strive to limit government action to fields in which it will not stifle individual enterprise and personal freedom, there seems to be little prospect of a real shrinkage. Big government appears to be with us to stay.

VI

The year 1945 was a year of great events. As it opened, the German counteroffensive of the Bulge in the snowy Ardennes was being turned back, while at the other end of the world General MacArthur's troops were storming through the Philippines. In March, American troops seized intact a bridge across the Rhine at Remagen, and the way was opened for an offensive across Germany. In April, when this offensive had just reached the Elbe, Franklin D. Roosevelt—who had proved himself a masterly war leader, well fitted to work in cordial partnership with the incomparable Churchill—died, exhausted by his long labors toward victory; and the massive burdens of the Presidency of the United States fell upon the shoulders of the inexperienced and unassuming Vice-President, Harry S. Truman. Later in the same month there began, at San Francisco, the international conference which set up the United Nations organization. By early May, Mussolini was dead, Hitler was dead, and Germany had surrendered. In July, the first atomic bomb explosion took place in New Mexico. In August, the bomb was used on two Japanese cities, and Japan surrendered—just after Stalin, like a football coach sending a senior into a game during the last minute of play to get his letter, had belatedly moved his troops against the Japanese. V-J Day brought wild rejoicing. Now for an era of peace!

As soon as possible we began bringing our troops home in response to a vociferous public demand. Whereupon we encountered two surprises.

The first was a happy one. There was no postwar depression such as innumerable people had expected. On the contrary, the new prosperity went right on, with the public spending money at such a pace that, with the relaxation of federal controls, there began a progressive inflation more severe than the wartime one. (From 1940 to 1945 the rise in the cost of living for moderate-income families had been 28.4 per cent; from 1945 to 1949 it was 31.7 per cent— with prices still going up.) A series of strikes brought a series of federal mediations, which usually gave labor at least a part of what it had asked for; and these wage increases were followed by price increases to absorb them—with, sometimes, a margin to spare. We saw a first round of wage increases, a second round, a third round— and then we lost track of the number. The rising cost of almost everything bore down heavily upon some businesses, and upon individuals with fixed incomes, but as to the continuing actuality of prosperity there could be no doubt whatever. With government expenditures continuing at a high level, the economic question of the day was not whether America could absorb all it could produce, but whether it could produce all it wanted to absorb.

The other surprise was deeply disturbing. With Hitlerism dead and done with, and with Japan docile under MacArthur's imperial rule, we no sooner started to relax than it was borne in upon us, with increasing ominousness, that Soviet Russia in her turn was bent upon world conquest. Not only must we keep large occupation forces both in the Far East and in Europe; we must also prop up exhausted Britain with a loan, come to the aid of Greece and Turkey under the Truman Doctrine, launch the Marshall Plan to the tune of billions a year for aid to the non-Communist governments and peoples of Western Europe; run for months a hazardous airlift to Berlin to prevent the Soviets from starving that city into submission; forge an Atlantic Pact to protect Western Europe, and contribute heavily to its defense; and, in 1950, hold off a Communist attack upon South Korea—meanwhile confronting, at every session of every council, assembly, and commission of the new United Nations organization, an unremitting barrage of obstruction and vilification from the Soviet representatives.

So our dreams of victorious relaxation ended almost as soon as they began. The draft had to be continued. The military establishment had to be built up again—at a cost which unhappily prolonged inflation. We found ourselves the uneasy proprietors of a big atomic-power industry, government controlled (how strange to American experience!) and supersecret. We made intermittently successful efforts at bi-partisan management of our foreign policy, but under the strain of our bewildering responsibilities there were constant political frictions and recriminations over the blunders or alleged blunders that had given communism the initiative in so many parts of the earth. We discovered that the American Communists had infiltrated into the management of many labor unions, many supposedly liberal public-service organizations, and some government departments; and so intense had the anti-Soviet feeling become that this discovery led —as we shall see in another chapter of this book—to the besmirching, often on the flimsiest or falsest of evidence, of the reputations of many estimable citizens. But on the other hand, our very distrust of the Soviets led to the passage, by large majorities, of measure after measure for the relief, upbuilding, and defense of Europe. In our deep anxiety we were carrying through a policy of aid which—however it might be resented by people in Europe who knew well that we had never suffered as they did, and whatever the final outcome of it might be—was generous and statesmanlike.

As the international tension mounted again, still another surprise became manifest. Real isolationism had virtually disappeared.

What had happened, paradoxically, was that most of those Americans who had formerly been isolationist, or would have been isolationist had the international skies been clearer, had become interventionists in a special area, the Far East. When they looked across the Atlantic Ocean, they looked with the old eyes of skepticism, voting against appropriations for Britain, paring down appropriations for the Continent. But when they looked across the Pacific Ocean, their mood was not skeptical, but full of faith in Chiang Kai-shek, whom they wanted to support fully; and they were angry at American officials, not because these officials had been too lavish in aid to a foreign government, but because they had been too lukewarm and too niggardly. Some of the critics even pushed their attack upon these officials to the point where it was implied that anyone who was not a wholehearted interventionist in Asia was suspect of Communist sympathies—an implication which they would hardly have accepted if it had been applied to full support of, let us say, the Marshall Plan.

What did this all add up to? To the fact that we had interventionists-in-Europe and interventionists-in-Asia, but few true isolationists any more—at least for the time being. However acrid the disputes over foreign policy, there was general agreement that the United States faced an inescapable assignment as chief guardian and financial helper and adviser of the non-Communist world.

That was a development which the American of 1935, had he been able to foresee it, would have regarded with complete incredulity.

Because it was so new, it was a development for which we ourselves were unprepared. The United States was gravely lacking in experts who knew China, Korea, Indo-China, Iran, Egypt, and other lands where crisis loomed; we had to begin hurriedly training them. Foreign-policy problems were new and strange to most of us. By nature we resented having to engage in government propaganda abroad. Emotionally we were unready for the commanding role that had been thrust upon us; for our inherited instincts—and most of our acquired instincts—told us that where we belonged was in the United States, looking after our own affairs. More than ever, we were the reluctant world power.

Chapter 12

Ole Ark A' Moverin'

By THE mid-century—as a small army of technicians, diplomats, exchange scholars, and journalists left the country to administer its new world responsibilities —Americans abroad found that they were repeatedly asked the question (partly as a result of persistent Communist propaganda): "What about your race relations in the United States?" To the Asiatic, to the African, to the men of color in every land, it made a great deal of sense to judge American promises of a Brave New World against American performance at home.

To this stock question the new missionaries of Fulbright, Point Four, ECA, and the technical assistance programs of the United Nations could find no stock response. They were unable to deny that a degree of discrimination continues to exist in the United States. Yet they were also aware that the impressions in men's minds abroad were outdated, and to that extent at least were distorted. And they found themselves wanting to tell the world, "But you must understand how much these things have changed in the past few decades."

In 1900 there were not quite nine million Negroes in the United States (as compared with some fifteen million in 1950) and they were overwhelmingly concentrated in the South. Not only did nearly nine-tenths of them live there, but nearly three-quarters of them were to be found in the *rural* South. For a generation they had enjoyed the nominal status of free men and women; but they were desperately handicapped by poverty, ill health, bad housing, inadequate education, scanty opportunity, and—in the South—an inferior position before the law. No less than 44.5 per cent of them were illiterate. By and large they held the most servile, heaviest, dirtiest, and worst-paid jobs; and their most characteristic occupation was as cotton-pickers, victims of an uneconomic and demoralizing system of farm tenantry which a cynic might have imagined to have been deliberately devised in order to inculcate in the tenants the very traits of shiftlessness and irresponsibility which were attributed to the Negroes. Many of them lived in virtual peonage by reason of debt.

The prevailing view of them among the Southern whites was that they were virtually subhuman and incapable of profiting by educa-tion; when a Negro manifested exceptional intelligence, this was taken to be a sign that he must have white blood in his veins. The colored people were to be regarded with affection and amusement so long as they kept their place, but must be intimidated the moment they showed any signs of stepping out of it; for underlying the enjoyment which the Southern whites took in their agreeable deport-ment, their gentle humor, their gift of song, their zest for rhythm, their instinct for courtesy, was a profound fear of them—a fear heightened by long memories of Reconstruction days, and by the realization that in many parts of the region they outnumbered the whites.

This fear had brought about their gradual disfranchisement by such devices as the "grandfather law": in 1900 it was estimated that out of 181,471 Negro males of voting age in Alabama only 3,000 were registered. Lynchings were numerous: in 1900 no less than 115 were recorded, and in 1901 the figure rose to a record 130 (as com-pared with an average of less than four a year during the nineteen-forties).

The million or so Negroes who lived outside the South fared on the average much better, partly because the wage level tended to be higher in the North and West, the schools better, the sanitary condi-tions less primitive, but also because there was as yet little fear of them in these regions; in some smaller communities the few resident Negroes were highly regarded and occupied positions of virtual social equality with their neighbors. But even in the North, Negroes in general were customarily regarded as comic or picturesque minor characters in the drama of American life, and the latest quaint saying of a colored servant played a part in the conversation of the well-bred, somewhat like that of the latest quaint saying of an amusing child.

There had long been a tendency to move northward among those Negroes who could afford the trip, but it was not until about the year 1915 that the northward migration reached flood proportions. What accelerated it was a rising demand for unskilled workers in northern industry by reason of the war boom. Year by year it continued, as word spread through county after county in the South that colored friends and relatives in Harlem or Philadelphia or Chicago were eating regularly and appreciating the absence of Jim Crow restrictions. But as the Negro population in the North swelled—especially in the big cities which absorbed an overwhelming majority of the migrants—the same sort of fear that had previously been acute only in the South began to possess many Northerners. Efforts to keep Negroes out of jobs which whites might want, and to pen them within their own slum districts, lest their presence elsewhere lower real-estate values, became more deliberate, more organized; during the mid-twenties the vicious Ku Klux Klan flourished not only in the South but in many parts of the North too. The colored people were learning to their cost that the amount of organized discrimination against any group considered alien is likely to be proportionate to the relative size of that group in the community, and that as they moved north they brought their problems with them.

Then came the Great Depression, and its impact upon the Negro population was appalling. In those days when apprehension over the loss of one's job became an obsession with millions of Americans, inevitably the worst sufferers were those who traditionally had been the last to be hired, the first to be demoted, the first to be fired. If the northward migration continued—as it did—this was largely because the chances of getting on relief were on the whole better

in the North than in the South. In the year 1935 the median incomes
of colored families were computed in a number of cities; in the
northern ones, they averaged about half, or a little less, of the
median incomes of white families (which themselves were nothing
to brag of in that Depression year); in southern cities they averaged
even less. In Mobile, Alabama, for example, the median Negro
family took in only $481 during the year, as against $1,419 for the
median white one. And in that same year *something like half of all
the Negro families in the North were on relief!*

The Communists made terrific efforts to capitalize upon this situation, and no wonder: was there not here a proletariat made to their
order? They signally failed to make more than a small number of
Negro converts, however; partly, perhaps, because the Negroes
constituted something closer to a caste than to a class, and had stratifications in their own communities which made such an appeal
unpalatable to many, including most of their natural leaders; partly
because communism was unpopular and, as one Negro put it, it was
"bad enough to be black without being red too"; and partly because
they were by nature allergic to the alienness of Communist theory and
action.

The approach of World War II brought a sharp economic improvement. As the general level of wages rose, Negroes could hardly
escape getting some of the benefits. These reached them laggingly,
however, for the desire of white workers to keep the best of the new
jobs for themselves had hardened into an attitude much more
conscious and deliberate than during the industrial boom of World
War I.

By this time another factor was at work. Innumerable white
citizens were becoming uncomfortably aware that the existence of an
underprivileged caste in the United States was a blot upon the record
of a nation enlisted in a fight for democracy. Negro leaders took every
opportunity to add to their moral discomfort by reminding them
that Negroes, drafted into the armed forces like whites, were segregated there and assigned to menial duties. The agitation against this
segregation, and for a code of "fair employment practices" in war

manufacturing plants, won strong backing among whites in the North; and even in the South, though there remained Rankins and Talmadges to shout the old battle cries of "white supremacy," there was manifest among great numbers of decent people the same sort of stirring of the conscience. They were becoming aware of how heavy an economic load weighs upon any community which deliberately condemns a part of its consuming public to poverty; and they were making a conscientious effort to find, by quiet accommodation, sympathetic solutions for the ancient problems of Negro poverty and misery in the Southern States.

For a time the upshot was uncertain. Wrote Gunnar Myrdal, completing during the war his massive, dispassionate study of the condition of the colored people, *An American Dilemma*: "Reading the Negro press and hearing all the reports from observers who have been out among common Negroes in the South and the North convinces me that there is much sullen skepticism, and even cynicism, and vague, tired, angry dissatisfaction among American Negroes today." And expecting—as most people did during 1943, 1944, and 1945—that the war would be followed by another depression, Myrdal wondered whether the friction that would result might set back Negro progress. For a time it looked as if the mutual antipathy of Negroes and whites might not remain within peaceful bounds, especially when, shortly after the war, some colored leaders advised their fellow Negroes to resist the draft so long as the armed forces of the United States did not put the two races on a footing of equality.

II

But there was no postwar depression. And all this time the uneasy American conscience was steadily at work. The result was that the postwar years saw a change that would have seemed unbelievable only a decade earlier.

A series of Supreme Court decisions set aside many of the laws and practices which had kept Negroes from the polls and from educational opportunity. One decision weakened the force of racially restrictive real-estate covenants. A number of Southern states repealed the poll-tax laws which had prevented great numbers of poor people, white and black, from voting; in the election of 1948 over a million Southern Negroes went to the polls. The Air Force and Navy officially ended segregation and the Army modified its former segregation practices. The pressure of "fair employment" laws in several Northern states, combined with the eagerness of many employers to set an example of enlightened employment policy, brought about the entry of colored workers in many fields of employment new to them. In New York, for example, anybody returning to the city after a long absence would have been struck by the large numbers of colored men and women in the midtown busses and on the midtown streets, traveling to jobs that had previously been for whites only, or to shop in stores where colored customers had previously been few and far between. In Northern and Western cities generally there was a noticeable breakdown of Jim Crow restrictions in hotels, restaurants, and theaters.

Ever since the nineteen-twenties there had been a rising appreciation, among intellectuals, of the Negro contributions to the arts, and especially to jazz music; and as time went on there developed among the more ardent students of jazz such a reverence for the pioneering contributions of the original jazz musicians of New Orleans and Memphis, and for the inheritors of the traditions of Basin Street and Beale Street, that men like Duke Ellington and Louis Armstrong found themselves the objects of a deep and deferential respect among thousands of music lovers. Meanwhile, in quite another area, the statesmanship and dignity of Ralph Bunche, as mediator in the Near East, was winning for him the admiration of innumerable whites. But still more important for Negro prestige, because it involved such an enormous public, was the prowess of Joe Louis, the great heavyweight champion, of whom Jimmy Cannon said that he was a credit to his race—the human race; and also the performance of a number of colored baseball players after the Jim Crow restrictions in professional baseball were broken down in the late nineteen-forties. Not only did the remarkable playing and exemplary behavior of men like

Jackie Robinson make the earlier color line in baseball seem preposterous to the fans, but by 1950 most of the enthusiasts for baseball seemed to choose their favorite players with almost no regard
for the color line; and so carefully did radio reporters of baseball
games refrain from mentioning the color of the players that there
were actually stay-at-home fans who could tell you Roy Campanella's
approximate batting average but were not aware that he was a Negro.

"Probably the most important thing that has happened in the
United States in the field of race relations," wrote Mrs. Eleanor
Roosevelt, "is that so many things are now taken for granted where
the integration of the two races is concerned. This was brought home
to me at the Inauguration of 1945 in the White House when a group
of newspaper women who had been watching the receiving line came
to me at the end of the day and said: 'Do you realize what twelve
years have done? If at the 1933 reception a number of colored people
had gone down the line and mixed with everyone else in the way
they did today, every paper in the country would have reported it.
We do not even think it is news and none of us will mention it.' "

No longer did magazines, newspapers, and moving pictures show
Negroes almost exclusively as comic or menial characters. Those
ancient stereotypes had been largely eliminated.

Most striking of all the changes, perhaps, was a new attitude on
the part of younger white Americans, both North and South—a very
widespread resolve to accept Negroes as people without regard to
their color. This attitude was manifest when, following Supreme
Court decisions, a number of universities in the southern and border
states admitted Negroes to unsegregated standing. University admin-
istrators were uneasy: would some hothead whites among the students
raise a ruckus? Up to the end of 1951 there had been no ruckus
anywhere. Uniformly, the students took the innovation in their stride.

Meanwhile a profound change in the economic pattern of the Old
South was having a further effect upon Negro fortunes. The invention of the cotton-picker and cotton-stripper was bringing an end
to the reign of King Cotton in the Southeast and was slowly under-

mining the ancient institution of farm tenantry. Little by little the former cotton plantations of Georgia, Alabama, and the Carolinas were being abandoned as cotton planters in the Mississippi Delta, Texas, Oklahoma, New Mexico, and Arizona proved themselves able to harvest cotton economically on large tracts of land fully adapted to mechanized operations. Little by little the southeastern states were shifting from cotton to dairy farming, livestock raising, vegetable raising, and the growing of pine trees for cellulose. And the result was a further drift of the former tenant farmers, black along with white, to the industrial cities and towns the country over.

The census figures of 1950 showed the extent of the shift. In 1900, as we have seen, nearly three-quarters of the Negroes in America had lived in the rural South; by 1950, *less than one-fifth of them did.* (And less than half of these were tenants.) In several Southern states —Alabama, Arkansas, Georgia, and Mississippi—the total colored population showed an actual decline since 1940; and although South Carolina registered an increase, it was exceedingly small. Meanwhile the figures for various Northern states illustrated how widely the Negro population was becoming distributed. In Connecticut, for example, the number of colored residents had leaped in ten years from 33,835 to 54,953; in Wisconsin, from 24,835 to 41,884. The northward tide was not simply flooding into the biggest and most congested centers; it was seeping out into other parts of the land.

And what of the economic fortunes of the colored people? During World War II Gunnar Myrdal had written:

The economic situation of the Negroes is pathological. Except for a small minority enjoying upper or middle class status, the masses of American Negroes, in the rural South and in the segregated slum quarters in Southern and Northern cities, are destitute. They own little property; even their household goods are mostly inadequate and dilapidated. Their incomes are not only low but irregular. They thus live from day to day and have scant security for the future. Their entire culture and their individual interests and strivings are narrow.

By the mid-century there was still a degree of truth in this generalization. Yet there were signs that during the nineteen-forties the rising tide of prosperity had to a very considerable extent carried the Negro population with it.

True, it was estimated in 1948 that the median Negro family income was 47 per cent lower than the comparable white family income. But in the *National Economic Review* for the year 1950, published by the President's Council of Economic Advisers in January, 1951, there was an estimate of the proportion of Negroes in various income groups which put the situation in somewhat different terms. Among those "spending units"—which means families and individuals—whose money income before taxes was less than $1,000 for the year, 83 per cent were found to be white; 15 per cent, Negro (leaving two per cent classified as "unascertainable"). Among the next higher group, with annual incomes between $1,000 and $2,000, 89 per cent were white, 10 per cent Negro. In the $2,000-$3,000 class, 92 per cent were white, 7 per cent Negro. And in the large group with incomes of $3,000 or over, 97 per cent were white, 3 per cent were Negro. When you examine those figures, remember that the Negroes of the country constitute just about one-tenth of the population. Therefore par for each of these classifications would be 10 per cent. The figures reveal a marked shortage of colored people in the more well-to-do groups, and an excess of colored people in the lowest group. But I wonder if many readers will not feel, as I did when I first saw those figures, some surprise that the overloading in the lowest brackets was not more extreme. The movement of Negroes away from tenant farming and into industry, and out of the Old South into other parts of the country, was combining with the general change in public attitudes to mitigate the deplorable situation described by Myrdal.

There were other favorable signs. Negro illiteracy had been cut in fifty years from 44.5 per cent to 11 per cent, and Negro expectancy of life had been increased by nearly 26 years. Lynchings—the endless topic of Communist propaganda the world over—had virtually ceased: in the entire United States only one lynching was recorded in 1945; six in 1946; one in 1947; two in 1948 (of which one of the victims was white); three in 1949; and two in 1950 (of which one victim was white). One would find it hard to find a disease so rare, or a type of accident so unusual, that in a land of a hundred and fifty million people they would not produce death rates larger than those.

By the mid-century there were 94,000 Negro students in American colleges and universities. And a colored woman who had been serving as an exchange professor in France told me that she was constantly having to explain to French audiences that there were a great many people like herself who were able to lead their professional lives with a minimum sense of belonging to a special caste. "Are you allowed to walk on the sidewalk in Washington?" she would be asked; and would have to explain that of course she was. One noted an increasing number of Negro policemen in Southern cities—often arresting white lawbreakers; and such symbolic events took place as the election of a Negro to the city council in Richmond, Virginia. All in all, the evidence was strong, not only that the status of the Negro had risen far above what most Europeans—influenced despite themselves by Communist rantings and also by the writings of earlier rebels against the American color line—imagined it to be, but above what most Americans still imagined it to be.

There was little prospect that this major American problem would move toward a solution without further friction and mutual antagonism. No era of amiable harmony was in sight. Yet at least the battleground of opinion was moving slowly toward a location less disadvantageous to the Negro. As Walter White wrote in the summer of 1951, America was making progress toward rubbing out the darkest blot on its democratic record—"often painfully slow, but it is still progress."

Chapter 13

Faster, Faster

WRITING in the year 1904, Henry Adams—"an elderly and timid single gentleman in Paris," as he described himself—recorded his astonishment at the year-by-year expansion of steam power and electric power, and at the discovery of radioactivity; and he propounded a "law of acceleration." The amount of force at the disposal of mankind was increasing faster and faster, he noted. "The coal output of the world, speaking roughly, doubled every ten years between 1840 and 1900, in the form of utilized power, for the ton of coal yielded three or four times as much power in 1900 as in 1840." And he looked forward to a fantastic future, in which the forces available to man would multiply until "the new American—the child of incalculable coal power, chemical power, electric power, and radiating energy, as well as of new forces yet undetermined—must be a sort of God compared with any former creature of nature."

At the rate of progress since 1800, continued Adams, "every American who lived into the year 2000 would know how to control unlimited power. He would think in complexities unimaginable to an earlier mind. He would deal with problems altogether beyond the range of earlier society. To him the nineteenth century would stand on the same plane with the fourth—equally childlike—and he would only wonder how both of them, knowing so little, and so weak in force, should have done so much."

At the mid-century a thoughtful observer of the startling progress of American technology is likely to feel a bewilderment akin to that which Adams felt in 1904. For the application of power to the circumstances of American life has not only increased at a dizzy pace since Adams's time, but has seemed to be accelerating sharply, with the promise of further leaps ahead. In the latter nineteen-thirties many economists had come to the conclusion that the United States had arrived at a "mature economy"; instead, we have been witnessing a technological revolution comparable to that which followed the introduction of steam, and far more rapid. During the fifteen years from 1935 to 1950 American technology took a stride forward at least as impressive as that which Henry Ford's assembly line dramatized in earlier years; and from all appearances this was not the culmination, but merely a preliminary phase, of a process of change which in time would profoundly alter the working and living conditions of the people.

We have already noted, in Chapter 11, how the coming of World War II unlocked the productive powers of American industry; how the manufacturers, when asked to go ahead and produce with little regard for cost or for anything else except quantity and speed, went into a burst of activity which astonished the world. But we have given only passing mention to the way in which the war stimulated invention and technological change. What the government, through its Office of Scientific Research and Development and other agencies, was constantly saying during the war was, in effect: "Is this discovery or that one of any possible war value? If so, then develop it and put it to use, and damn the expense!" The result has been likened to a team of experts combing through a deskful of scientific papers, pulling out those which gave promise of usefulness, and then commandeering all the talent and appropriating all the money that might be needed to translate formulae into goods of military value.

The classic example, of course, is the way in which, following the splitting of the atom in 1939 and the confirmation of this event by American experiments in 1940, the government presently launched the Manhattan Project, at a cost of billions, and compressed into less than five years of research and engineering and manufacturing experiment and development what might otherwise have taken a generation to accomplish. But there were other examples innumerable. For instance, it was in 1929 that Alexander Fleming first described penicillin. Long years went by before the possibilities of what he had discovered were realized. Not until the war came was penicillin adapted for medicinal use. But then the work was pushed with such speed that before the end of the war the drug was being supplied in vast amounts. Still another example was the pioneer work done by Robert Watson-Watt and other British investigators in the development of radar, under the awful necessity of protecting England from German bombs; the utilization of their findings in the American manufacture of radar equipment on the grand scale; and the resulting education of thousands of young Americans in the principles and possibilities of electronics.

Each of these developments which I have cited was based, in large part, upon scientific discoveries made abroad. We should remember that the metaphorical deskful of papers of which I have spoken was international; much if not most of the fundamental work out of which grew the new wartime products and devices was European. What the United States contributed most effectively was a capacity for the organization of research, especially in applied science; the ability to set up brisk production lines; and a zest for doing big things at top speed.

The war crisis brought together as never before the pure scientist, the applied scientist, the manufacturing executive, the military officer, and the government administrator, and put them into a partnership which mightily affected their future understanding of one another. The physicist or chemist who had been cloistered in a university laboratory, and had taken a special pride in paying no heed to the possible practical application of his findings, was thrust into emergency work of the most lethally practical sort, and hauled off to Washington to consult with generals and admirals and bureaucrats and engineers and manufacturers; and these others acquired a new respect for his scholarly ardor, now suddenly so vital to them. The question has been raised whether the quality of disinterested academic investigation was not somehow tarnished in the process, and especially whether the continuing diversion of much scientific talent into specific projects for the government even after 1945 may not have slowed our advance in pure science. But certainly there took place during the war a cross-fertilization of thinking which was stimulating to all concerned. Many a professor was enlivened by his new contacts, and many an industrial executive went home from Washington with a new insight into the future potential of scientific research.

All in all, during the war American technology underwent a hothouse growth.

II

Meanwhile the war-induced prosperity was speeding technological change on a quite different level. The jingle of cash in the pocket was preparing innumerable ordinary Americans to buy and use more machines just as soon as these became available. And after V-J Day the rush was on.

Everybody, to begin with, seemed to want new automobiles, which had been unavailable for purchase during the war. There was hot competition for the joy of getting a new car fresh from the assembly line; people talked about the number of months or years that they had "had their name in" with dealers; there was a lively racket in ostensibly used cars; and it was years before the automobile manufacturers could catch up with the demand. After they had done so, in the single year 1950 they sold more than eight million vehicles —which was more cars than had existed in the entire United States at the end of World War I.

But that wasn't the half of it. During these postwar years the farmer bought a new tractor, a corn picker, an electric milking machine; in fact he and his neighbors, between them, assembled a formidable array of farm machinery for their joint use. The farmer's wife got the shining white electric refrigerator she had always longed for and never during the Great Depression had been able to afford, and an up-to-date washing machine, and a deep-freeze unit. The suburban family installed a dishwashing machine and invested in a power lawnmower. The city family became customers of a laundromat and acquired a television set for the living room. The husband's office was air-conditioned. And so on endlessly.

Few of these machines for working and living were new in principle. Many had been on the market and in use for a long time. Essentially it was prosperity which put these and other machines into widespread use—prosperity plus a variety of sometimes mutually antagonistic forces, such as, for example, the electric-utility industry, enemy-to-the-death of the New Deal, and the Rural Electrification Administration, offspring of the New Deal, which between them were at least partly responsible for the remarkable progress in the electrification of American farms. In 1935 only about 10 per cent of American farms were electrified; by 1950, more than 85 per cent were.

A one-time resident of Arkansas, returning to Fayetteville at the mid-century after a prolonged absence, remarked that the most eye-opening thing about the farms he saw in the neighborhood was that almost all were electrified; in his boyhood an electric-lighted farm had been a rarity. At about the same time the editors of a popular magazine planned to publish a picture story on the daily routine of a farmer's wife; they abandoned the project because the farmers' wives that their correspondents and photographers had encountered had so much mechanical kitchen equipment that they could hardly be distinguished photographically from other housewives. In 1950 a British "productivity team" visited America to study the agricultural methods in use, and visited a large number of farms from New Jersey to Nebraska, with their interest focused, not on the spectacularly large farm with its intensive mechanization, but on the family-size farm run by the farmer and his family with the aid, perhaps, of one hired hand. They noted not only the widespread and increasing use of such things as tractor plows, disk harrows, corn planters, corn pickers, combine harvesters, milking machines, self-unloading trailers, and so on, but also the fact that on farm after farm the work was

being reorganized to take advantage of machinery. The farmer no
longer thought of a machine simply as an efficient and untiring substitute for a horse, or for human effort, but as a device which would
enable him to go about his business in a new way—using a hay dryer
to preserve the vitamins in his cattle feed, for instance, or substituting
for the electrical milking of cows in a traditional stanchion barn the
building of a "milking parlor" adjacent to an open cattleshed or
"loafing barn."

During the nineteen-forties the number of farm workers shrank
from 9½ millions to only a little over 8 millions. Nevertheless farm
production increased by 25 per cent. This was partly, of course,
because prosperity at home and food shortages abroad had broadened
the market; but partly it was because farmers, like other Americans,
were using more and more machines, old and new, in their daily life.

III

Simultaneously the rising wage rates in American factories were
prompting a restless search for labor-saving methods of production.
These took innumerable forms, some of them based upon sheer
elementary common sense—"Can't we dream up a machine to do the
work that those unskilled workers are sweating over?" or "Why
not redesign this floor of the factory so that the work won't have to
be lifted by hand from this point to that, but will move smoothly
from job to job by conveyor belt?"—while others involved scientific
formulae and mechanical assemblies of the utmost complexity.

The common-sense labor-saving devices would make a long list—
overhead cranes, conveyors of all sorts (gravity rollers, skate rollers,
belt conveyors), power grabs for picking up unit loads, power-driven
hand tools, the use of compressed air for cleaning, and so forth.
Typical, perhaps, in its simplicity and its significance is the use of
the fork truck and pallet: the fork truck being a sturdy little truck
equipped with a fork—or pair of metal fingers—with which it can
pick up goods, lift them high, and carry them from point to point;
and the pallet being simply a double-bottomed tray on which cartons
or bundles of goods can be piled for such transportation. The fork

truck can insert its metal fingers between the two layers of a loaded pallet on a freight car, lift it, carry it to its appointed place in the factory, put it carefully in place, and then withdraw the metal fingers and return for another load. All very simple; nothing abstruse about it. But anybody who has watched the laborious unloading of trucks across a city sidewalk—one man lifting cartons out of the truck, another man toting them indoors, to be taken by a third man to their proper place in the building—can realize the amount of human heaving and hauling that the fork truck and pallet eliminate. For all this effort is substituted the work of one man, driving about in his fork truck and manipulating with precise skill the metal fingers of his fork. Such contraptions are symbolic of a whole class of labor-saving devices in that they regard human labor as expensive and therefore to be conserved, while the wood or plastic that goes into the making of pallets is plentiful and comparatively expendable.

Anybody can understand the basic principle of a fork truck. But the layman can only stand in awe before some of the complex electronic machines which came into use during the period between 1935 and 1950—machines for measuring materials with microscopic exactitude, or for watching the performance of a machine and automatically correcting flaws in its performance. The language used by engineers in talking about them is quite unintelligible to him, as are the processes involved. But at least he can appreciate the miraculous results they achieve. They can count and inspect the goods coming off an assembly line, passing or discarding them as faithful or unfaithful to the specifications. They can check, with incredible precision, the exact thickness of a sheet of steel, or discover the hidden flaws inside a mass of metal. They can watch the work of a machine with an eye of superhuman vision, and start, stop, regulate the machine in accordance with their observations. Here again, though the scientific principles at work are far beyond lay comprehension, the symbolic significance is clear: you can not only dispense with even a reasonably skilled workman by building into a machine all the foreseeable motions with which he might react to variations in the task before him, but you can even provide the machine with eyes much sharper and reactions much prompter than his. With such appliances coming into use, no wonder the most striking thing about many a factory floor, today, is the multiplicity of machines and the almost total absence of machine tenders.

Another innovation which came into use during this same period has a somewhat different significance. It does not eliminate the workman; instead, it makes him a less wasteful and more responsible performer. This is "quality control"—a system of taking an occasional sample of the work produced by a given machine, submitting this sample to the most minute electronic inspection, and recording on a chart just how it deviates from absolute perfection. The workman, consulting this chart, can thereupon regulate the adjustment of his machine, not by guesswork, but with exact knowledge of just how it is functioning. This device—which in many a factory has saved large amounts of money by reducing the number of defective products —has the effect of raising the status of the workman by making him in a special sense his own boss, the informed critic and judge of his performance.

What has been the cumulative effect of the introduction of such varied machine methods? First, it has reduced sharply the demand for unskilled labor. In 1900 there were some eleven million "common laborers" (including those on the farms) in the United States; by 1950 there were less than six million. At the other end of the spectrum it has increased tremendously the demand for engineers and technicians. At the beginning of the century, according to President Conant of Harvard, chemical engineering had not developed as a profession; "today [he was speaking in 1951] there is a great shortage of chemical engineers in spite of the fact that more than 15,000 have been trained in the last five years." As for engineers in general, they increased in number from about 40,000 in 1900 to about 400,000 in 1950, and still there was such a furious demand for them—intensified by the Korean war—that in 1951 the students graduating from engineering schools were being looked over by talent-scout teams from over four thousand companies, and one university placement officer declared, "Even our worst students have had at least three offers."

The economist Colin Clark has called attention to the fact that as an industrial civilization becomes more advanced, there tends to be a movement of people out of farming into industry, and then out of industry into what he calls the "services"—meaning business, trade, transportation, entertainment, the professions, etc. This movement has certainly been taking place in the United States. Since 1900 the proportion of Americans engaged in farming has taken a big drop; the proportion engaged in industry, overall, has changed very little; the proportion engaged in the "services" has jumped upward. Take this fact in conjunction with the facts about the shift within industry and we emerge with a general finding: At the mid-century there are fewer and fewer people working with their hands, more and more people working at desks; fewer workers with brawn, more workers with brain; fewer whose jobs require only a limited education, more who need an advanced education.

There are still many dark satanic mills in the United States. There are still numerous jobs of grinding effort or wearisome monotony. Even the most automatic factory has to employ maintenance men, sweepers, cleaners; these men's work has been very little mechanized, and they tend to form a sort of new proletariat of the machine age. Yet the general trend is toward an enhancement of the dignity of labor.

Ever since Henry Ford set up his assembly line we have been hearing lamentations over the tendency of the factory to turn a man into a robot, to make him a mere mechanical bolt-tightener, hour upon hour. Dreadful pictures have been drawn of the completely mechanized future day when man would be dehumanized by such labor. But what has actually been happening, increasingly, is that a machine has been put to work tightening those everlasting bolts; that the man who formerly tightened them, or his counterpart, is either managing a more intricate machine, or sitting at a desk studying engineering reports; while the man who formerly broke his back lifting bundles of goods is sitting at the controls of a conveyer. For the principle that has been at work is this: If the job is unendurably heavy or monotonous, that's a pretty good sign that you can get a machine to do it.

IV

Like scouts moving before an advancing column of troops, the investigators and engineers of pure and applied science have meanwhile been moving ahead. For well over a generation, now, the chemists and chemical engineers have been ringing the changes on an idea mentioned in an earlier chapter of this book, the idea that "synthetic" materials can do better than merely imitate nature: they can actually improve on nature. It was before World War II—on October 25, 1939, to be exact—that they produced the climactic demonstration of this idea; that was when nylon stockings first went on sale. During the nineteen-thirties and the war years, other pioneers of technology succeeded in adapting the Diesel engine—that long-neglected source of power—to widespread use on the railroads and in industry. They developed high-octane gasoline into a plentiful source of power for airplanes. They brought the production of synthetic rubber to a point where it served, not merely as a war substitute, but as a product of continuing value for a nation on wheels. They found out how to use tungsten-carbide cutting tools for immensely rapid machine-tool operations. And they made medical history by discovering the merciful possibilities of the antibiotics.

As for atomic power—their most imposing achievement—we already have been shown its deadly possibilities; what its beneficent ones may be is still uncertain, in view of the fabulous cost of producing it, but they might well, in time, make man—in Adams's words —"the child of incalculable power."

In the field of aviation the working of Adams's law of acceleration has been strikingly exemplified. In 1935 there was no transoceanic flying except on an adventurous and experimental basis; scarcely a dozen years later, the first question asked of anybody who said he was leaving for Europe was, "Are you going to fly or go by boat?" By the end of the war we saw the arrival of the jet plane; within a few years thereafter, the speed of planes was reported to have passed the supposedly impassable sonic barrier; by 1950 the exploration of the upper air had reached a point where sober men of science were talking in matter-of-fact tones about the chances for space travel.

In quite different fields one encounters startling evidence of the way in which the advance of research has been transforming American businesses—as when one hears from an official of the Corning Glass Works that more than 50 per cent of Corning sales in 1950 was in products which did not exist commercially ten years earlier.

The nineteen-forties were a heyday for the chemists and chemical engineers. The oil industry, for instance, happily discovered that, as Carroll Wilson has put it, "there were things more valuable than fuel in a barrel of crude oil," and, beginning about 1942, built a number of continuous-flow chemical plants which rivaled the wildest fantasies of an H. G. Wells. In these strange new factories with their shining fractionating towers and their latticeworks of bright-colored pipes, "the raw material, fluid or gas, flows continuously in at one end, passes through intricate processing stages, and debouches in a twenty-four-hour stream of products at the other," wrote the editors of *Fortune* in their 1951 book, *U.S.A., the Permanent Revolution.* And what a variety of products—ranging from fertilizer to detergents, from cosmetics to refrigerants, from synthetic rubber to printer's ink! Nowadays the petrochemists, sitting in their laboratories and drawing pictures of arrangements of molecules that look like diagrams of football plays, see themselves as the architects of a multifold new industrial era.

But perhaps it is not to the chemists, but to the physicists, that one should look for the most startling future discoveries; or to co-ordinated efforts by physicists, chemists, biologists, and mathematicians. In the year 1948 chemistry gave us cortisone, that minister of comfort and shaker of medical theory; in the same year physics produced the transistor, a tiny device which may well supersede the vacuum tube. The half century was hardly over before co-ordinated researches developed krilium, a soil conditioner of unguessed potentialities. And there are hardheaded men who believe that the joint efforts of physicists, chemists, and biologists may be taking us to the threshold of accomplishing the miracle of photosynthesis—of producing food from light as plants produce it.

Perhaps Henry Adams was not so far wrong with his prediction that "every American who lived into the year 2000 would know how to control unlimited power." Certainly things have been accelerating at the mid-century.

Chapter 14

More Americans, Living Longer

DURING the year 1932 a
huddle of social scientists put the finishing touches on a massive
study of American life which they called *Recent Social Changes,*
and in this book some of them made cautious estimates of the probable increase in the future population of the country. Noting that the
rate of growth appeared to be slowing down, they figured that a
"continuation of present trends" would produce a 1940 population
of 132 or 133 millions. In the event they were not far wrong; when
the year 1940 rolled round, the actual figure proved to be a trifle
smaller—presumably because of the discouragements of the Great
Depression—yet only a trifle: it was 131,669,275. But on the same
tentative basis the social scientists made a prediction for 1950, and
on this one they were spectacularly wrong. Their prediction: between
140½ and 145 millions (which, you will agree, allowed considerable
leeway for error). The actual 1950 figures: 150,697,361 people—
more than five millions more than their outside estimate! There had
been a huge, unexpected, and altogether astonishing increase.

The chief reason for the increase was a big jump in the birth rate
during the nineteen-forties. To ascribe this flatly to "war and prosperity," as some people have done, seems a little oversimple; for
World War I had brought no such big bulge, and during the reasonably prosperous nineteen-twenties the birthrate had not risen but had
declined a little. Yet undeniably the draft regulations, deferring

husbands with children, were a factor. Another was the natural tendency of young people facing the prospect of being separated for months or years—or perhaps forever—to plunge into marriage in a hurry. Still another was the eagerness of young men returning from the notably undomestic life of the armed services, and of girls who had been waiting for them, to want to begin to enjoy domesticity just as soon as possible, with terminal pay and in many cases the G.I. Bill of Rights to help finance the venture. And at a time when wars and rumors of wars seemed to jeopardize one's career and threaten one's very life, there was not only a human need for seizing whatever satisfactions were within reach but also, perhaps, a desire to make some sort of contribution to the future, to perpetuate one's blood—or if not an outright desire (since most births are in some degree accidental) at least a slackening of the resolution not to perpetuate it for the time being.

In any case the birth rate, which—after a long decline—in the nineteen-thirties had hovered in the neighborhood of 17 or 18 per thousand of population, went to 20.9 in 1942 and 21.5 in 1943; declined a trifle to 20.2 in 1944 and 19.6 in 1945 (when a good many million potential fathers were in Europe or on Pacific islands or at sea); and then rose abruptly to 23.3 in 1946 and 25.8 in 1947—after which it declined, but only very slightly, to 24.2 in 1948, 24.1 in 1949, and 23.5 in 1950.

Surely here was a very interesting reaction to the dislocations and carnage of war. It came at a time when many of the more articulate intellectuals appeared to have reached the conclusion that the hazardousness of life, the helplessness of the individul in the grip of blind destiny, and the general decline of firm convictions as to the value of human effort, were reducing mankind to despair. What happened to the birth rate would seem to give grounds for wondering whether the population in general was not taking a cheerier view of the future. Even among American college graduates as a group (who for a long time had been reproved for not reproducing themselves) the trend in the birth rate was upward; records of the alumni and alumnae of 167 colleges showed that the class of '41 had produced, by 1951, more children per graduate than the class of '36 had done when ten years out.

Was the institution of the family taking on a new lease of life in America? This notion may seem odd to one who notes that while the marriage rate, which had lagged during the Great Depression, rose during and after the war to a lofty peak in 1946, so did the divorce rate. But the large number of divorces at that time was surely due in part to repentance at leisure from hasty wartime alliances. For if it is true, as a cynic has said, that proximity and opportunity are responsible for most marriages, so a lack of proximity and a variety of opportunity will break up many marriages. And even though during the rest of the nineteen-forties the divorce rate remained higher than in prewar years—2.6 per thousand population in 1949, for example, as against the high figure of 4.3 in 1946 and a mere 2 in 1940, 1.6 in 1930, 1.6 in 1920, 0.9 in 1910, and 0.7 in 1900— this gave evidence, perhaps, of a declining conviction that marriages should be durable, but not of any doubt that they were desirable.

The figures seem to bear out one's impression that most American young people of the nineteen-forties had no such cynical or disillusioned reservations about marrying and bringing up a family as had possessed many of the bright young people of earlier decades. They did not want to prolong indefinitely the delights of single adventure. They did not regard marriage as a bourgeois expedient for enforcing a conventional monogamy upon free spirits. Nor did they, despite many warnings of the forthcoming collapse of civilization, regard with undue dismay adding to the number of human creatures who must allegedly confront that collapse. No, they wanted to marry and have babies, preferably in a ranch-type house with a dishwashing machine for the joint use of husband and wife, and with a TV set which would entertain them right beside the conjugal hearth. They had been around a lot and had decided that east, west, home was best.

II

Another reason why the population of the country grew so startlingly during the nineteen-forties was that fewer people were dying. The nation had never before been so healthy.

Indeed the cumulative change in this respect since 1900 had been prodigious. The death rate for a number of diseases which in 1900 had struck dismay into people's hearts had been cut way down: for influenza and pneumonia, from 181.5 (per 100,000 people) to 38.7 in 1948; for tuberculosis, from 201.9 to 30; for typhoid and para-typhoid, from 36 to 0.2; for diphtheria, from 43.3 to 0.4; for scarlet fever, from 11.4 to a small fraction of 0.1—a figure which in 1948 represented only 68 deaths in the entire country. Since immortality is denied to mankind and in the end people usually die of something, it was natural that startling reductions such as these should have been accompanied by increases in the death rate from degenerative diseases, notably heart diseases and cancer, which took the places formerly occupied by pneumonia and tuberculosis as the leading causes of death. But the net change in an American's expectation of life be-tween 1900 and 1950 could hardly have been more impressive: it went up from 49 years to 68 years!

What had brought this miracle about? An interlocking series of advances in medical knowledge, medical training, medical practice, sanitation, public health measures, and general popular understand-ing of the principles of health. According to Dr. Alan Gregg, "The Harvard biological chemist Lawrence J. Henderson once remarked that somewhere around 1910 the progress of medicine in America reached the point where it became possible to say that a random patient with a random disease consulting a physician at random stood better than a 50-50 chance of benefiting from the encounter." Since then the medical profession had not only learned a vast lot about the treatment of numerous ailments, but had acquired for use such extraor-dinarily effective drugs as sulfanilamide (dating from 1935), penicillin (discovered in 1929, but not put to clinical use until the early forties), antibiotics such as aureomycin (even more recent), and the revolutionary ACTH and cortisone (not clinically used until 1948). So effective were public health measures such as mosquito control for the prevention of malaria that in 1950 the State of Missis-sippi offered a bonus of $10 to any doctor who could find a new case of malaria, and not a single case was reported. Nor should one overlook the contribution to general public health made through the discovery of the vitamins (beginning with vitamin A in 1913) and through popular education about them; by the mid-century it was a rare family which had not yet heard that there were special virtues in tomato juice, fruit juices, green vegetables, and salads, to say nothing of milk.

Let Brigadier General Simmons, dean of the Harvard School of Public Health, produce a neat statistical comparison of the gain in the effectiveness of the medical services of the armed forces since the days when young Dr. Harvey Cushing, meeting at Baltimore a trainload of typhoid victims of the Spanish-American War, was horrified by the dirt and squalor that he witnessed: "In the Spanish-American War the rate for deaths from disease among our troops was about 25 per thousand per annum. . . . In World War I the rate was reduced to about 16. . . . In World War II . . . [it] was only 0.6 per thousand per annum."

The increasingly successful war against infectious diseases had brought about during the nineteen-forties a great increase in the number of old people, a new interest in pension plans, and—since the tendency of business concerns to lay off employees at sixty-five or even sixty was still gaining headway—an acute question whether pensions beyond that age would not constitute a burden too heavy for most companies to carry. Meanwhile the jump in the birth rate was beginning by 1950 to swamp an already overcrowded elementary school system, and threatened to do so increasingly for many years to come. So it was that as the nineteen-fifties began, Americans in their wage-earning years were faced with the prospect of having to support, in one way or another, more human creatures senior and junior to themselves than ever before in recent history.

III

Not only were Americans, by and large, much healthier; they were also physically bigger. This was not readily demonstrable by reference to the medical records of the two world wars, for the average height of registrants for the draft in the first two years of Selective Service

for World War II was exactly the same as that of recruits examined
during World War I—5 feet, 7½ inches—though the men of 1941-
1942 averaged 8 pounds heavier than those of 1917-1918—150
pounds as against 142 pounds. (Registrants classed by local boards
as available for general military service in 1941-1942 averaged 5
feet 8⅒ inches in height and were heavier still—152 pounds.) Such
comparisons were bound to be somewhat misleading, however, since
they involved men selected under differing conditions and representing differing proportions of men of various ancestries. Comparisons made for reasonably comparable groups among well-to-do
old-stock Americans indicated a lively increase in size. For instance,
Harvard students of the eighteen-seventies and early eighties averaged
5 feet 8.12 inches tall and 138.40 pounds in weight; Harvard students of the nineteen-twenties and early thirties averaged over two
inches taller—5 feet 10.14 inches—and over ten pounds heavier—
149.05 pounds. And there was almost precisely the same degree of
difference between the measurements of Vassar students of the class
of 1885 and of the class of 1940: the younger girls averaged 5 feet
5.1 inches tall, as against 5 feet 3.1 inches for the earlier group;
weighed 126⅓ pounds, as against 115.7 pounds for the earlier ones;
and incidentally had slightly larger waists—25¼ inches as against
24⅞ inches. (The Vassar female waist, incidentally, reached its
minimum in girth in 1905—23⁷⁄₁₆ inches—and its maximum in the
belt-around-the-hips era of 1927—26³⁄₁₆ inches.)

Whatever may be the difficulty of securing precisely comparable
statistics, it was certainly a common observation throughout the half
century that sons tended to be taller than their fathers, daughters than
their mothers, and that young girls especially, at the mid-century,
were requiring shoe sizes that struck their mothers with dismay.
During the nineteen-forties a graduate of an eastern preparatory
school for girls, returning as a teacher, remarked with surprise to the
school doctor on the dimensions of her young charges. "But they're
so *big*!" she said. "Big?" said he. "That's the tomato-juice generation
you're seeing. Wait till you see the grapefruit-juice generation!"

By the mid-century the population statistics showed an impressive drift westward—especially to California and the Pacific Northwest. They showed also a steadily continuing movement from the farms and the smaller towns toward the centers of population. However much devotees of the character-building value of homespun living might lament the urbanization of American life, there seemed to be no stopping it. Behind it was economic logic, for farm production was requiring fewer and fewer workers, and the service occupations flourished best in big communities; behind it, too, was the irresistible centripetal pull of opportunity—or fancied opportunity—for the talented. Did the automobile, the telephone, the popular magazines, the radio, and TV enhance the life of farmers and villagers by enabling them to keep in touch with the great world? Yes, but they also brought to the girl or boy in Hagerstown or Paducah or Grand Forks an almost irresistible invitation to taste the delights of Los Angeles or Chicago or New York, where the doings of people were news, where the lights were bright, and where glamour had its recognized headquarters.

Finally, the melting pot had long been successfully at work. Since immigration had been sharply limited in the early nineteen-twenties, the number of foreign-born Americans had been steadily shrinking as one by one men and women who had come across the seas by steerage during the flood tide from Europe came to the end of their lives. Less and less often did one hear foreign languages spoken in American cities and industrial towns. The sons and daughters of the immigrants had resolutely acquired American customs and manners; the third generation—who possessed, as one New Yorker of Italian parentage put it, the "great advantage of having English-speaking parents"—were as American as Mayflower descendants, though to the latter their names might still seem foreign. During the nineteen-twenties, sports writers had been wont to comment with amusement on the European names that were showing up more and more frequently in the lineups of winning football teams; but by 1950 the cosmopolitan origins of the American people had become so thoroughly taken for granted that one would have been uttering a cliché to comment on, for instance, the interesting combination of names possessed by the men who played in the World Series of that most American of sports, baseball. Here is the batting order of the winning nine of 1950 in the first game of the Series: Woodling, Rizzuto, Berra, DiMaggio, Mize, Brown, Bauer, Coleman, Raschi —Yankees all!

PART **THREE**

THE NEW AMERICA

Chapter **15**

The All-American Standard

A_S WE enter upon the second half of the twentieth century and pause to take stock of our situation, let us look to see, first, what has happened to the gap that once yawned so widely between rich and poor.

In money terms—income terms—the change has not been overwhelming. There are still islands of deep poverty in the United States, and there are families and individuals by the millions who through illness, age, adversity, or marginal ability, live on the ragged edge of want. And the average represents nothing like affluence. Yet even so, what has happened over half a century, but most impressively since 1940, has been striking enough to be described by the definitely unhysterical director of research of the National Bureau of Economic Research as "one of the great social revolutions of history."

Nobody should produce figures on the current distribution of income among the American people without warning the reader that they are approximations merely. Different groups of conscientious economic investigators, working with different sets of data—such as income-tax returns, census returns, and various special surveys—produce very different calculations. Nevertheless our statistics today are far more accurate than any that could have been produced at the turn of the century, when there was no income tax, when Andrew Carnegie's income was something like twenty thousand times greater than that of the average American workman, when the slums were full of miserable immigrants living in stench and filth, and when many a thoughtful citizen shared with Edwin Markham a vague apprehension of the day when the toiler—"the emptiness of ages in his face"—would rise to judge the world.

The figures I shall cite here are based upon the data reported by a subcommittee of the Joint Committee on the Economic Report of the Congress of the United States, which dealt with the distribution of income in 1948; they are roughly parallel to the figures included in the January, 1951, report to the President by his Council of Economic Advisers, and probably come somewhere near the truth.*

According to them, in recent years some 10.6 per cent of all the families in the United States have been living on individual or family incomes of less than $1,000 a year. That is about one family in ten, trying to make out on a dismally inadequate money intake.

About 14.5 per cent have been living on incomes of between $1,000 and $2,000—approximately one family in seven.

About 20.6 per cent—say one family in five—have had incomes of between $2,000 and $3,000.

A very much larger number, about 33.6 per cent, or something like a third of all our families, have had between $3,000 and $5,000.

Only about 17.9 per cent—say one family out of seven—have had between $5,000 and $10,000.

And a very small group—about 2.9 per cent, or only one family in thirty-four—have been in the over-$10,000 bracket.

There are also a great many individuals not living in any family;

* The Council of Economic Advisers, figuring in terms of "spending units"— which may be families or individuals—say that in 1949 the lowest fifth of these spending units were scrimping on incomes of under $1,280 a year; the next fifth, on incomes of between $1,280 and $2,289; the middle fifth received incomes of between $2,290 and $3,199; the next-to-the-top fifth, incomes of between $3,200 and $4,499; the top fifth, $4,500 and over.

If you compare the Council's figures with those of the Joint Committee's sub-committee, remember that the Council's calculations are loaded downward by the fact that in the lower brackets there is a heavy concentration of single people (as distinguished from families). But you should then bear in mind another fact: that what is a deplorable income for a family of five may be a manageable one for a single person. If you will also meditate upon the infinite diversity of human circumstance, and the difficulty of drawing a clear line, even among your own acquaintances, between dependents and separate spending units, you will begin to realize why such figures give us only a very smudgy outline of the actual state of affairs.

in 1948 there were estimated to be some eight million of them in all. Their incomes follow more or less the same pattern, except that they are more numerously represented in the lowest brackets.

Now let us look for a moment at the lowest of these groups: the 10.6 per cent of the families (or thereabouts), and also the individuals, who are living on annual incomes of less than $1,000. Who are they?

They include, to begin with, some farmers and private businessmen who have simply had a bad year—have had to sell crops or goods at a loss, let us say. But some or most of these have savings enough to tide them along. (No grinding poverty there, in most cases.) They include a great number of rural poor: people working poor and worn-out land, tenants, sharecroppers. (A good many of these— we don't know how many—may be able to raise enough food for their own use so as to manage somehow on even a grimly small money income.) Another group, not quite so large, consists of old people, who in some cases have families depending on their meager savings or earnings, and in other cases are fending for themselves alone, with or without old-age relief. (One out of every four families dependent on elderly people and two out of three single elderly men and women had to get along in 1948 on less than $20 a week, said Robert L. Heilbroner in a study of American poverty in *Harper's Magazine* for June, 1950.) Others of the lowest group are victims of broken families—women, for example, who have been divorced or deserted and are unable to support themselves properly. Some are disabled people—the crippled, the mentally ill. (Many of these, to quote Mr. Heilbroner, "will be wards of the community as long as they live.") Some, probably, are chronic ne'er-do-wells, useless derelicts of society, seldom hired and then not for long. One should add that among the rural poor and the stranded old people and such-like a disproportionate number are Negroes.

Step up into the next lowest rank of poverty, the group with family or individual incomes of between $1,000 and $2,000 a year, and we find more businessmen who have been encountering tough sledding, more marginal farmers, more old people, more divorced or deserted wives, more disabled people, more marginal laborers who have been laid off again and again, and also some members of another group: those whose wages, even in this time of plenty, have been so low as to keep them in a constant struggle with poverty. Again, among most of these groups there is an unduly large representation of Negroes.

Perhaps the most striking thing about the make-up of these two groups, comprising the lowest third of the nation, income-wise, is that —with the partial exception of the Negroes whose special situation I have discussed in Chapter 12—these are not "the masses." They are not a proletariat. They are a great number of people, very widely scattered, who are in very different sorts of trouble, economic and otherwise.

They may range all the way from the elderly man who lives so neatly and proudly that you would never guess, to see him, that he sometimes goes hungry, and the upstanding farmer whose crops for this year have been ruined by storm, to the bum who panhandles to buy himself another drink, and the moron who hasn't the wit to hold a job. Our facilities for helping these misfits and victims of adversity are far from ideal, heaven knows, but they are far more adequate than they were at the beginning of the century. And there are no such huge pools of mass misery as existed then.

During the Depression Stuart Chase once wrote something to the effect that in a fluid society there would always be people climbing up the economic staircase and others tumbling down it, but that if it was a decent society there should be some way of preventing the latter from falling all the way to the cellar. What with the helpfulness of relatives and neighbors, and the efforts of private charitable organizations, and our city and county relief organizations, we succeed nowadays in catching most of them at the ground floor.

It is when we examine the next two or three brackets—those representing incomes of $2,000 to $10,000—that we encounter the central fact of our present prosperity. This is that millions upon millions of families have risen out of the under-$2,000 class and the

$2,000-$3,000 class and have climbed a bracket or two. These fortunate families have been getting their money from a wide variety of occupations; among them have been farmers, office workers, professional people, semiskilled and skilled industrial workers; but it is the industrial workers who as a group have done best—people such as a steelworker's family who used to live on $2,500 and now are getting $4,500, or the highly skilled machine-tool operator's family who used to have $3,000 and now can spend an annual $5,500 or more. Consider a single salient statistic: that the *average* earnings of workers in all manufacturing industries in America in 1950 were $59.33 a week. During the past decade these earnings, as they climbed, have been pursued by rising prices, but on the average they have kept well ahead.

What do these figures mean in human terms? That millions of families in our industrial cities and towns, and on the farms, have been lifted from poverty or near-poverty to a status where they can enjoy what has been traditionally considered a middle-class way of life: decent clothes for all, an opportunity to buy a better automobile, install an electric refrigerator, provide the housewife with a decently attractive kitchen, go to the dentist, pay insurance premiums, and so on indefinitely.

Whether these industrial workers, farmers, and other assorted people have been the ones most deserving of such a lift in fortune is uncertain. One might have wished that intellectual workers—teachers, for example—had been among the principal beneficiaries of the new order. (They certainly have not.) Nevertheless the effect upon the rest of us of the dwindling away of what used to be the lower class has been impressive. For as the families which have moved up a bracket or two have been able to buy more goods, their expanded purchasing power has given an immense lift to business in general. America has become more prosperous by making the poor less poor.

At the top of the scale there has likewise been a striking change. The enormous lead of the well-to-do in the economic race has been considerably reduced.

Let us see what has happened to the top five per cent of the population, income-wise—roughly speaking, the people who have been living on incomes of $8,000 or over.

According to the elaborate calculations of Simon Kuznets of the National Bureau of Economic Research, during the period between the two wars the people in this comparatively well-off group were taking a very big slice of the total national income—no less than 30 per cent of it, before taxes; a little over 28 per cent after taxes. But by 1945 their slice had been narrowed from 30 to 19½ per cent before taxes, and from 28 to 17 per cent after taxes. Since 1945 this upper group has been doing a little better, relatively, but not much.

As for the top one per cent, the really well-to-do and the rich, whom we might classify very roughly indeed as the $16,000-and-over group, their share of the total national income, after taxes, had come down by 1945 from 13 per cent to 7 per cent.

A question at once arises. Have we, in reducing the slice received by these upper groups, and increasing the slice received by lower groups, simply been robbing Peter to pay Paul? (It often looks that way to Peter, especially around March 15.)

The answer is that Peter has been getting a smaller relative slice of a much larger pie. Even after one has made allowance for rising prices, one finds that the total disposable income of *all* Americans went up 74 per cent between 1929 and 1950. That is a very considerable enlargement. So that although the well-to-do and the rich have suffered *relatively*, it is much less certain that they have suffered *absolutely*.

And one might add at this point an interesting footnote. The big hike in wages that we were speaking of a moment ago has not, by and large, reduced profits. In fact when we compare the 1929 totals with the 1950 ones, we discover that total profits rose in the interval a little more sharply than total wages and salaries! To quote the apt slogan of the New England Council: "The rising tide lifts all the boats." (And why did the rich not gain heavily thereby? Because the profits were in part retained for business expansion; because dividends were more widely distributed; and also, of course, because taxes were much higher.)

Nevertheless the shift in the position of the rich has been very striking. It has been cynically said that there are no legitimately rich men any more; there are only tax-dodgers and people who live very well on expense accounts. That is by no means true. One can hold on to most of the profit from some financial deals by adroit and quite legal use of the capital-gains provisions of the federal income-tax law. Oil men have made out very affluently indeed with the advantage of the 27½ per cent allowance for depletion in the same law. And there are still some tax-exempt securities which are very useful to those whose capital is large enough to provide them with a goodly income even at low interest rates. But by and large, the big incomes are hacked to pieces by the Collector of Internal Revenue.

To offer a somewhat hypothetical example, the highest compensation listed in the public records of the Securities and Exchange Commission for the year 1950 was $626,300 earned by Charles E. Wilson, president of General Motors. Part of this was in stock and cash which he was to receive over the next five years; but let us suppose that it had all been handed to him in cash in 1950 and that he had had to pay a federal income tax on the whole $626,300, and on nothing else—without any exceptional deductions. The government would have taken some $462,000 of it, leaving him only some $164,300. That is not exactly penury, but it is not the sort of income on which one puts aside many millions.

As for those who possess large inherited fortunes, or self-acquired fortunes piled up in a day when taxes were lower, and have big establishments to keep up, and have acquired in the course of time all manner of moral obligations to less well-heeled relatives and friends—and who know furthermore that it is upon the likes of them that colleges and schools and hospitals and charities depend for sizable gifts (since the tax-dodgers, the gamblers, and even many of the worthiest of the newly prosperous recognize no such duty and opportunity)—their plight, as taxes and prices both rise, may often be summed up in the words of one of them who said, "There is no such thing as being rich; there is only being poor on a much larger scale."

Hence the affection of the rich for state and municipal bonds, which bring in a small but tax-exempt return; for the capital-gains tax, which is much lower than the regular income tax; for extra remuneration in company stock, which may appreciate in value; and for various devices by which remuneration is spread over a long term of years. (You make a thirty-year contract, let us say, which includes payment for your full services for ten years and for "advisory" services after that, so that you will still be keeping the wolf a long distance from the door long after your active services have ended.)

Hence, too, the disposition of many people whose winnings are stronger than their consciences to live as far as possible on a cash basis in the hope of eluding the eye of the tax collector—which, if their prosperity is new, they can do for a time. (The known rich, the inheritors of wealth and the executives of big corporations, can scarcely do it, for the eagle eye of the tax collector is upon them.) If I were an investigator for the Bureau of Internal Revenue, I should want to follow up people who pay for fur coats or diamonds by peeling bills off a roll, and I do not wonder that these investigators watch the papers for news of big jewel robberies.

Hence, also, the briberies and implicit briberies of tax collectors which have been such a stench in our nostrils in recent years.

Hence, furthermore, the growing practice, not only among members of the wealthiest class but among many others who consider themselves only modestly well off, of living partly on the company.

You wouldn't need to get any salary at all if everything you might need or want—housing, transportation, entertainment, for yourself and your family and guests unlimited—were provided for you without charge. Some approximation of this enviable state is apparent in the lives of many company executives. They get about by company car, when needed, or company-bought railroad accommodations, or company plane; and if the plane takes them and their guests to the Kentucky Derby or a Rose Bowl game, why that's all right too: that's "making contacts." They hold prolonged business conferences at delightful resorts, with golf or bathing for relaxation, and of course the company pays for everything. They may enjoy holidays at a company camp, or play golf at a company country club. If they want to throw a cocktail party at a fashionable hotel for a couple of hundred people, the company foots the bill for that, too: that, too, is making contacts. The proprietor of a big New York hotel described to me during World War II the lavish parties—shocking, for wartime, in their extravagance—that were thrown in his ample rooms; and I asked him whether they were paid for by individuals or by companies. "Oh, all of them by companies," he said. In the May, 1950, issue of *Flair*, John O'Hara, describing what he aptly called "the new expense-account society," spoke of the difficulty that ordinary visitors to New York had in getting tickets to *South Pacific* except at preposterous prices, and added, "There are customers at $100 a pair, and the customers are the big corporations. . . . The big corporation has first claim on everything, from restaurant tables to Pullman reservations home."

Even somewhat smaller fry can do very well on expense accounts. In the restaurant life of midtown New York, where there is a heavy trade in the prestige that goes with eating or drinking in the immediate neighborhood of movie actresses, advertising big-shots, senators, gossip columnists, successful authors, publishers, ex-champion athletes, and television comedians, there is a wide circle of men and women, some of them on modest salaries, who lunch day after day, and dine often, on expense accounts. Sometimes they are dazzling out-of-town clients; sometimes they are just taking one another to lunch. In either case the company pays. I asked the proprietors of two of the most exalted of these restaurants what proportion of their guests, from day to day, were eating and drinking on expense accounts. One said nearly half at lunch, and also for dinner in his most favored room; fewer for dinner elsewhere in the establishment. The other said three-quarters of the guests at lunch, fewer at dinner, very few in the late evening; but he guessed that at a night spot with entertainment the ratio would again be high. It is quite possible that a good many clients and prospects are really snared by such entertaining; but in any case the theory that this is how clients and prospects are snared makes for delightfully lavish living on the part of both hosts and guests for at least part of the twenty-four hours, at no cost to themselves.

The wife of the Cleveland machine-tool executive or Pittsburgh steel executive who lives so grandly away from home may sometimes find there is something a little lopsided in their family scale of living. "The company has spoiled Jim terribly," said a businessman's wife quoted by William H. Whyte, Jr., in *Life* magazine for January 7, 1952.

Even when he was only earning $7,500 a year he used to be sent to Washington all the time. He'd go down in a Pullman drawing room and, as J. R. Robinson of the General Company, take a two-room suite. Then he used to be asked by some of the company officers to a hunting and fishing lodge that the company kept in the north woods. When he went to New York, he'd entertain at Twenty-One, the Barberry Room, and the Chambord. Me, meanwhile I'd be eating a 30-cent hamburger and, when we went away together on vacation, we would have to go in our beat-up old car or borrow my sister's husband's. This taste of high life gives some of these characters delusions of grandeur.

There are many highly placed businessmen, of course, who will not take advantage of such opportunities. An executive with an income of well over two hundred thousand a year (before taxes) told me that when he was in Florida he was constantly amazed by the number of people who were obviously paying for things on a scale that he couldn't afford. As for himself, his taxes and obligations were such that it was all he could do to keep out of the red for the year. Some of the men and women he had been seeing in Florida may have enjoyed living on a minimum scale for fifty weeks and on a grand scale for two; others may have been tax-dodgers; but it is more than likely that a good many of them had discovered, and were exploiting, the current substitute for real wealth: a company that is willing to foot the bills.

II

Much more impressive, however, than the narrowing of the gap in *income* between rich and poor has been the narrowing of the gap between them in their *ways of living*.

For instance, consider the matter of personal appearance, remembering that in 1900 the frock-coated, silk-hatted banker and his Paris-gowned wife were recognizable at a distance, if they ventured among the common herd, as beings apart. Forty or fifty years ago the countryman in a metropolis was visibly a "hayseed"; the purchaser of inexpensive men's clothing was betrayed by his tight-waisted jackets and bulbous-toed shoes. Today the difference in appearance between a steelworker (or a clerk) and a high executive is hardly noticeable to the casual eye. Not long ago, at a tennis tournament, I sat two or three rows behind the chairman of the board of one of the most famous banking houses in the world, and looking at his veteran Panama hat and his ordinary-looking sack suit I wondered how many of the people about him would have guessed that he was anybody of great financial consequence. And there is many a man with an income in six figures (before taxes) and with thousands of employees who, though his suit may be a little better cut than those of most of the men about him on a New York subway train or a transcontinental plane, attracts no curious notice at all; he looks just about like everybody else.

As for women, the difference in appearance between the one who spends $5,000 a year on clothes and the one who spends only a small fraction of that is by no means as conspicuous as the difference between the woman who has good taste and the woman who lacks it. The fact that the wealthy woman has thirty dresses to the poor woman's three is not visible on the street, and the fact that her dresses are made of better materials and are better cut is observable only by the expert eye at close range. Fashion used to be decreed by Paris, imported by the most expensive dress shops, then modified by the more expensive American dress manufacturers, and finally—after an interval of six months to a year—modified still further, almost beyond recognition, by the manufacturers of cheap dresses. The process is now quicker and the differences much less sharp. Unless the poor woman is exceptionally poor—or indifferent—she like the rich woman has a permanent—probably in her case a home one. And women of every income group wear nylon stockings.

Consider for a moment a contrast with regard to those stockings. At the turn of the century silk stockings were a mark of luxury. In the year 1900, in a nation of 75 million people, only 155,000 pairs were manufactured. In the year 1949 the American sales of nylon stockings—considered by most people at least as fine as silk, if not finer—were not 155,000, but 543 *million* pairs: enough to provide every female in the country, from the age of fourteen up, with between nine and ten pairs apiece. How is that for an example of the dynamic logic of mass production producing luxury for all?

A generation ago the great mail-order houses produced different clothes for the Western farmer's wife and for the city woman in the East; today there is no such distinction, and a friend of mine whose train stopped recently at a small Oklahoma town remarked that the girls on the railroad platform there were virtually indistinguishable in appearance from girls on Madison Avenue or Michigan Boulevard. It could almost be said nowadays that the only easily visible mark of wealth which a woman can put on is a mink coat.

At this point an explanatory word is in order. The trend that I am describing is not a trend toward uniformity. Among both men and women there is a great diversity in attire. The point I am making is that the diversity is more a matter of preference, or of custom among the members of a local or vocational group, than of economic class.

Does this trend toward the breakdown of class lines in clothes seem unimportant? I do not think it is. The consciousness that one is set apart by one's appearance is a great divider; the consciousness that one is not set apart is a great remover of barriers.

Let us proceed from clothes to the equipment of daily living. As Professor H. Gordon Hayes pointed out in *Harper's* in 1947, the rich man smokes the same sort of cigarettes as the poor man, shaves with the same sort of razor, uses the same sort of telephone, vacuum cleaner, radio, and TV set, has the same sort of lighting and heating equipment in his house, and so on indefinitely. The differences between his automobile and the poor man's are minor. Essentially they have similar engines, similar fittings. In the early years of the century there was a hierarchy of automobiles. At the top were such imported cars as the Rolls-Royce, Mercedes-Benz, and Isotta Fraschini; to possess one of these was a mark of lively wealth. There was also an American aristocracy of the Pierce Arrow, Peerless, and Packard. Then came group after group, in descending scale, till you reached the homely Model-T Ford. Today, except for a few survivals such as the obstinately rectangular Rolls-Royces of the old school, and a few oddities such as the new British sports cars, which to the American eye would seem to have been constructed for exceptionally dashing midgets, there is a comparative absence of class groupings. And, although the owner of a big, brand-new car probably has a large income, he may merely be someone who adjusts a slender income to cover the costs of the machines that entrance him.

In the matter of running water and plumbing, the breakdown of distinctions has proceeded much more slowly but nevertheless steadily. There have been, it is true, some injuries to Southern mountaineers who at their first glimpse of a water closet decided that one was supposed to stand in it to wash one's feet; but today only the older and poorer tenements and dwellings in American cities and towns lack running water, bathtubs or showers, and water closets, and these conveniences are fast being installed in farmhouses the country over.

Meanwhile the servant class has almost vanished, especially in the North and West, although servants' wages have a purchasing power today from five to ten times or more greater than in 1900 (and, if the servants live in, offer an exceptional opportunity for saving). Their virtual disappearance, which has imposed upon all but a tiny fraction of American families the chores of cooking and cleaning and washing, not only marks the absorption of the immigrant proletariat of yore into general American society, in which domestic service has been regarded as humiliating, but also removes another contrast between the ways of living of the prosperous and the poor. Today the daughter of comfortably circumstanced parents had better know how to cook well—and their son, too, may find the knowledge pretty nearly essential.

What has been responsible for this convergence between the ways of living of rich and poor? The causes are numerous and complex, as we have seen in previous chapters; some are economic and political, like the income tax and trade-union pressures, or political and social, like the development of public parks and playgrounds. The dynamic logic of mass production is a leading cause, of course; it accounts for the virtual disappearance from the market of one sort or another of luxury goods, whose makers and vendors have found themselves in hopeless competition with the makers and vendors of mass-produced goods of adequate quality. For example, the tailor, bootmaker, and shirtmaker wage an uphill fight for existence. I have a perverse liking for wearing pumps with evening clothes. Of recent years they have been almost unobtainable, and a couple of years ago I had to pay through the nose for a new pair. When next I want one, which would be in about 1960, I shall not be surprised to find they are no longer made—that there has been no market for them that would justify making them. Mass production rules us; and mass production permits diversity only within limits.

Another important factor in the change has been the immense spread of education. In 1900 less than one American boy or girl out of ten of high school age was actually at high school; now over four out of five are. This means not only book learning for them; it means also a considerable social education in the ways of living of a variety of families of the community. Also the number of students at American universities, colleges, and teacher-training institutions has increased eightfold.

Still another factor in the change was World War II, which sent several million young men on foreign travels, gave the teachable ones remarkable chances to learn about other modes of life, and provided some of them—such as flying officers—with opportunities to live on a scale they had never before known. I remember during the war going to a shabby little photographer's shop to get a passport photograph taken, and hearing from the proprietor that his son was a pilot flying planes across the South Atlantic. And I wondered whether, two or three years earlier, that boy would have dreamed that he would ever have a chance to see Brazil and Liberia while enjoying the favored status of an army officer.

Nor should we overlook the immense influence of the mass-circulation magazines, the movies, the radio, and television in imposing upon Americans of all income levels the same patterns of emulation: in other words, making them want to be the same sort of people.

Take, for example, the women's magazines and the magazines of what the publishing trade calls the "shelter field," meaning those devoted to houses and gardens. For decades they have been educating millions of women, month after month, in the techniques of better living—telling them how to tend the baby, how to care for children, how to entertain guests pleasantly, how to prepare well-balanced meals, how to decorate a house prettily, how to make the lawn and garden attractive, and so on. Some of their advice may sometimes have seemed amusing to the experienced; some of the information given has been perverted to the flattery of advertisers, or has been superficial or complacent; but the net educational effect upon people whose horizons have been hemmed in by circumstances has been remarkable. And the mass-audience magazines, with their national circulations, have also done much to break down parochialism; to give the housewife in a dingy city apartment, or the boy and girl growing upon a remote farm or in a factory town, glimpses of worlds outside their routine rounds. It would be interesting to know how many people there are in the United States today who got from popular magazines their first acquaintance with, let us say, vitamins.

The advertisements in these magazines and elsewhere, furthermore, have constantly been providing incentives to work hard in order to be able to buy more goods. There are some workers, in America as elsewhere, who, when they get a wage increase, respond by taking things easier on the ground that they can now afford to relax. But to the extent that this is not the general rule—to the extent that workers keep on driving in the hope of being able to afford even more—we can point to mass advertising as one of the great incentive makers.

This form of journalistic mass education has been a purely twentieth-century phenomenon. At the turn of the century there was no American magazine with a circulation of anywhere near a million; by 1947 there were no less than 38 with circulations of over a million apiece; and the *Reader's Digest* alone, with its plethora of cheerful suggestions on how to live better, had reached by 1951 a total circulation in the United States of over 9½ millions.

Likewise the movies, which date only from about 1905, and the radio, which as an instrument for popular broadcasting dates only from 1920, have been bringing together in their audiences men, women, and children of all income levels to enjoy the same emotional excitements, and have shaped their films and programs to a common denominator of American experience.

In the movies, popular stars like Cary Grant, Humphrey Bogart, Gregory Peck, Montgomery Clift, and Farley Granger may play the parts of men who are supposed to be rich and stylish, or men who are at the end of their economic rope; but whatever role any one of them assumes, his popularity depends upon his representing a kind of charm that any young American male can appreciate and at least approach; in other words, upon his conforming to what old-fashioned people would call middle-class standards of speech and behavior. I prefer to call them classless, or all-American, for that, essentially, is what they are. The Hollywood actresses are subject to the same compulsion; they may be cast in queenly or in humble roles, but their publicity advisers know that if the public is to adore them they must be represented in the film magazines as ready to make a salad, mop the kitchen floor, and hang out the wash—after which they may be shown enjoying some lucky leisure in well-designed bathing suits beside sumptuous swimming pools.

On the radio Jack Benny, for all his big income, plays the part of a Jack Benny who lives in a modest house, owns a wheezy old car, and has for his sole servant a jack-of-all-trades helper with whom he is on the breeziest of terms. And Ozzie and Harriet Nelson find themselves in a series of comic situations which one might label as middle class, but which are common in their essence to the experience of millions of young parents and children of various income levels.

And what is the result? Both the rich man's fourteen-year-old son, who dismays his conservative parents by trying to talk like Humphrey Bogart, and the truck driver's son, who cherishes the same hope, will grow up to be more like their idols—and thus, more like one another—than they would have otherwise. And something else happens. Half a century ago a coal miner who found himself at a fashionable restaurant would not have had the faintest notion of how to behave; nowadays he has only to ask himself, "How would Gregory Peck do it?" In short, the social distance between the extremes of American society is shrinking.

Whenever I think of this change, I think of something I saw not long ago in New York City. A street was being torn up for repairs, and while the workmen were standing waiting for the arrival of new equipment, one of them, who had in his hands an iron rod presumably used for prying off manhole covers, was enjoying a little relaxation. I looked twice to see what he was doing with that rod. He was practicing a graceful golf stroke.

III

To say that the reduced resources of the rich and the trend toward an all-American standard of living have done away with Society would be an exaggeration. Social emulation is a perpetual force in human affairs; in any community, social lines tend to be drawn and snobberies to flourish; in most towns and smaller cities there is an easily discernible social pattern with a local society on top, though its composition may be forever shifting. But as one proceeds from the smaller communities to the larger ones, the pattern becomes today much more complex, multiple, and elusive. It is complicated by the variety of professional and business groupings which are to be found in a big community; and by the special hierarchies within large businesses which impose upon social relationships a set of distinctions which have little to do with the old ones based upon family, fortified by wealth (these business hierarchies I shall refer to again in the next chapter). It is affected, too, by the prestige which attends not only successful business executives regardless of their social status but also, much more dazzlingly, entertainers and other newsworthy or photogenic characters.

In the constantly growing suburbs it is confused by the rapid shift in personnel, as well as by the division of people's attention between the concerns and entertainments of the suburb and those of the city of which it is a satellite. The Sheridans, who gave such delightful parties last year, move to Detroit; the Stanleys are lovely people but go to town for their real social life; the young Edwardses are mighty attractive, but just moved out to the suburb last year when their eldest child was arriving at school age, and may move elsewhere if their income rises, and will probably go back to town anyhow when the youngest child is grown up. The pattern is kaleidoscopic, to the confusion of organized snobbery.

Society—the old Society, with a large capital S—used to center in New York. But it is in New York that the present-day pattern reaches its utmost complexity. Here the well-to-do are in heavy concentration, and few of them know more than a tiny fraction of the others. They form vaguely defined, overlapping groups. There are, for example, the bankers, brokers, and downtown lawyers and their families. There are the publishers, writers, advertising people, radio and television people—a series of groups which in turn overlap a series of Broadway ones. There are substantial business groups operating in wholesale and retail trade. There are the people associated with churches of various denominations—the local Catholics forming an exceptionally distinct set, though it overlaps those whose primary concern is with politics. There are ties of acquaintance between men and women connected with the backing of different sorts of charitable and public-service organizations. There are further ties between New Yorkers who have come from one part of the country or another, or whose summer and week-end life brings them together in local communities on Long Island or in Connecticut or New Jersey or elsewhere. Each of the arts has its devotees and supporters, linked loosely by mutual acquaintance. In some of these areas of interest Jews intermingle with non-Jews; in others, Jews are quite separate. At any dinner party or cocktail party one is likely to meet some people of one's own group along with others, probably previously unknown to one, whose association with the host and hostess has been based upon some other ties of common interest.

To say that in this variegated scene Society is no more would be by no means correct. There are many families of noteworthy lineage and substantial means to whom such a statement would seem preposterous. But that this Society still exists is pretty nearly their secret.

Its assemblies and coming-out parties attract limited public attention. It still offers, for a select number of debutantes, a brief and furious round of social activity, and tries to provide for them the most carefully selected male companionship—the selective process being somewhat vitiated by the necessity of importing for the larger festivities considerable numbers of students, not so scrupulously chosen, from such nests of the young elect as New Haven and Princeton. But as the young men and women grow older, their other interests make such claim upon their time and attention that the status of most of them as members of Society becomes somewhat blurred. And though the more loyal of the elders of Society might turn up their noses at that less ancient emulative group known as Café Society, and at the glare of publicity which surrounds Tallulah Bankhead or Joe DiMaggio or Van Johnson, the fact remains that many of their progeny would rank membership in the Knickerbocker or the Links or the Brook or the Colony Club below membership in the group favorably known to the attendants at the Stork Club or Twenty-One. And the society columns tend to concern themselves largely with the café crowd. One of the things that gave glitter to Society in the old days was that its festivities were brilliantly costly; nowadays a big corporation can throw a party at the Waldorf which few private families could afford. In short, to the extent that Society exists, it is virtually unknown to the general public, and unnoticed.

The advertisers in their turn have taken heed of the change. "It is a sign of our times," Agnes Rogers wrote in 1949, "that glamour is now generally advertised as attainable by all American women, and as very easy to come by—you buy it in a jar. Few manufacturers feel today that to sell their products they must make women identify themselves with the wealthy or socially elect. The snob appeal has become less potent than the appeal of glamour arrived at through purchase of the right products and through careful schooling in their appropriate use. Anybody can have it, whatever her background, for a little money and some effort. Glamour has been democratized."

As for the great houses of an earlier day, those mighty castles in which the rich and fashionable lived on a princely scale, they too have mostly succumbed to the estate tax and the supertax. Some are still occupied, especially in Newport, where the old guard of the socially elect stubbornly try to conduct themselves as if nothing much had happened. But in New York the most famous of the mansions that once made Fifth Avenue the avenue of millionaires —such as those of William H., William K., and Cornelius Vanderbilt—have been razed to make way for business buildings or apartment houses. In Newport itself, Ochre Court is a Catholic college and The Breakers is leased year by year for use as a museum, where one may see if one wishes what it was like to be a Vanderbilt in the grand days. The Frederick W. Vanderbilt house at Hyde Park is likewise a museum. At Lenox, the Henry White house is an inn. Outside Philadelphia, Whitemarsh Hall, the 130-room E. T. Stotesbury house, is a research center for Pennsalt—the Pennsylvania Salt Manufacturing Company. At Palm Beach, the Flagler mansion is part of the Whitehall Hotel. Others have become nunneries, boys' and girls' boarding schools, hospital institutions. And nothing like them has been built for a good many years, not only because of the colossal expense of upkeep at present labor costs, but also because the taste of the prosperous today is for a less princely—or pseudo-princely—kind of living.

One views the passing of these private palaces with mixed feelings. There always tended to be something bogus about the grandeur of the most imitatively European of them. One thinks of the rise in labor costs that has made them so ruinously difficult to maintain today, and reflects that it has brought new comfort and opportunity to a host of men and women. One grants that there is a subtle affront to human dignity in the accumulation of great staffs of personal attendants and flunkies. And yet there was a glitter about some of these great houses that one misses in the less stratified community of today.

Last summer I went through one of the lesser of them—lesser in terms of the number of people it once housed, for it had no more than eight or ten master bedrooms, but sumptuous in the way of life that had once flourished there. It stood vacant, waiting for a purchaser. The tall columns of its portico stood on stucco bases now cracked and chipping away. The wooden columns of a side porch were cracked, the old paint peeling from them. The garden outside had grown up to weeds; the view over a smiling valley was partly cut off by rising undergrowth. Inside the house, vandals had ripped off a telephone box here, left piles of litter there in their hunt for valuable loot. The carved ceiling of the great central hall—three stories high, some sixty feet long—had partly come away as the result of a leak in the roof; there were little heaps of fallen plaster on the hardwood floor. One could scarcely believe that the drawing room and dining room had once been lit of an evening only by scores of candles as men and women in evening clothes gathered in a ritual strange in its graceful formality to the folkways of the present. And one wondered whether the passing of such a way of life was the price of democracy, and whether that price was inconsiderable or high.

IV

Today the cult of informality is pervasive. Its advance has been so long-continued that one would momentarily expect a reaction toward elegance; but for every step taken in the direction of formality, two steps are presently taken in the direction of an easier code of manners.

Look at the male American of today. The cutaway coat is obsolescent, except for borrowed or rented wear at weddings. (At a recent wedding I noted that one of the duties of the groom and best man was to attend to the business of renting cutaways for the ushers, with no more embarrassment than would attend the hiring of a caterer to serve the wedding breakfast.) The tail coat is worn only by a very few of the well-heeled young, at a very few parties; the elder citizen of means seldom takes out of mothballs that full dress suit that he acquired in 1926. The dinner coat is worn less and less, and the number of families whose males customarily dress for dinner has dwindled to the vanishing point. The hard collar has likewise almost completely departed. The waistcoat (or vest, if you prefer) is going; if a man under forty wears one he is marked as conservatively inclined in dress. Hats of any sort are in gradual retreat, especially in summer. As for the hard straw hat, it is virtually a period piece—worn chiefly by elderly gentlemen with unalterable habits, or by young bloods with a zest for the picturesquely antique. And in a recent survey by the National Office Management Association, three quarters of the companies responding to questions about office rules said they allowed men employees to remove their coats at any time, an additional 13 per cent allowed this in warm weather only, and over 58 per cent allowed sports shirts.

Sports attire is gradually on the way in, ranging from the separate tweed jacket and flannel or khaki slacks to the fancy-patterned shirt and slacks favored in California and Florida. Work clothes of various sorts tend likewise to be popular for easy-going wear. Young men shun neckties except as occasional concessions to formality, and the standard costume of an undergraduate out for a day with a girl at a girls' college is likely to be a shirt or T-shirt and slacks, with wool socks and unpolished shoes. If he wishes to follow the very strictest code of aristocratic propriety, he may insist upon wearing a plain white or plain blue shirt with buttoned-down collar (left open, of course) rather than anything of Hawaiian aspect, and dingy white shoes rather than dingy brown ones; but he won't get into a regular two-piece suit, with necktie, until dinner. And on many a campus the two-piece suit plays today almost, though not quite, the part that the dinner coat played in the early years of the century: it is what one wears on a formal occasion. Otherwise one is happy in khaki slacks and a T-shirt, sports shirt, sweater, lumberman's shirt, or windbreaker, the combination chosen depending on the weather. So steady is the campaign of attrition against the formerly orthodox male costume, in fact, that one suspects that its one-hundred-and-twenty-five-year reign may be approaching its end.

Among women the trend toward informality of attire is not so clearly defined. Yet it is amusing to note with what enthusiasm the supposedly omnipotent moguls of the dress trade and the advertising trade decree from time to time the return of elegance, and how widely spaced and brief are their triumphs; while the majority of the younger women, and many older ones too, go hatless all year round, go stockingless in summer, and wear flat-heeled loafers or ballet shoes and peasant kerchiefs.

This informality is well suited to the prevalent code of easy-going companionship between the sexes. Husbands and wives spend more time in one another's company than they used to; with cooking and dishwashing and baby-tending to share, and with the high cost of labor virtually forcing the husband to make a hobby of amateur cabinet-making and of painting the kitchen and repairing the household equipment, they could hardly avoid this even if they chose, and there is not much occasion to dress up for one another. With the steady spread of co-education, boys and girls become accustomed to seeing the opposite sex at work as well as at play, and costume themselves accordingly. Men's clubs succumb one by one to a demand for ladies' dining rooms, or even for the admission of females to club precincts sacred in earlier days to the male; no one appears to fear that feminine eyes or ears will be offended by anything brutish, and there is a general feeling that it is good fun to have the other sex around. In this matter there is, of course, a sharp divergence between the custom of one community or social group and another. In general, the more sophisticated the group, the less do the men and women tend to separate to enjoy themselves. But that the general trend is toward a more relaxed companionship seems beyond a doubt.

Gradually, as servants become rarities, the dinner party at which guests are seated about a table is supplanted by casserole entertaining, buffet style. The hour for dinner becomes more elastic as the hostess waits until the last guest has arrived before putting the finishing touches on the meal—with the result that those who were so injudicious as to come at the hour appointed may have had an unduly prolonged bout with the cocktails. Little by little the formal introduction, in which the identity of Mr. Jones is made known to Miss Robinson, gives way to an introduction of Henry Jones to Barbara Robinson; to which, in all but a few remaining islands of social rigidity, he may respond with, "Hi, Barbara." I have heard a waiter at a metropolitan restaurant with three- and four- and five-dollar entrees on its à la carte bill of fare put diners at their ease with the greeting, "What'll it be, folks?" Rare is the dance given in a private house; and though it is possible to take a group of young people to dance at a hotel or night club, such entertainment is likely to be so crowded and expensive that when the young people are on their own they are likely to go to a roadside tavern, where they can drink beer or soft drinks, dance, play the jukebox, and discuss life at a reasonable cost in a congenially relaxed atmosphere. Square-dancing, once the sport of yokels, enjoys high popularity among various economic groups, and the more rustic and romping it is, the better they like it. "Come in your blue jeans," said the invitation to boys to attend a recent square dance at a highly select girls' school in New York. On a Saturday, in a suburb, one will occasionally see a Catholic girl headed for confession in blue jeans with a fancy hat—the only one she owns. In aspect after aspect of American life, ceremony appears to be in continuous retreat.

Why? Primarily, perhaps, because informality seems to people to be democratic, unpretentious, friendly. Among the sons and daughters of the rich there is a vague, surviving guilt complex: an embarrassed consciousness that during the Depression great numbers of people were resentful of their way of life and suspicious of the origin of the funds that made it possible. This guilt complex takes many forms, and one of them is a preference for the sort of entertainment which won't seem to involve putting on airs. The same is true in some degree of many people in the upper echelons of a business organization: so aware are they of the distrust of them which unionism fosters that they go out of their way, at a company party, to show that they have no princely delusions. Among large numbers of people in other income brackets there is, perhaps, a sort of mystic satisfaction in what appear to be democratic ways; among others there is simply a feeling that formality is a big bore, and outdated, and they are relieved that they don't have to make the effort.

Whatever one's view of the cult of informality, it is distinctly a manifestation of the all-American standard of living and behavior.

Chapter 16

Corporations, New Style

 F_{EW} things are harder than to observe clearly the life and institutions of one's own day. Newspapers do not help much, for they record the unusual, not the usual. Magazines help from time to time, but they too are under a compulsion to concentrate on the surprising; and the same, by and large, is true of the radio and TV. Photographers tend to seek out either the exceptional or the picturesque; as a producer of books of pictures-and-text on recent history I have often been struck by the scarcity of pictures which show the ordinary, everyday aspect of things, or the generally accepted way of doing things, at any given period. And even when we look about us with our own eyes, we tend to be conditioned by the ideas which we picked up when young, either from our parents or at school or college, as to the supposed nature of the things we see. It is still worse when, after looking, we begin to generalize about our observations, for as often as not we have no vocabulary to describe them which is not loaded with terms which have outdated historical connotations.

Such as the word "capitalism," for instance. We customarily say that our economic system is capitalistic; yet the word connoted half a century ago, and connotes today in Europe, a way of doing business quite different from the current American way. Or the contrasting terms "free enterprise" and "socialism," each of which carries an overload of traditional meaning which is not very helpful in defining what we may intend to convey about the exact state of economic and political affairs today.

And take the corporation. Most American business is done by corporations, ranging in size from virtually one-man affairs to massive enterprises like General Motors, which today spends more money annually than the United States Government used to spend in the nineteen-twenties (even including the expenses of the Army and Navy). Nearly half of all gainfully employed Americans are on the payroll of a corporation; if we exclude farmers and other self-employed people from our reckoning, the proportion is much larger. Yet the very nature of American corporations, especially the big ones, has so changed since the days when most of us first heard the term—or since the textbooks were written that first introduced us to the corporate concept—that we have difficulty in grasping the reality of what we actually see when we look at them.

The change has been very important to all of us. Let us therefore try to see the corporate institution of today with fresh eyes.

To begin with some generally familiar facts: A corporation is traditionally supposed to be controlled by the people who put up the money to launch and develop it; they take shares of stock in it, and as stockholders they elect directors to look after the running of it for them, and the directors select and supervise the managers who do the actual running. Thus, in theory, and in the letter of the law, the stockholders are the ultimate authority. This is still true in most young companies, which need capital to get going, and in many small ones anyhow. But in most successful American concerns which have grown to maturity, and especially in the very big ones which between them do a very large proportion of American business, the stockholders are no longer in control in any real sense: they are subordinate in authority and importance to the management.

It is the management which determines policies and makes decisions. Important decisions must be ratified by the directors, to be sure; many if not most directors feel a heavy sense of responsibility, and there is some evidence that this sense of responsibility has been growing in recent years; yet their contribution to the actual running of the corporation tends to be somewhat negative, if only because few of them are living from day to day with the problems laid before them. As for the stockholders, the law still says that they must ratify some sorts of major decisions, so a legal rigmarole has to be gone through by which the stockholders will say OK at their annual meeting. But this annual meeting is ordinarily a farce.

The officers of the company, exuding a synthetic affability, may be faced with a few embarrassing questions and a few adverse speeches, but the great majority of stockholders have sent in proxies favorable to the management, and the protesters are therefore annihilated by a gentleman who rises to cast several million votes against them. I myself have attended an annual meeting in which, in the absence of any opposition, the proceedings were even more cut-and-dried: the minutes of the meeting had been prepared in advance, they were read aloud slowly, and at the appropriate moments various directors responded to their various cues and offered the appropriate resolutions and passed them, fortified by the knowledge that the bundles of proxies which lay on the table between them gave them full legal authority to act on the stockholders' behalf.

Suppose a stockholder doesn't like the way the corporation is being run? Only if he is eccentric, or a special sort of crusader, or a politician (union or otherwise) trying to make a stir, does he try to oppose the management of a really big company. What he does, instead, is to sell his stock and get out.

His General Motors stock, or Goodyear stock, or United Airlines stock does not in the great majority of cases represent to him a part ownership and control of the mighty enterprise; it represents a way of getting some income (or profit), his right to which is attested by a prettily decorated sheet of paper which he keeps in his safe-deposit box; and his interest in the corporation's fate is likely to take principally the form of looking at the stock-market page from time to time to see how the price is doing. If he doesn't like what he sees, he sells.

The management regards him with far more respect than it

regarded its minority stockholders at the turn of the century, when it might tell them nothing at all about the company's progress, or at the most produce for them a batch of bloodless statistics. Now he is given full and lively reports, full of photographs of the company's more picturesque operations, and graphs in which the amount of money spent in this and that way is represented by pretty piles of coins. I haven't yet seen an annual report with a picture of a smiling bathing-suit girl in it, but I am sure there must have been such: it is hardly possible that any concentrated effort of salesmanship at the mid-century could long do without this standard symbol of delight. But just there is the nub of the situation. The stockholder is viewed very much as the customer is viewed: not as an owner but as someone who had better be wooed lest he take his patronage elsewhere.

With potential opposition melting away through the sales exit, the management is very much in the saddle—and in most of these larger companies it is virtually self-perpetuating. How else could things be run in, let us say, the American Telephone Company, which has over a million shareholders, no one of whom owns more than one-tenth of one per cent of the stock?

Looking at this segment of American business, we would almost find it appropriate to call our present economic system "managementism" rather than "capitalism."

All this has been familiar to a great many observers for a great many years. But there is another change which is not quite so widely recognized, though it too has been known to the knowledgeable for a considerable time.

This is that the corporation of today, and especially the big one, is not only not run by the stockholders but is in most cases not nearly so dependent upon the purveyors of money—in short, the bankers—as it used to be. In the old days the managers of companies went hat in hand to Wall Street—or State Street, or Chestnut Street, or LaSalle Street—when they needed funds for the salvation or reorganization or expansion of their businesses, and the bankers proffered money on terms which usually involved their having a say in the future management of those companies. As a result, a great banker to whom other bankers kowtowed and of whom big investors stood in awe could become, as did Morgan the Elder, something very close to a supreme boss of much of American business. Today bankers are indeed needed for help in the rescue or reorganization or new financing of many businesses, and their aid may be very valuable indeed, and their influence strong; but their chance to throw their weight around is limited. In the first place, the terms on which they may deal with their clients are now closely restricted by law. In the second place, rival candidates for the role of rescuer have appeared on the scene, such as the government's Reconstruction Finance Corporation (some of whose officials in recent years have been discovered to have taken a highly personalized view of their function). When a corporation needs money for expansion, it may go to Madison Square rather than to Wall Street—in other words, to a big insurance company—or may be able to enlist the interest of one of those rising aggregations of capital, the investment trusts. Or it may use its own money.

For to a very large extent successful corporations today are self-financing. They roll their own capital, by paying out only part of their earnings in dividends and using the rest to buy new machinery, build new plants, acquire new subsidiaries. This method of superseding the banker was rare among big corporations at the turn of the century, but it became very popular in the nineteen-twenties, and it is standard among them today. The head of a large and successful corporation with ample funds is therefore likely to regard Wall Street somewhat as he does his doctor: better be polite to him because the awful day might come when he could give one orders, and anyhow his occasional services and check-ups are useful; but in the meantime the doctor is not one's master. Similarly, nobody in Wall Street is the successful corporation head's master, Mr. Vishinsky and his like to the contrary notwithstanding.

In this as in many other matters, the Soviet propagandists—and many foreign observers of America who are far less unsympathetic—

not only distort the truth about America but distort a truth more than twenty years out of date.

Is the big and successful corporation its own master, then? Not quite.

To begin with, it is severely circumscribed by the government. As Professor Sumner H. Slichter has said, one of the basic changes which have taken place in America during the past fifty years is "the transformation of the economy from one of free enterprise to one of government guided enterprise. . . . The new economy," says Dr. Slichter, "operates on the principle that fundamental decisions on who has what incomes, what is produced, and at what prices it is sold are determined by public policies." The government interferes with the course of prices by putting a floor under some, a ceiling over others; it regulates in numerous ways how goods may be advertised and sold, what businesses a corporation may be allowed to buy into, and how employees may be paid; in some states with Fair Employment laws it even has a say about who may be hired. "When a piece of business comes up," writes Ed Tyng, "the first question is not likely to be 'Should we do it?' but 'Can we do it, under existing rules and regulations?' " He is writing about banking, but what he says holds good for many another business. Furthermore, in the collection of corporate income taxes, withholding taxes, social security taxes, and other levies the government imposes upon the corporation an intricate series of bookkeeping tasks which in some cases may be as onerous as those it must undertake on its own behalf. Thus the choices of enterprise are both hedged in and complicated by government.

Management is severely limited, too, by the power of labor unions. This is almost wholly a negative power: the union can tie the corporation up, but cannot run it, or even administer the provisions of a contract arrived at between it and the company: this it has to leave to the management. But the obstructive power of union leaders may be very great; the people who say that the man who in recent years has come closest to Pierpont Morgan in the exercise of personal

power in the national economy is John L. Lewis are not very far off
the beam. In unionized plants a series of contracts have served, in
effect, to enact what has been well described by Peter F. Drucker as
"the new common law of the industrial plant and office" as to hiring
and firing, seniority rights, the handling of grievances, overtime
work, vacations, and a lot of other things. In many cases this body
of common law may be beneficial in the long run to the corporation
as well as to its employees, but it certainly reduces the independence
of the management.

Finally, the management must always steer its course with an eye
to how its actions will look, not only to its employees, its stockholders,
its customers, and the government, but also to the general public.
The heads of little businesses may engage in deals which will not
stand public scrutiny, and sometimes get away with grand larceny;
the heads of big businesses are aware that this is exceedingly risky.
For they know they are under close critical observation. Detailed
reports to the Securities and Exchange Commission, detailed reports
to the tax gatherers, and the possibility at any moment of being in-
vestigated by the Federal Trade Commission or by a congressional
committee, leave them with about as much sense of privacy as a
goldfish. A goldfish has got to be good. These men have acquired,
too, for the most part, a healthy respect for the commercial value of
general popularity, and feel that it is incumbent upon them to win
friends and influence people. And this obligation, too, diminishes
their opportunities to do as they personally please.

So while the managers of our corporations continue, within limits,
to hire, fire, pay, buy, manufacture, and sell as they choose to do, and
after they reach a successful maturity are in large degree free from
interference by stockholders and financiers, and are thus very differ-
ently placed from the managers of nationalized industries or businesses, nevertheless the limitations are so numerous and severe that to
speak of these men as engaged in "free enterprise" is more picturesque
than accurate. They are managing private institutions operating under
a series of severe disciplines, and committed to doing so with an eye
to the general welfare.

But that isn't the quarter of it.

II

For the very nature of corporate business has been undergoing a change.

To pick out one word that comes as near as any other to describing the change, one might say that business is becoming professionalized, in the sense that more and more men in business are engaged in doing the sort of thing that we associate with the professional man (lawyer, doctor, engineer, professor) and doing it more and more in a spirit resembling that of the professional man.

When at the end of the first decade of this century the president of Harvard University, composing the citation for the degree given by the new Harvard Graduate School of Business Administration, called business "the oldest of the arts and youngest of the professions," there was considerable levity among the hard-shelled—and not simply because the language he used reminded people of the identity of the oldest of the professions. They thought the whole idea preposterous. Business, a profession! What an innocent notion! Business was a rough-and-tumble battle between men whose first concern was to look out for number one, and the very idea of professors being able to prepare men for it was nonsense. As a matter of fact, many a tough-fibered tycoon of those days was dubious even about employing college graduates, whom he regarded as toplofty, impractical fellows who had to unlearn a lot before they were fit for the business arena. One rough measure of the change that has taken place since then is to be found in the fact that this very professional school of business at Harvard has won widespread respect, and financial backing as well, from among big corporations; and that many of these corporations, at their own expense, send some of their most promising officials, at the age of forty or thereabouts, to fit themselves for enlarged responsibilities by taking the school's thirteen-week course in Advanced Management. This does not mean that a great university has departed from its scholarly traditions to shelter a trade school; it means rather that an important part of American business, as now operated, requires of its leading men what are essentially professional skills and abilities.

Heaven knows there are large areas of trade where a shrewd eye for a quick buck is dominant. There are businessmen aplenty to whom money-making is the sole criterion of performance—money-making at anybody's expense. Yet today the officers of most corporations of consequence have to cope with so many intricate technical problems of various sorts, have to bear in mind so constantly their interlocking relations with their employees, the government, their consumers, and the general public, and have to concentrate so hard upon keeping a complex of operations in effective balance, that there is a growing demand for men with highly trained and flexible minds.

Business is absorbing into itself a host of functions of a professional or semi-professional nature. It employs engineers in profusion; as the authors of a volume on *Executive Action* have put it, "There is no longer such a person as 'the engineer,' but there are a multitude of specialized engineers, many of whose skills are not interchangeable." It employs statisticians, cost accountants, auditors, economists, quality-control experts, motion-study experts, safety engineers, medical directors, personnel men, labor-relations specialists, training executives, public-relations men, advertising men, market analysts, research consultants, foreign-trade consultants, lawyers, tax experts —the list could be continued at length.

Take a single element in the modern corporate picture: that of research. In the early years of the century it was a rare company which had its own research laboratory; and even after such laboratories began to multiply fast during the nineteen-twenties, one old-line executive, asked if his company had a research department, said, "Yes, but we just sort of subsidize it as a publicity front." Even during the Great Depression, however, the multiplication continued; and by 1947 the "Steelman report" issued by the President's Scientific Resources Board estimated that of the 137,000 scientists and research engineers in the country, 30,000 were working for the government, 50,000 were working in colleges and universities, and 57,000—a group larger than either of the other two—were working in industrial research laboratories.

Take another element in the picture: the wide variety of responsibilities, quite apart from traditional business ones, that a corporation may find itself saddled with. Tharon Perkins, writing about the American oil companies operating in Venezuela, has noted that each one has had to build a whole new town near each oil field before it could begin to do business—and that this has meant "having to provide a house for each employee, an education for the children, hospitals and medical care for the entire family, paved streets, garbage collection and a sewerage system, stores where food can be bought (much of it below cost), power plants to supply electricity, water systems with pure water, laundries and ice plants—and even amusement centers with baseball diamonds, movies, and club houses for dancing and billiards"; and that "an oil company district manager or area superintendent has to *run* this civilization after he has built it." That sort of town building and town managing requires a bevy of experts with highly diversified professional talents.

The various specialists who are drawn into the employ of a big corporation are not, in most cases, by any means shut away from others of their kind who work for other employers. No, they go to meetings of the National Society of Sales Training Executives, or the National Association of Cost Accountants, or the American Society of Corporate Secretaries, or what not, there to swap notes on progress in their particular fields and to pick up ideas. And when some of these groups assemble—when, for instance, the industrial chemists meet with government chemists and university chemists at sessions of the American Chemical Society—they find common ground in devotion to the broadening of their particular area of learning. I have before me a report of a recent conference on aviation health problems. It was conducted by the Harvard School of Public Health (a private institution of learning and teaching), and it brought together professors from Harvard and other institutions, representatives of the Navy, Air Force, and U. S. Public Health Service, and representatives of airlines, aircraft manufacturing companies, and insurance companies. That sort of collaboration goes on every day the country over. Said Dr. J. Robert Oppenheimer before a congressional committee in 1945. "The gossip of scientists who get together is the lifeblood of physics, and I think it must be in all other branches of science. . . ." And so it is with personnel men, market analysts, and cost accountants too, he might have added, and with all those other corporation employees who take a truly professional interest in their specialties.

This swapping of ideas brings us to one of the most significant facts about American business today—a fact which never ceases to amaze European and even British businessmen when they confront it: that there are few secrets in American business. Rather there is a continual cross-fertilization through the pooling of facts and ideas.

This takes place in a number of ways. Take one upper-level way. When the directors of the Manufacturing Chemists' Association, representing scores of chemical concerns, meet monthly, there is laid before them a tabulation of the safety record of the whole industry —not only as a whole, but firm by firm, so that the man from du Pont or Monsanto learns the exact safety figures of Merck or American Cyanamid. Why do they do this? Obviously because safety is a matter of such common concern to them that the necessity for sharing whatever knowledge can be accumulated takes precedence over the competitive impulse.

Similarly the magazine publishers set up many years ago the Audit Bureau of Circulations, to make periodically a thorough and unbiased inspection of the circulation records of each magazine, and to publish the figures in detail. In some other countries these figures would be jealously guarded secrets; here the assumption is that it is to the advantage of all that the advertiser who buys space shall know exactly what he is buying, even if this means that the competing concerns in the industry shall each know just how the others are faring.

The pooling of information takes place through trade journals too. Their number is legion, and each one is full of ideas on how to do more effective business. I have been told, not unreasonably, that one reason why Italian military aviation was so backward during World War II was that Mussolini's Fascist government had banned the importation into Italy of aeronautical trade journals from the United

States and Britain, thus depriving the Italian engineers of a vast deal of information which we here make available to all.

But the most characteristic of all American institutions for the pooling of information are trade conventions. In 1930, according to the *Wall Street Journal*, there were 4,000 trade associations in the United States; now, believe it or not, there are no less than 12,000 —1,500 national ones and 10,500 state or local ones. And so many of these organizations have salaried managers that the logical, climactic development has taken place: two hundred of the managers gathered in Chicago in 1951 to consult together as a trade association of managers of trade associations!

When one of these organizations holds its annual or semi-annual convention—whether at the Waldorf or Commodore in New York, or the Stevens or Edgewater Beach in Chicago, or the Chase in St. Louis, or in Atlantic City or French Lick or White Sulphur—the ritual is well-nigh standard: the green-baize-covered registration desk for new arrivals, where they are handed a lapel badge and a schedule of meetings and festivities; the formal meetings in the Palm Room or Ballroom (sometimes ill-attended in the mornings); the formal dinner at which some grand panjandrum of the industry makes a speech concocted by his ghost-writer on the glories of free enterprise and the insidious menace of socialism; the back-slapping, highball drinking, poker playing, and general skylarking that makes the members feel like boys again; the bridge or canasta tournaments for wives —if these are invited; and, if they are not, the tendency of executives to return home in such a depleted condition as to confirm the local legend that New York, or Chicago, or Atlantic City, or whatever the convention place happens to be, is a sink of iniquity. Yet though the serious purpose of these gatherings sometimes seems submerged in a tide of alcohol, it nevertheless is vital. Information is pooled— about buying conditions, selling conditions, the nature of the market, the latest technical advances. The conferees may not tell each other quite everything; nevertheless the characteristic answer to the question, "How's your paper supply holding up in quality?" is emphatically not, "None of your business." These men have learned that it is to the long-range interest of all to pass information around, very much as the members of the American Historical Association have learned that it is to the long-range interest of the science and art of history to pass information around.

III

Surveying the current business scene and the complex of problems pressing upon the modern large-scale executive, the editors of the magazine *Fortune* recently declared in their book, *U.S.A., the Permanent Revolution,* that "management is becoming a profession"; and in an advertisement they put it even more flatly: "THE TYCOON IS DEAD. . . . The mid-century business man has had to go to school —in labor, in politics, in social welfare. The engineer's a business man, the salesman's an economist, the research man knows advertising, the finance man knows law."

The tycoon dead? The report may be exaggerated. Nevertheless there is a striking difference between the type of men now rising to the top in big business and those of an earlier day.

Take, for example, the eight men whom I mentioned in Chapter 4 as among the most influential in American economic affairs at the turn of the century: J. Pierpont Morgan, John D. Rockefeller, Andrew Carnegie, Edward H. Harriman, James Stillman, George F. Baker, William Rockefeller, and H. H. Rogers. I noted that of all these men, none had been to college except Morgan, who had spent two years at the University of Göttingen in Germany. Nowadays it seems quite natural to us that the great majority of big business executives should be college graduates and that many should have been trained in engineering or law.

For example, in the automobile industry—regarded by many as a pretty tough one—the chief executive officer of General Motors, Charles Erwin Wilson, a graduate of the Carnegie Institute of Technology, began his career as an electrical engineer. The president of Chrysler, Lester Lum Colbert, went to the University of Texas and the Harvard Law School, after which he became a specialist in labor law. And though Henry Ford II, head of the Ford company, constitutes a somewhat special case, being one of the few leading executives who may be said to have inherited his job (an increasingly unusual thing today, when there is a marked trend away from the family-run firm), he at least spent some years at Yale.

Frank Whittemore Abrams, chairman of the board of Standard Oil (New Jersey), the biggest of all American concerns in terms of total assets, is a Syracuse man, class of 1912, and was trained as an engineer; the president of the same company, Eugene Holman, holds a master's degree from the University of Texas and began his career as a geologist.

Among the recent top executives of General Electric, the other Charles E. Wilson (Charles Edward), who was president until he took over the national mobilization assignment in 1950, is an exception in not having gone to college, but the chairman of the board, Philip Dunham Reed, got an engineering degree at Wisconsin and a law degree at Fordham; Wilson was succeeded in the presidency by Ralph J. Cordiner, Whitman College '22. At U. S. Steel the recent chairman of the board, Irving S. Olds, Yale '07, Harvard Law School '10, is a lawyer. And at American Telephone & Telegraph, upon the retirement of Walter S. Gifford, Harvard '05, a statistician (who later became the American Ambassador to Great Britain), he was succeeded in the top position by Leroy Wilson, Rose Polytechnic Institute '22, an engineer, and on the latter's death the place went to Cleo F. Craig, University of Missouri '13, an electrical engineer.

The mention of Gifford's ambassadorial service suggests another interesting thing about such men as these: that many of them have at one time or another held government jobs. Among those I have just listed, for instance, Charles Edward Wilson was not only the chief officer of the national mobilization effort in 1950-1952, but in World War II was executive vice-chairman of the War Production Board, where Cordiner also was for a time vice-chairman. Reed worked for the government from 1941 to 1945 in a variety of assignments, one of which carried the rank of Minister. Holman put in a number of years with the U. S. Geological Survey before he went into the oil business. One might add parenthetically that when Gifford went to the Court of St. James's, he succeeded Ambassador Lewis W. Douglas, who had been at various times a congressman, the U. S. Director of the Budget, chancellor of McGill University, and president (later chairman) of the Mutual Life Insurance Company.

If in our list of automobile companies we had included Studebaker, we might have noted that it was the head of Studebaker, Paul Hoffman, who took over one of the biggest political tasks of our time, the administration of the Marshall Plan—and then became head of the Ford Foundation. And speaking of foundations, it should be noted that in 1948 Devereux C. Josephs, who was head of the Carnegie Corporation, a foundation which deals extensively with professors, moved over to become president of the New York Life Insurance Company, where the chairman of the board, George Leslie Harrison, had been trained as a lawyer and had been governor of the Federal Reserve Bank of New York, a semigovernmental organization.

These men are characteristic of a shift even more pronounced among many of their juniors: a shift toward the rise, in big business, of men to whom government service and public service of other sorts come naturally, complementing their professional and business training to prepare them for the wide range of techniques and public responsibilities which present-day business confronts. New style corporations are getting new-style leaders.

We need not pause here more than a moment to note another aspect of American life that most of us so take for granted that we are astonished when Europeans express surprise at it: the fact that America is crammed from end to end with private organizations and associations—national, state, and local—designed to look out for one aspect or another of the common good; and that in most of these, businessmen play active and often leading roles.

In their book, *U.S.A., the Permanent Revolution,* the editors of *Fortune* have hammered hard at the significance of this fact, driving home their argument by showing how these organizations are run in a specific city—Cedar Rapids, Iowa: how Keith Dunn, executive vice-president of the Century Engineering Company, presides at a luncheon meeting of the Cedar Rapids Chamber of Commerce, of which he is president, and then moves on immediately afterward to a meeting of the Community Chest; and how Van Vechten Shaffer, president of the Guaranty Bank & Trust Company, is not only head of the Chamber's Co-ordinating Committee, but is a trustee and secretary of Coe College, president of the Cedar Rapids Community Foundation, chairman of the local Health Council, a member of the Iowa Health Council, and a money raiser for St. Luke's Hospital, the local symphony, and the amateur theater—and in all gives a third of his time, and often more, to the local community. There is nothing new about businessmen being on hospital boards, school and college boards, or charitable boards, or about their wives being active in the women's clubs and federations thereof and the Parent-Teacher Associations. But some of the organizations that have developed in recent years with active business support do strike a somewhat new note in this picture of what Erwin D. Canham of the *Christian Science Monitor* has called "voluntary collective action . . . a kind of collectivism which has a potency incomparably more dynamic than Marxist collectivism could ever be."

Let me mention only two out of a great many. There is the Committee for Economic Development, an organization for economic study and political recommendations based upon this study, which does not simply try to promote the interest of business management but takes a much broader view of economic affairs, and brings together on its committees and research groups a mixture of company heads and academic economists which would astonish an old-time tycoon. And there is also the Advertising Council, described by Lewis Galantière as "a voluntary organization of professional men who donate to the nation the copy, the designs, and the technical skill that go into our public campaigns for better schools, road safety, fire prevention, government bond sales, the war against tuberculosis and other diseases." Listening to a radio commercial on the importance of adequate support of our schools, and realizing that it was written and distributed for free by the Advertising Council, and is incorporated in an expensive radio show because the sponsors of Bob Hope, let us say, feel that its inclusion adds to the public appeal of their show, one feels as one does when listening to a Metropolitan Life Insurance Company commercial on the treatment of arthritis: "Yes, I suppose this is just good business in a way—but where does one draw the line between good business and the promotion of the common weal?" These days they seem to overlap considerably.

And not only do they overlap, but there is a constant effort to build bridges over whatever gaps remain between them. At the mid-century the desire for synthesis and reconciliation—between various sciences, between science and industry, between sociology and business, between this element in our society and that—is widespread and contagious. It has become the fashion to hold conferences at which representatives of supposedly contrasting interests in American society put their heads together and try to arrive at common counsel. One of these conferences, recently, was organized by the Advertising Council, with the idea of throwing light on what aspects of American life were least understood abroad. It was held at the Hotel Waldorf-Astoria in New York on April 16, 1951; the panel of talkers included an author, a magazine editor and author, a foreign radio consultant and author, a newspaper editor, a professor, a college president, a foundation head, a manufacturer, and a manufacturer turned statesman and foundation head. What these men said was interesting, but not half so interesting as that at the mid-century it seemed to be important to get them together to discuss the meaning of America. That is a sample of the way in which men engaged in business and in other kinds of effort are constantly drawn together to arrive at mutuality of ideas in the common interest.

Another trend in American business is toward the supplanting of one-man management by team management. The tycoon may not be dead, but such autocrats as the late table-pounding George Washington Hill of American Tobacco and the rambunctious Sewell Avery of Montgomery Ward are in increasingly short supply. One corporation head summed it up to me this way:

A lot of the companies in my industry were started in the early years of the century as one-man shows: there was a fellow with an idea and some capital, and the business was his personal business. Then the thing grew, and in the twenties the sales problem was uppermost, and this man was succeeded by a big salesman. Later we began to see the importance of research, and a research man, or at any rate a research-minded man, would get the nod. But now research has become so complicated that it's a specialty, and what you need is a team of people each one of which knows one or more of these various specialties, and the chief thing required of the head fellow is that he be able to keep this team working as a well-balanced unit. He's got to be a good captain of the team. As chairman, I don't pretend really to know what the research people are doing; it's my job to keep them going in harmonious balance with the rest of the outfit.

The organization of Standard Oil (New ᵀᵉ⸗ y) is exceptional in that the directors are full-time salaried men ᴜ ᵣs of the company staff, meeting as a board once a week, while an e ᵣecⁿtive committee of five of them meets every day; but it offers an interesting—if extreme— case of the current emphasis upon teamwork. C. Hartley Grattan has described in *Harper's* how the men at the top work:

The Board is indisputably the core of the management of the company. Its decisions are group decisions. Unanimous consent is always sought and when there is sharp division of opinion which cannot be overcome by the usual methods of persuasion, the matter is laid over with a request for more facts. As a Board member the President participates in discussions as an equal, just as the Chairman of the Board does also. It seems likely, the members being only human, that the views of the Chairman and the President carry more weight than those of ordinary members; but this, it is insisted, does not give either domination of the Board. Their position is simply *primus inter pares*.

What of the attitude of such new-style managers as these toward the general public interest? Here one should walk very warily indeed, recognizing that speeches by a corporation head may be window-dressing arranged by a public-relations department and that, in general, protestations of virtuous intent cannot always be taken at face value. Nevertheless something seems to have happened.

The Great Depression had much to do with it. The top men of America's big corporations remember the doghouse which they inhabited in those days; and though some of the elder ones are still unreconstructed Washington-haters, and there is hardly a man in authority today who does not on occasion splutter at some of the restrictions—and monumental paper work—imposed upon him by the government, a great many of the younger and more nimble-minded of them have acquired a genuine distaste for the shenanigans of the nineteen-twenties, a firm intention not to butt their heads against the political and social facts of life as their predecessors did, and a hard-learned but unfeigned awareness of the principle that, in the long run, as Peter F. Drucker has put it, "No policy is likely to benefit the business itself unless it also benefits the society." The war had something to do with the change, too, bringing together as it did businessmen, government men, labor leaders, physical scientists, social scientists, and assorted professional men in government under-takings in which they learned to appreciate one another's competence and point of view. I do not mean that our business executives have put on haloes; I prefer the way in which the attitude of these men was described by Ralph Coghlan of the St. Louis *Post Dispatch* at the Corning conference of 1951—a conference, by the way, which dealt with "Living in Industrial Civilization," and brought together in a two-day powwow businessmen, sociologists and other scholars, journalists, and government officials, and was staged by a business concern, the Corning Glass Company. Said Mr. Coghlan:

"When I was growing up, the word 'soulless' corporation was a very common term. . . . Well, in my lifetime I have seen a remarkable change in this. I don't know whether it could be said that corporations have obtained souls, but at least they have obtained intelligence."

IV

The American corporation of today, large or small, is not only an economic unit. It is a political unit too, in the sense that most of those who work for it are much more conscious, during most of their working hours, of being under its governance than of being under the governance of the regular political officials. The boss—whether president, or department head, or supervisor, or foreman—is an executive authority closer to them than any governor or mayor; and the code of practices of the firm—that body of common law of which we have spoken—seems to them to condition their lives and fortunes more urgently than the ordinances of the city or the laws of the state and nation. For it defines the extent of their property rights in their jobs, which may mean more to them than any of their tangible possessions, and it also determines in large degree the amount of satisfaction that these jobs give them from day to day. Whether this code of practices has been built up by management alone, or by contract between management and union, it regulates not only them but, indirectly, their families too, so that when Mr. Jones or Miss Miller shifts from a job in one company to a job in another, the wrench to their daily mode of life and their view of the world about them may be as sharp as if they had moved from town to town.

And the corporation is a social unit too, a community. The girl who comes from an Ohio town to Philadelphia to take a job is acutely aware that among her new fellow employees and their friends she may find the man she will marry; as she begins to go out to lunch with other girls in her department she is being introduced by degrees into a new society. The young man who is transferred from the Cleveland plant to the Kansas City plant knows that his social life in Kansas City will be built in large part about the friendships he makes within the plant there.

The extent to which the corporation constitutes a community depends of course upon many factors—the social homogeneity of the employees as a group; whether the company dominates the town in which it is located or is a small unit among many; whether or not most of the employees separate at night to go to different dormitory suburbs; and whether there is felt to be official pressure for or against a concentrated association with other members of the corporation's staff. (One recalls the remark attributed to Ben Sonnenberg, the New York public relations man, a believer in the importance of outside contacts, that lunching with colleagues is "career suicide.")

But on the whole the social life within the corporation is a more important element in the American scene, I believe, than one would gather from most of our fiction—which is likely to be produced either by self-employed people who do not know this life at first hand or by people who have experienced it but are such natural-born individualists that they look upon it with a bilious eye. General awareness of its importance may account, at least in part, for the steady movement toward the cities, where people obscurely feel that they will be guaranteed some social opportunities through office contacts—many more than a small community would offer—but will not be as wholly dependent upon these, as imprisoned within the corporate community, as they might be in a one-company town.

In some corporations the social pattern takes curious forms. *Fortune* published late in 1951 two articles dealing with the pressures upon wives of executives in some concerns to conform to a rigid code of executive-wifely conduct. These articles—later summarized in a single article in Life—revealed that in some corporations executives are not chosen, or promoted, until their wives have been approved as suitable members of the company community; these wives are expected to have social ease, to refrain from injudicious talk or alcoholic indiscretion, to guide other wives toward seemly behavior, and to help their husbands put the company's interest before any other. Indirectly the articles also revealed how delicate a pattern of conformity, echelon-mindedness, and snobbery such a custom may impose upon the community, turning the concept of teamwork among executives and the concept of the corporation as a community into caricatures.

From the comment which these articles occasioned it was clear that there are corporations in which no such gentle conspiracy to erase individuality takes shape. Yet in one way or another both the management and the union, if any, are likely to tend, for their own reasons, at least to encourage the employees' sense of belonging.

Thus in the urbanized society of the mid-century the company or union paper serves as the equivalent of the old-time country weekly. "Angela Filson in Accounts Payable is sporting a new ring these days. The lucky man is Jerry Cassidy of the Des Moines office. Congratulations, Angela and Jerry!" . . . "Agent Win Winget won enough in two football pools to keep his twins in new shoes for the next three years." . . . "Our deep sympathy goes to Lillian Gerchar, Helen Debreceni, and Pearl Anthony in the recent loss of loved ones." . . . "Eleanor Rich, twelve-year-old daughter of Howard Rich, employed in the pipe mill at Gadsden, recently won the Alabama State Spelling Championship. In cinching the crown she correctly spelled 'baccalaureate' and 'eleemosynary.' In the photo Eleanor is shown with her proud dad." What are these but the sort of personals that have been the traditional seasoning of small-town community life? And does not the office party serve the corporate society as the sort of saturnalia that other communities have needed and have not always been able to devise—as occasions where the salesmen kiss the secretaries, and the office boy tells the department head that his routing system is all wrong, and the community code tells them that none of this is to count on the official record?

In this corporate community the labor union plays today an anomalous part. By its very nature it is divisive, required to be anti-management, anti-company, anti-industry, a sort of His Majesty's Opposition that will never, like an opposition political party, be required—or be able—to take office and show that it can do better. The union leader is in a curious spot. Unable, himself, to put into practice any of the changes for which he campaigns, he is compelled by his very position to make the most of grievances, to whip up mistrust, and in some cases to keep alive the threat of a strike which may paralyze not only the company or industry against which he is campaigning but many another which has had no part in the dispute. When inflation threatens, the position he occupies almost forces him to keep on pushing for increases which will add to the inflationary pressure; if he doesn't, he may lose his job to someone who shouts more loudly and consecutively than he. For he is cast in the role of a crusader, and if the time comes when the need is not for rebellion but for reconciliation and reconstruction, he is in danger of losing status. Furthermore, his search for able subordinates is complicated by the tendency of management to promote some of the ablest potential candidates into ineligibility. He is required almost inevitably to be an underminer of that loyalty to the company which offers one of the deepest satisfactions of corporate work. And the one really strong weapon in his arsenal, the strike, is an exceedingly blunt one, which hits a great many people at whom it is not aimed.

That the right to strike remains one of the fundamental liberties in an industrial society one may agree. One may agree, too, that unions and their leaders have played and are playing a vital part in the raising of the general standard of living; and that, by and large, the codes of practice which they have written into the statute books of industry (always excepting the featherbedding codes imposed on certain industries) have done and are doing much to make for decent conditions of life which would not otherwise be attained. It seems undeniable, furthermore, that some method of providing an uncringing representation of the rank and file of corporate employees in the contest over the disposition of corporate funds is essential to our general well-being. Yet it remains an anomaly of our industrial life that this deep division of loyalties is built into it in a day when the trend toward a general American standard of living is otherwise such a unifying force.

Under these circumstances it is noteworthy that we have so many ably managed and responsible unions as we have today, and that patience and good will are so often to be found on both sides of the table in management-labor relations. Strikes, like airline accidents, make news; reasonable agreements, like the hundreds of thousands of airline flights that arrive safely, do not. In the reports of the British productivity teams there has been frequent mention of the extent to which managements and unions have been found to be working together toward the improvement of manufacturing and administrative methods. One reason would seem to be that common-sense people recognize that they work better, and are happier, when their loyalties are not in head-on conflict, but overlap.

That already the strike itself is tending to change its character in response to this recognition has been manifest in recent years. Though some strikes have been bitter and violent, these have been the exception; and the contrast of the rest with the strikes of earlier years has been very sharp. Mary Heaton Vorse, who as a reporter deeply sympathetic with labor observed the steel strikes of 1919 and 1937 and then that of 1949 at close range, visiting some of the same mill towns and attending strikers' meetings, was astonished at what she saw in 1949: the absence of violent goon squads; the sympathy of the townspeople generally with the strikers, who seemed to them not a mob of red revolutionaries, as they had seemed in 1919, and even in 1937, but a collection of respectable fellow citizens to whom it was reasonable to extend financial credit in the emergency; the action of some company officials in serving coffee to the pickets; the manifest interest of almost everybody in maintaining order. The contrast with the old days has been even cleaner-cut in some other recent strikes, during which there has been noted in the local community an air of friendly excitement something like that at the close of a lively political campaign, or at the time of a big football match; in such communities the strike has been regarded not as class warfare but as a sort of game played between two teams, one of which has numbers on its side while the other has authority and money.

Meanwhile there are further signs, here and there, of a further evolution toward a lessening of the anomaly, toward a conceivable new order of things. Recent contracts tying wages to productivity are one sign. Such innovations as the Scanlon system of rewards, which again emphasizes productivity, are another. The widening group of companies which have introduced profit-sharing—some of them, like Lincoln Electric, with astonishing results—constitute still another. The intense preoccupation of many company officials with the art of communicating with employees and the public, and the studies which are constantly being made of the satisfactions and dissatisfactions of the workers' lot, are likewise encouraging. It may be that one of the changes we shall see during the next generation will be a transformation of the very nature of the union from an instrument of counter-loyalty and coercion into a less emotionally divisive though equally effective part of the organizational machinery of American business. For as it exists today it is becoming something of an anachronism in the more enlightened industries.

The corporation has come a long way, but there is still much unfinished business ahead of it.

Chapter 17

The Spirit of the Times

THE late President A. Lawrence Lowell of Harvard was an extempore speaker so brilliant that he could go to a public dinner quite without notes, listen to three preliminary speakers, and then, rising to speak himself, comment aptly on the remarks of those who had preceded him and lead easily into an eloquent peroration of his own. One of the reasons why he could do this was that he had almost by heart a number of suitable perorations on which he could construct variations suitable to the particular occasion. His favorite one dealt with the difference between two ancient civilizations, each of them rich and flourishing—Greece and Carthage. One of these, he would say, lives on in men's memories, influences all of us today; the other left no imprint on the ages to follow it. For Carthage, by contrast with Greece, had a purely commercial civilization in which there was little respect for learning, philosophy, or the arts. "Is America in danger of becoming a Carthage?" Lowell would ask—and then he would launch into an exposition of the vital and enduring importance of universities.

There are a great many people today, there have been a great many people throughout American history, who have in effect called the United States a Carthage. There are those who argue that during the past half century, despite the spread of good living among its people, it has been headed in the Carthaginian direction; that it has been producing a mass culture in which religion and philosophy languish, the arts are smothered by the barbarian demands of mass entertainment, freedom is constricted by the dead weight of mass opinion, and the life of the spirit wanes. There are millions in Europe, for instance, to whom contemporary American culture, as they understand it, is no culture at all; to whom the typical American is a man of money, a crude, loud fellow who knows no values but mechanical and commercial ones. And there are Americans aplenty, old and young, who say that achievement in the realm of the mind and spirit has become ominously more difficult in recent years, and that our technological and economic triumphs are barren because they have brought us no inner peace.

Some of the charges against contemporary American culture one may perhaps be permitted to discount in advance. Thus one may discount the laments, by people with twenty thousand a year, that other people whose incomes have risen from two thousand to four are becoming demoralized by material success; or the nostalgia of those who, when they compare past with present, are obviously matching their own youth in pleasantly sheltered circumstances with the conditions and behavior of a much more inclusive group today. One may also point out a persistently recurring error in European appraisals of the American people: many Europeans, being accustomed to thinking of men and women who travel freely and spend amply as members of an elite, have a tendency to compare certain undeniably crude, harsh, and unimaginative visitors from the States with fellow countrymen of theirs whose social discipline has been quite different—who belong, in European terms, to another class entirely. It is extraordinarily hard for many people, both here and abroad, to adjust themselves to the fact that the prime characteristic of the American scene is a broadening of opportunity, and that the first fruits of a broadening of opportunity may not be a lowered voice and a suitable deference toward unfamiliar customs.

So let us begin by giving the floor to a man who may be relied upon not to slip into these pitfalls, yet who nevertheless takes a hard view of what the past half century has done to his country.

"At the beginning of 1950," writes Bruce Bliven in his introduction to the book *Twentieth Century Unlimited,* "many newspapers and magazines . . . published elaborate reviews of the years since 1900, liberally illustrated with the quaint costumes of the McKinley era, with bicycle parades, barber-shop quartets with handlebar mustaches, and the earliest automobiles struggling along highways deep in mud. None of them, so far as I am aware, discussed what seems to me the most significant fact about the changes in the past half century—the alteration in the moral climate from one of overwhelming optimism to one which comes pretty close to despair.

"Half a century ago, mankind, and especially the American section of mankind, was firmly entrenched in the theory that this is the best of all possible worlds and getting better by the minute. . . . There was a kindly God in the heavens, whose chief concern was the welfare, happiness, and continuous improvement of mankind, though his ways were often inscrutable."

Today, continues Mr. Bliven, we have lost this faith and are "frightened to death"—of war, atom bombs, and the looming prospect of a general brutalization and deterioration of the human species.

Have we, then, become an irreligious and rudderless people?

Church statistics do not help us far toward an answer to this question. They show steady gains in membership for most church groups, roughly comparable to the gain in population; but they are suspect because of a very human tendency to keep on the rolls people who never go to church any more except for weddings and funerals, and there is no way of knowing whether the compilers of church statistics have become more or less scrupulous in the past few decades. My own definite impression is that during the first thirty or forty years of the half century there was a pretty steady drift away from church attendance and from a feeling of identification with the church and its creed and institutions, at least on the part of well-to-do Americans (except perhaps among the Roman Catholics, who were under an exceptionally rigid discipline). It became customary among larger and larger numbers of the solid citizenry of the land to sleep late on Sunday morning and then grapple with the increasing poundage of the Sunday paper, or have a 10:30 appointment at the first tee, or drive over to the Joneses' for midday cocktails, or pack the family into the car for a jaunt to the shore or the hills. I myself, making many week-end visits every year over several decades, noted that as time went on it was less and less likely that my host would ask on Saturday evening what guests were planning to go to church the next morning; that by the nineteen-twenties or thirties it was generally assumed that none would be. And although the households in which I visited may not have been representative, they at least were of more or less the same types throughout this whole period. Today I should imagine that in the heavy out-of-town traffic on a Friday afternoon there are not many people who will be inside a church on Sunday morning.

It has been my further observation that during at least the first thirty and perhaps the first forty years of the century there was an equally steady drift away from a sense of identification with the faiths for which the churches stood. Among some people there was a feeling that science, and in particular the doctrine of evolution, left no room for the old-time God, and that it was exceedingly hard to imagine any sort of God who was reconcilable with what science was demonstrating and would at the same time be at home in the local church. Among others there was a rising moral impatience with an institution which seemed to pay too much attention to the necessity of being unspotted by such alleged vices as drinking, smoking, card playing, and Sunday golfing, and too little to human brotherhood; the churches, or many of them, made a resolute effort to meet this criticism by becoming complex institutions dedicated to social service and the social gospel, with schools, classes, women's auxiliaries, young people's groups, sports, and theatricals, but not many of them held their whole congregations—at least on Sunday morning. Still others felt that the clergy were too deferential to wealthy parishioners of dubious civic virtue, or too isolated from the main currents of life. And among many there was a vague sense that the churches repre- sented an old-fashioned way of living and thinking and that modern- minded people were outgrowing their influence. And as the feeling of compulsion to be among the churchgoers and church workers weak- ened, there were naturally many to whom the automobile or the country club or the beach or an eleven o'clock breakfast was simply too agreeable to pass up.

Whether or not this drift away from formal religion is still the prevailing tide, there was manifest during the nineteen-forties a counter-movement. In many men and women it took no more definite form than an uneasy conviction that in times of stress and anxiety there was something missing from their lives: they wished they had something to tie to, some faith that would give them a measure of inner peace and security. The appearance on the best-seller lists of such books as *The Robe, The Cardinal, Peace of Mind,* and *The Seven Storey Mountain* indicated a widespread hunger and curiosity. Some returned to the churches—or entered them for the first time. In families here and there one noted a curious reversal: parents who had abandoned the church in a mood of rebellion against outworn ecclesiastical customs found their children in turn rebelling against what seemed to them the parents' outworn pagan customs. The Catholic Church in particular made many converts, many of them counter-rebels of this sort, and spectacularly served as a haven for ex-Communists who swung all the way from one set of disciplinary bonds to another. Whether the incoming tide was yet stronger than the outgoing one, or what the later drift would be, was still anybody's guess at the mid-century; but at least there was, and is, a confusion in the flow of relogous feeling and habit.

Meanwhile, in quantities of families, the abandonment of church allegiance had deprived the children of an occasionally effective teacher of decent behavior. Some parents were able to fill the vacuum themselves; others were not, and became dismayed that their young not only did not recognize Bible quotations but had somehow missed out on acquiring a clear-cut moral code. Looking round for someone to blame for what had happened, such parents were likely to fasten upon the public schools, arguing that to all their other duties the schools must add the task of moral instruction. There were other parents whose conscientious study of psychological principles, including the Freudian, and whose somewhat imperfect digestion of the ideas of progressive educators so filled them with uncertainty as to what moral teachings to deliver, and whether any sort of discipline might not damage young spirits, that these young spirits became—at least for the time being—brats of a singular offensiveness. And even if there had always been brats in the world, it was easy for observers of such families to conclude that moral behavior was indeed deteriorating, and that basketball scandals and football scandals and teen-age holdup gangs and official corruption in Washington were all signs of a widespread ethical decay.

This conclusion was and is of doubtful validity, I am convinced. There has probably never been a generation some members of which did not wonder whether the next generation was not bound for hell in a handcar. It may be argued that at the mid-century the manners of many teen-agers have suffered from their mothers' and fathers' disbelief in stern measures; but that their ethical standards are inferior, by and large, to those of their predecessors seems to me doubtful indeed. As for today's adults, there are undoubtedly many whose lack of connection with organized religion has left them without any secure standards; but as I think of the people I have actually known over a long period of time, I detect no general deterioration of the conscience: those I see today do a good many things that their grandparents would have considered improper, but few things they would have regarded as paltry or mean. And there has been taking place among these people, and in the country at large, a change of attitude that I am convinced is of great importance. During the half century the answer to the ancient question, "Who is my neighbor?" has been receiving a broader and broader answer.

There are still ladies and gentlemen who feel that they are of the elect, and that the masses of their fellow countrymen are of negligible importance; but their snobbery is today less complacently assured, more defiant, than in the days when Society was a word to conjure with. The insect on the leaf is less often found "proclaiming on the too much life among his hungry brothers in the dust." There are still business executives with an inflated sense of their own value in the scheme of things, but the "studied insolence" which Mark Sullivan noted among the coal operators of 1902 when confronted by the union representatives and the President of the United States, and which magnates often displayed on the witness stand in those days, is no longer to be seen (except perhaps among such underworld gentry as Mr. Frank Costello).

I recall a college classmate of mine who in 1912 said that he knew about a hundred of the five hundred members of his class, and although he knew it sounded snobbish, weren't those after all about all that mattered? His equivalent today might say such a thing, but pretty surely he would recognize as he did so that he was flying in the teeth of accepted opinion. People who today look at what were originally the servants' quarters in an old mansion, or even in a swank apartment of the 1920 vintage, are shocked at their meagerness: is it possible, they ask themselves, that decent men and women could have had such disregard for the human needs of men and women living cheek by jowl with them?

The concept of the national income, the idea of measuring the distribution of this income, the idea of the national economy as an entity affected by the economic behavior of every one of us, the very widespread interest in surveying sociologically the status of this and that group of Americans the country over, in the conviction that their fortunes are interdependent with ours: all these have developed during this half century. The ideal of equality of educational opportunity never before commanded such general acceptance. In previous chapters of this book I have tried to show that in recent years there has been a marked shift of attitudes toward our most disadvantaged group, the Negroes, and no less noticeably in the South than elsewhere; and that the concept of responsibility to the general public has become more and more widespread among the managers of pivotal businesses. The amount of time which individual men and women give to good works in the broadest sense—including church work, volunteer hospital work, parent-teacher associations, the Boy Scouts, the Red Cross, the League of Women Voters, local symphony orchestras, the World Federalists, the American Legion, the service activities of Rotary, and so on endlessly—is in its total incalculable.

(There are communities, I am told, where the number of people who engage in money raising for the churches is larger than the number of churchgoers.) In sum, our sense of public obligation has expanded.

The change has had its amusing aspects. There comes to one's mind Anne Cleveland's cartoon of a Vassar girl dining with her parents and exclaiming, "How can I explain the position of organized labor to Father when you keep passing me chocolate sauce?" One thinks of a banker's daughter of one's acquaintance, who in her first job was much more deeply interested in the plight of the file clerks, whom she regarded as underpaid, than in helping the company make money. And of the receipt by Dr. Ralph Bunche, in the spring of 1951, of no less than thirteen honorary degrees in rapid succession, the singular unanimity of his choice by so many institutions undoubtedly reflecting in part a delight at finding an unexceptionable opportunity to pay tribute to a Negro.

That the change should meet, here and there, with heated resistance, is likewise natural. The democratic ideal imposes a great strain upon the tolerance and understanding of humankind. So we find a conscious and active anti-Semitism invading many a suburban community which once took satisfaction in its homogeneity and now finds it can no longer live to itself; or a savage anti-Negro feeling rising in an industrial town in which Negroes were formerly few and far between. And here one should add a footnote about the behavior of our armed forces abroad. For a variety of not easily defined reasons —including undoubtedly the traditionally proletarian position of the foreign-language-speaking immigrant in the United States—there is an obscure feeling among a great many Americans that the acceptance of the principle of human dignity stops at the water's edge: that a man who would be fiercely concerned over an apparent injustice to a fellow private in the American Army may be rude to Arabs, manhandle Koreans, and cheat Germans, and not lose status thereby—and this, perhaps, at the very moment when his representatives in Congress are appropriating billions for the aid of the very sorts of people of whom he is so scornful.

Yet in spite of these adverse facts there has been, I am convinced, an increasing overall acceptance in America of what Dr. Frank

Tannenbaum has called "the commitment to equality . . . spiritual equality." Whether this rising sense of identity of interest with our fellow citizens should be labeled as religious, as Dr. Tannenbaum and other speakers seemed to feel at the Waldorf Round Table of April, 1951, seems to me a matter of playing with words. Whether, as Walter H. Wheeler, Jr., suggested at that meeting, we may be "depleting and living off inherited spiritual capital, to put it in business language," is far from certain. Yet at any rate this may be said: If we as a people do not obey the first and great commandment as numerously and fervently as we used to, at least we have been doing fairly well with the second.

II

We come now to another question to which the answer must be even more two-sided and uncertain. Does the all-American standard, the all-American culture to which I devoted Chapter 15, threaten quality? Are we achieving a mass of second-rate education, second-rate culture, second-rate thinking, and squeezing out the first-rate?

The charge that we are indeed doing this comes in deafening volume. To quote no less a sage than T. S. Eliot: "We can assert with some confidence that our own period is one of decline; that the standards of culture are lower than they were fifty years ago; and that the evidences of this decline are visible in every department of human activity." And if this seems a rather general indictment, without special reference to the United States, it may be added that Mr. Eliot has given abundant evidence that he is out of sympathy with the American trend, preferring as he does a "graded society" in which "the lower class still exists."

One could pile up a mountain of quotations by critics of the American drift, playing the changes upon the two notions that, according to C. Hartley Grattan, account for the *Katzenjammer* of American writers today:

(1) a feeling . . . that the values by which men have lived these many years are today in an advanced state of decomposition, with no replacements in sight; and (2) that whatever a man's private values may be, he

cannot expect in any case consistently to act on them successfully because
the individual is, in the present-day world, at the mercy of ever more
oppressive and arbitrary institutions.

In other words, that the man of original bent—the writer, painter,
musician, architect, philosopher, or intellectual or spiritual pioneer
or maverick of any sort—not only faces what Eugene O'Neill called
the "sickness of today," which in Lloyd Morris's phrasing has
"resulted from the death of the old God and the failure of science
and materialism to give any satisfactory new one," but must also
confront a world in which the biggest rewards for literary creation
go to manufacturers of sexy costume romances; in which the Broadway theater, after a glorious period of fresh creation in the nineteen-
twenties, is almost in the discard, having succumbed to the high cost
of featherbedding labor and the competition of the movies; in which
the movies in their turn, after a generation of richly recompensing
those who could attract audiences by the millions and stifling those
whose productions had doubtful box-office value, are losing ground
to television; in which the highest television acclaim goes to Milton
Berle rather than to Burr Tillstrom; and in which the poet finds his
market well-nigh gone. One might sum up the charge in another way
by saying that the dynamic logic of mass production, while serving
admirably to bring us good automobiles and good nylons, enforces
mediocrity on the market for intellectual wares.

This is a very severe charge. But there are a number of matters
to be considered and weighed before one is ready for judgment
upon it.

One is the fact that those who have most eloquently lamented the
hard plight of the man or woman of creative talent have chiefly been
writers, and more especially *avant-garde* writers and their more appre-
ciative critics, and that the position occupied by these people has been
a somewhat special one.

During the years immediately preceding World War I the in-
venters and innovators in American literature were in no such prevailing mood of dismay. On the contrary, they were having a high

old time. In Chicago, such men as Vachel Lindsay, Edgar Lee Masters, Sherwood Anderson, Ring Lardner, and Carl Sandburg were experimenting with gusto and confidence. In New York, the young Bohemians of Greenwich Village were hotly and rambunctiously enamored of a great variety of unorthodoxies, ranging from free verse, imagism, post-impressionism, cubism, and the realism of the "ashcan school" of art to woman suffrage, socialism, and communism (of an innocently idealistic variety compared with what later developed in Moscow). When Alfred Stieglitz preached modern art at "291," when the Armory Show was staged in 1913, when Max Eastman and John Reed crusaded for labor, when Floyd Dell talked about the liberation of literature, they saw before them a bright new world in which progress would in due course bring triumph to the wild notions of such heralds of the new enlightenment as themselves.

But World War I brought an immense disillusionment. No longer did the millennium seem just around the corner. And the prevailing mood shifted.

The novelists of the Lost Generation concentrated their attention upon the meannesses and cruelties of contemporary life, and often their keynote was one of despair. Mencken led a chorus of scoffers at American vulgarity and sentimentality, not indignantly but cynically; when asked why he continued to live in a land in which he found so little to revere, he asked, "Why do men go to zoos?" Sinclair Lewis lampooned Main Street and George F. Babbitt; Scott Fitzgerald underscored the baseness of respectable folk who went to Jay Gatsby's lavish parties and then deserted him in his hour of need. And many of the *avant-garde* and their admirers and imitators went to Paris, where Gertrude Stein said that "the future is not important any more," and Hemingway's characters in *The Sun Also Rises* acted as if it were not. But in a world without hope one could still cherish art, the one thing left that was worth while, keeping it aloof from politics and business; and one could particularly cherish that art which it was most difficult for the vulgarians of politics and business to comprehend. To these refugees from twentieth-century America "difficulty itself became a primary virtue," as Van Wyck Brooks has remarked: they paid special homage to the aristocratic elaborations of Henry James, the subtleties of the recluse Marcel Proust, the scholarly allusiveness of Eliot, and the linguistic puzzles of Joyce. And a pattern was set, quite different from the pattern of 1910. To have a literary conscience was to take a bleak view of American life, human life in general, and the way the world was going; and also of the ability of any readers but a few to understand and appreciate true literary excellence.

This credo was to prove astonishingly durable. During the nineteen-thirties it had to contend with another emotional force. The economy had broken down, revolution was in the wind (or so it seemed to many at the time), and many writers felt a generous urge to condemn the cruelty of capitalism to "one-third of a nation," and to espouse the cause of embattled labor. Thus they abandoned hopelessness for militance. There was an outpouring of proletarian novels by writers whose first-hand knowledge of factory workers was highly limited. Yet even among many of the writers and critics who were most valiant in support of the common man there remained a conviction that the man of sensibility and integrity must inevitably write in terms intelligible only to the very uncommon man; and we beheld the diverting spectacle of authors and students of advanced composition returning from mass meetings held on behalf of sharecroppers and Okies to pore over the sacred texts of Henry James, who would have ignored sharecroppers, and Eliot, who was certainly out of tune with the Okies.

During World War II the impulse to defend labor turned into an impulse to defend the G.I. against the military brass. The older impulse to depict the world as a dismal place turned into an impulse to show how brutal men at war could be (including, often, the very G.I. who was supposed to engage the reader's sympathy); and the belief that quality was bound to go unappreciated by all but a very few turned into a general pessimism over the future of culture, a pessimism that seemed almost to welcome defeat for any sort of excellence.

"It must be highly embarrassing (at least I hope it is)," wrote W. H. Auden in 1948, "for living American novelists to be told . . .

that they have produced the only significant literature between the two wars. . . . Coming from Europe, my first, my strongest, my most abiding impression is that no body of literature, written at any time or in any place, is so uniformly depressing. It is a source of continual astonishment to me that the nation which has the world-wide reputation of being the most optimistic, the most gregarious, and the freest on earth should see itself through the eyes of its most sensitive members as a society of helpless victims, shady characters, and displaced persons. . . . In novel after novel one encounters heroes without honor or history; heroes who succumb so monotonously to temptation that they cannot truly be said to be tempted at all; heroes who, even if they are successful in a worldly sense, remain nevertheless but the passive recipients of good fortune; heroes whose sole moral virtue is a stoic endurance of pain and disaster."

Could it be that such novelists have been following a fashion set longer ago than they realize? That one reason why sales of novels in very recent years have been disappointing is that, as Mr. Grattan has suggested, "contemporary writers appear to have given up before contemporary readers are ready to do so," and that perhaps the readers are today ahead of the writers? That the continuing notion among many advanced writers that only difficult writing is good writing has led them to pay too little attention to the art of communicating with numerous readers who may not be such oafs as they suppose? And that a sort of contagion of defeatism among literary folk today should lead one to accept with a certain reserve their unhappy conclusions concerning the state of American culture?

Let us note their laments and look a little further.

III

One like myself who has worked for a great many years for a magazine which nowadays can pay its authors no more than it did a decade ago, because it has to pay its typographers and shipping men so much more, is not likely to be complacent about the lot of the man of letters today. Nor is one who has felt he was waging a steady uphill fight on behalf of what he perhaps fondly considered distinguished journalism—uphill because there were constantly appearing

new magazines aimed at readers by the millions, and because advertisers tended to want to reach those millions—going to be complacent
about the condition of literary institutions. It seems to me undeniable
that the great success of the mass-circulation magazines and the rise
of the staff-written magazines have between them made it harder
for the free-lance author who lacks the popular touch and who will
not do potboiling, or cannot do it successfully, and who has no other
assured source of income, to live comfortably. But then he almost
never has had things very easy financially. And there is this to be
said: one reason why magazines with severely high standards find the
going difficult is that they have no monopoly of material of high
quality, for during the past few decades an increasing amount of
such material has been finding a place in the mass periodicals. (For
a couple of random examples, let me cite Winston Churchill's mem-
oirs, appearing in *Life*, and Faulkner's short stories, coming out in
the *Saturday Evening Post*.) Furthermore, the number of writers of
talent who made good incomes by writing for the mass magazines
without the sacrifice of an iota of their integrity is much larger than
one might assume from the talk of the *avant-gardists*. The picture
is a mixed one.

So too with regard to books. The market for the output of the
"original" publishers, meaning those who sell newly-written books
at standard prices, chiefly through the bookstores, is somewhat larger
than before the war, but it is manifest that price increases, reflecting
high labor costs, have deterred many buyers. The share of a few very
successful writers in the total authors' revenue increases; and it
becomes more difficult than it used to be for those whose books are
not likely to sell more than a few thousand copies (these include
nearly all poets) to get their work accepted. Yet here again the
situation is not as black as it has been painted. I agree with Bernard
DeVoto that no book really worth publishing fails of publication by
some unit of a very diversified industry; and I would add that while
there is trash on the best-seller lists, most of the books which reach
those lofty positions, with very pleasant results for their authors'
pocketbooks, are among the best of their time.

And there is more to it than this. For there are also numerous book clubs, at least two of which sell books by the hundreds of thousands each month. There are the quarterly Condensed Books brought out by the *Reader's Digest*—four or five novels or nonfiction books condensed in one volume—which, launched in 1950, were selling by early 1952 at the rate of more than a million apiece. And there are the paper-bound reprint houses, whose volumes, priced at twenty-five or thirty-five cents for the newsstand and drugstore trade, are bought in phenomenal lots. In the year 1950 the total was no less than 214 million; in 1951 the figure had jumped to 231 million.

Two-thirds or more of these paper-bound books, to be sure, were novels or mysteries—thus falling into classifications too inclusive to be reassuring as to the public taste—and some were rubbish by any tolerable standard (the publishers of such wares having learned, as one cynic has put it, that you can sell almost anything adorned on the cover with a picture connoting sex or violence, or preferably both, as in a picture of a luscious girl getting her dress ripped off by a gunman). But consider these sales figures (as of January 1952) for a few paper-bound books: Tennessee Williams' *A Streetcar Named Desire*, in play form, over half a million; George Orwell's *Nineteen Eighty-four*, over three-quarters of a million; Norman Mailer's *The Naked and the Dead*, over a million and a quarter; Ruth Benedict's *Patterns of Culture*, 400,000; and—to cite an incontrovertibly classical example—a translation of *The Odyssey* (with an abstract cover design), 350,000. And remember that these sales, which are above and beyond book-club sales and regular bookstore sales, have been achieved in a nation of avid magazine readers. It is true that the financial returns to the author from such low-priced books are meager: he gets less revenue from a million of them than from 20,000 sold at standard prices. Nevertheless there is an interesting phenomenon here. There is a big American market for good writing if it and the price are within easy reach.

Let us look at the market for art. The painter of today faces two great difficulties. The first is that his work is offered to the public at high prices (if he can get any price at all) because he can sell only his original work, to one collector or institution, and cannot dispose of thousands at a time; and collectors with ample money are scarce. The second is that the abler young painters of the day have mostly swung all the way to the abstract, which to most potential buyers is about as comprehensible as contemporary poetry. Yet the signs of interest among the public are striking. Forbes Watson is authority for the statement that there were more sales of paintings in the nineteen-forties than in all the previous history of the United States; that in the year 1948 there were a hundred exhibitions of American art in American museums; and that the total attendance at art exhibitions that year was over 50 million. One should also take note of the greatly enlarged number of local museums; of the lively promotion of an interest in art by many universities and colleges; the rising sale of reproductions, in book form and otherwise; and also the recent sharp increase in the number of Sunday amateur dabblers with a paintbrush. Lyman Bryson reports that the lowest estimate he has been able to find of the number of people who paint in the United States today is 300,000. And the Department of Commerce says that the sales of art supplies went up from four million dollars in 1939 to forty million in 1949—a tremendous leap. The suspicion comes over one that there is something stirring here, too, and that the plight of the contemporary artist, like the plight of the contemporary writer, may be partly due to the fact that the market for his output may not yet be geared to the potential demand.

We turn to music—and confront an astonishing spectacle.

In 1900 there was only a handful of symphony orchestras in the country; by May 1951 there were 659 "symphonic groups"—including 32 professional, 343 community, 231 college, and a scattering of miscellaneous amateur groups. Fifteen hundred American cities and towns now support annual series of concerts. Summer music festivals attract audiences which would have been unimaginable even thirty years ago. To quote Cecil Smith,

The dollar-hungry countries of Europe are setting up music festivals by the dozen, not to give American tourists the music they would not hear at home, but to make sure they do not stay at home because of the lack of music in Europe. The programs at Edinburgh, Strasbourg, Amsterdam, Florence, and Aix-en-Provence are designed as competition for Tanglewood, Bethlehem, Ravinia, the Cincinnati Zoo, and the Hollywood Bowl.

Mr. Smith cites further facts of interest: that the Austin, Texas, symphony recently took over a drive-in movie for outdoor summer concerts; that Kentucky hill people come in their bare feet when the Louisville orchestra plays in Berea; and that "an all-Stravinsky program, conducted by the composer, strikes Urbana, Illinois, as a perfectly normal attraction."

A good deal of the credit for this extraordinary state of affairs goes to the radio. The first network broadcast of a symphony orchestra was held in 1926, the first sponsored one came in 1929, the Metropolitan Opera was put on the air in 1931, and Toscanini was engaged as conductor of the NBC orchestra in 1937; by 1938 it was estimated that the Music Appreciation Hour, conducted by Walter Damrosch, was being heard each week by seven million children in some 70,000 schools, and that the Ford Sunday Evening Hour, featuring the Detroit Symphony, was fifth among all radio programs in popularity. Millions upon millions of people were getting music of all sorts— popular, jazz, and classical—in such quantity, year after year, that businessmen and housewives and school children who had never until a few years earlier heard a symphony orchestra or a string quartet were getting an ample opportunity to find out for themselves whether "Roll Out the Barrel" or "One O'Clock Jump" or Beethoven's Seventh sounded best on a fifth or tenth hearing. In the late nineteen-forties the radio network production of classical music began to weaken as television made spectacular inroads upon the radio business; but long before this another way of communicating music had jumped into prominence.

During the nineteen-twenties the phonograph record business had been threatened with virtual extinction by the rise of radio. But presently it began to expand: people who had developed a lively interest in music began to want it on their own terms. The expansion was accelerated by the wild vogue of jazz, whose more serious votaries

soon learned that if you were to become a really serious student of
what Benny Goodman and Duke Ellington were producing, you must
collect old recordings and become a connoisseur of Handy, Beiderbecke, and Armstrong. By the nineteen-forties, young people
who in earlier years would have gone off dancing of an evening were finding that it was very agreeable to sit on the floor and
listen to a record-player, with a few bottles of beer to wash the
music down. Many whose taste in books and in art was very limited
were not only becoming able to identify the most famous symphonies
by their first few notes, but were developing a pride in their acquaintance with the works of Bach's obscure contemporaries, and in their
connoisseurship of the comparative merits of recordings by various
orchestras. A very rough estimate of the sales of records during the
year 1951, made by *Billboard* magazine, put the grand total at some
190 million—more than one for every man, woman, and child in the
United States—and the total sale of records in the "classical" cate-
gory at perhaps ten to fifteen per cent of that 190 million: let us say
something like twenty to thirty million classical records. To give a
single example: as many as 20,000 sets of Wanda Landowska's
harpsichord recordings of the Goldberg Variations were sold during
the first three months after they were issued. And a shrewd student
of American culture tells me that as he goes about the United States
he keeps being told, in place after place, "Our town is sort of
unusual. I suppose the most exciting thing, to us, that's going on here
isn't anything in business but the way we've put over our symphony
orchestra (or our string quartet, or our community chorus)."

Verily, as one looks about the field of the arts, the picture is confused. Here is an incredible boom in public interest in music, along
with expanding audiences for the ballet, old-style and new-style. Here
is the Broadway theater almost ready for the pulmotor—and local
civic theaters and college theaters in what look like a promising
adolescence. Here are the movies, beloved by millions (and berated
by highbrow critics) for decades, losing audiences little by little to
television, which has not yet outgrown a preposterous crudity. Here

is architecture, which has outgrown its earlier imitation of old European styles and is producing superb industrial buildings along with highly experimental and sometimes absurd modern residences —while the peripheries of our great cities, whether New York or Chicago or St. Louis or Los Angeles, display to the bus traveler from airport to town almost no trace of the handiwork of any architects at all. Here are lovely (if monotonous) motor parkways—and along the other main highways a succession of roadtown eyesores (garages, tourist courts, filling stations, billboards, second-hand auto salesrooms, junk dealers, and more billboards) which make the motor parkways seem, by contrast, like avenues for escapists.

Is not the truth of the situation perhaps something like this: Here is a great nation which is conducting an unprecedented experiment. It has made an incredible number of people, previously quite unsophisticated and alien to art or contemptuous of it, prosperous by any previous standard known to man. These multitudes offer a huge market for him who would sell them equipment or entertainment that they can understand and enjoy. To compare them with the people who in other lands have been lovers and students of literature and the arts is grossly unfair. They are not an elite, but something else again. Let us say it in italics: *This is something new; there has never been anything like it before.*

The job before those Americans who would like to see the United States a Greece rather than a Carthage is to try to develop, alongside the media of entertainment and equipment which satisfy these people's present needs, others which will satisfy more exacting tastes and will be on hand for them when they are ready for more rewarding fare. The problem is an economic one as well as an artistic one. Whether it can be solved is still anybody's guess. But in a day when, despite the discouragement of many literati, much of the best writing in the world is being done in the United States; when the impoverishment of foreign institutions of learning has made American universities no mere followers on the road of learning, but leaders despite themselves, attracting students from many continents; and when, willy nilly, a burden of responsibility for the cultural condition of the world rests heavily upon America, it should do us good to look at the army of music lovers that we have produced. For if this is what auspicious economic conditions can bring in the area of one of the great arts, possibly the miracle may be effected elsewhere too, and the all-American culture may prove to have been, not the enemy of excellence, but its seed-bed.

Walt Whitman saw the possibilities when he wrote, fancifully depicting the arrival of the muse, a migrant from ancient Greece to the New World:

> By thud of machinery and shrill steam-whistle undismay'd,
> Bluff'd not a bit by drain-pipe, gasometers, artificial fertilizers;
> Smiling and pleas'd with palpable intent to stay,
> She's here, install'd amid the kitchen-ware!

IV

Yet there is still another question to ask.

The other day, running through some old papers of mine, I came upon a copy of a Commencement address I had once delivered. It was entitled "In a Time of Apprehension," and in it I had spoken of the fact that many people were feeling a "sense of doom, a sense of impending disaster." A good deal of what I had said then seemed to me, as I reread the address, to fit the mood of the mid-century. But the date on the manuscript was June, 1938—not only before the atom bomb and the Cold War, but before World War II.

Since much longer ago than that there has been from time to time in the minds of many Americans a feeling of uneasy tension, combined often with one of frustration: a feeling that mighty, unmanageable forces might be taking one toward that "impending disaster," and there was nothing one could do about it. In general one might ascribe this mental state to the difficulty of adjusting ourselves emotionally to life in what Graham Wallas called the "Great Society" —a complex society in which the fate of a Kansas farmer or a Syracuse druggist may be determined by a break in the New York stock market, or a government decision in Washington, or an invasion in Korea. But more specifically there was first the World War of 1914-

1918, with its demonstration that something that had happened in Sarajevo—where and what was Sarajevo?—could turn the lives of Americans upside down; then there was the Great Depression, with its solar-plexus blow to men and women who had thought that their personal industry and efficiency could not go without reward; then the march of Hitlerism and the coming of World War II, which involved young men in lethal battle in places they had never even heard of a year before; then the rise of that other distant but implacable menace, Soviet Russia, and the apprehension that a new war might break out at any moment, and the added terror of the atom bomb. And through all these latter years there were the uncertainties involved in government emergency regulations such as the draft, which as managed at the mid-century seemed to many young Americans to make a travesty of the idea of free will.

There is probably no one who has not had at one time or another this feeling of being as helpless in the grip of great events as a passenger strapped to his seat in an airliner roaring through a fog. The businessman making out his budget for the coming year, or signing a long-term contract; the young couple planning marriage; the undergraduate wondering whether to go on to law school—all are likely to feel that any decision they may make carries an implicit rider, "Unless all hell busts loose." And anyone presenting, as I have been doing in this book, the thesis that we in the United States during the past half century have on the whole made our country a better place to live in, can almost hear angry replies: "How can you say that, when about all we have succeeded in doing is to move from a time of assurance to one of perpetual emergency?" The fear of the unpredictable colors all our lives—and never more so than during the past few years.

In that Commencement address of 1938 I said that we were living in a time of panic and of irrational opinions born in panic, and remarked that what happens during such times is that people look for scapegoats on whom they can take out their anger at the invisible forces which keep them in jeopardy. This, too, has been happening since the aggressive intentions of the Soviet Government became transparently clear to most Americans—say about the year 1946 or 1947. We have been looking for American scapegoats on whom we can blame our present predicament, and whose discovery and punishment might make us feel secure again. And so panicky, irrational, and long-continuing has been the search, and so widespread have been the suspicions and fears that it has aroused, that Americans face in these mid-century years the disturbing question whether under such circumstances they can maintain the freedom that has been their most prized heritage.

This is not simply a question of the moment. For the contest with organized communism may, for all we know, last a decade—or two —or three—whether or not it flames into full-scale war. There are those who say that most living Americans may have to look forward to its continuance for the rest of their lives. That will mean continuing strain, suspense, uncertainty; and continuing danger of irrational reactions to that strain.

The specific form that our scapegoat hunting has taken in recent years has been due, first of all, to the peculiar history and nature of the Communist party in America. During the Depression years it ensnared some good and public-spirited men and women to whom it seemed simply an organization dedicated to radical action to solve the problems that were then racking the country. If it had Russian connections, this didn't bother many of them very much, for to them at that time Russia actually seemed a place which had found the cure for depressions; and besides, during the latter nineteen-thirties— until August, 1939—the Soviet Government was making common cause with the democracies against Hitler. If it was a secret organization, if it involved its members in constant deceit, this they innocently swallowed as a necessity for a hard-boiled militant group. Its converts were not very numerous, but many of them were strategically placed: they were mostly intellectuals who could be insinuated into positions of influence in government departments or in "front" organizations, and people who, as labor leaders, could get control of unions.

"The truth was," as I wrote in *Since Yesterday* in 1940, "that many of the young rebels had embraced—or at least dallied with—communism because they saw it as the end-station of the road of disillusionment. First one saw that the going order was not working right; then one progressed to the consideration of reforms . . . and decided that half-measures would not suffice to redeem America; one went on to the idea that nothing short of revolution would serve; and there at the terminus of one's journey sat Karl Marx waiting to ask one's unquestioning devotion, there was the Communist Party promising to make a clean sweep of all that was hateful in American life. How welcome to find the end of the road, how easy to be able to ascribe everything one disliked to capitalism!"

So things looked to most of those who got hooked. Many of them unhooked themselves when the 180-degree turns in Communist policy in 1939 and 1941 made it clear to anyone in his senses that the Party was in absolute subjection to a cynical foreign power; but others could not or would not, and continued their machinations under such clever disguises that so highly placed an innocent as Henry A. Wallace could as late as 1948 be deluded into imagining that he was not being used by them for their conspiratorial purposes.

Because the Communist party was conspiratorial and imposed secrecy upon its members, the job of ferreting them out of government departments, and organizations for the support of this or that public policy, and labor unions, was difficult. Because a great many fine, patriotic people had worked in these departments or organizations or unions, it was almost inevitable that some of these people too should come under suspicion. Because Communists were accustomed to lying about their connections, the question naturally arose whether these loyal citizens, too, might not be lying when they affirmed their loyalty. Because American foreign policy had not prevented the build-up of Soviet power, or the victory of the Chinese Communists over the Chiang Kai-shek government, a further question arose in many suspicious minds: were these people about whom they had their doubts responsible for the insecure plight of America and the uncertainty in which we were all living? Because most of the converts to communism had been radicals, and they had infiltrated most successfully into radical or liberal organizations, the suspicion took another form in undiscriminating minds: anybody who had any ideas which looked queer to his neighbors might be a Communist, or something like a Communist. And because these suspicions were rife, there was a wide-open chance for zealots (of whom the most furious were some of the very people who had got hooked in the nineteen-thirties, and were working out a savage atonement for their error) and for ambitious politicians to brand many decent and conscientious citizens as virtual traitors, thus placing upon them a stigma which they might never live down. The chain of circumstances that had begun with Communist secrecy reached very far indeed.

And it has reached even farther than that. For, as a result of the inquisitions of various congressional committees, and the government loyalty checks, and the strange drama of Alger Hiss, and the fulminations of Senator McCarthy, and the terrorization of parts of the entertainment world by the publication of *Red Channels*, and the charges made against many school and college teachers, a great many useful and productive people have been frightened into a nervous conformity. If a college instructor, lecturing on economic theory, reaches the point in his lecture where he should explain the respects in which Karl Marx was right in his economic diagnosis, he is in a dither: suppose some neurotic student should report that he is teaching communism? If a schoolteacher so much as mentions Russia, she wonders what tongues may start wagging in the Parent-Teacher Association. If a businessman gets in the mail an appeal for funds for European refugees, he looks uneasily at the letterhead and wonders if it may represent some group he'd rather not get entangled with. If a politician running for the city council campaigns for better housing, he knows well that his opponent will probably call his proposal "communistic," or at any rate "leftist"—an inclusive term which might be applied to almost anything, but has vaguely opprobrious overtones and may lose him votes by the thousands. At many a point in American life, adventurous and constructive thought is stifled by apprehension.

That behind this uneasy scapegoat hunting is the sense of frustration produced by living under the tensions of an uneasy day was manifest during the uproar over the removal of General MacArthur in the spring of 1951. For perhaps the most striking thing about that great debate was not the speeches and counter-speeches, or the interminable sessions of the Joint Congressional Committee which interviewed officials at length, but the floods of venomous letters received by newspaper editors and radio commentators who did not favor the great General. It was almost as if some wellspring of poison had been tapped. One realized then how many people there were whom the state of international affairs generally, and the war in Korea in particular, had strained beyond their endurance: they had to throw something at somebody, in a paroxysm of anger. The outright expression of this rancor was short-lived, and when Bobby Thomson hit his home run, and whole communities were all just Giant fans and Dodger fans again, one could recognize once more the familiar good humor of the American democracy. Yet the basic question remained: How can we maintain mutual trust, and an invigorating freedom of thought and expression, in a nation which for an indefinite time must carry heavy and uncertain responsibilities abroad, and meanwhile be unrelaxed in its armed strength?

We are by nature a sanguine people, but never before have we been subjected to the sort of prolonged strain that we feel today, and our patience, humor, and courage are being sorely tested.

Chapter **18**

What Have We Got Here?

FOR the March 4, 1951, issue of *This Week*, a magazine that goes as a supplement to over ten million readers of Sunday newspapers, the editor, William I. Nichols, wrote an article (later reprinted in the *Reader's Digest*) called "Wanted: A New Name for 'Capitalism.' " Arguing that the word is no longer the right one to fit our present American system, because in too many people's minds, especially in other parts of the world, "it stands for the primitive economic system of the nineteenth century," Mr. Nichols asked: "How shall we describe this system— imperfect, but always improving, and always capable of further improvement—where men move forward together, working together, building together, producing always more and more, and sharing together the rewards of their increased production?" He said he had heard various suggestions, such as "the new capitalism," "democratic capitalism," "economic democracy," "industrial democracy," "distributism," "mutualism," and "productivism," but wondered if there might not be a better term. And he invited readers to write in their own suggestions in a coupon printed in the magazine.

Fifteen thousand coupons came back with suggestions. "Never in my whole editorial experience," said Mr. Nichols afterward, "have I touched so live a nerve."

Perhaps one reason for this extraordinary response was that the idea of asking readers to do something simple and easy about an idea thrown at them—"as if it were a box-top contest," as Mr. Nichols said—was an apt journalistic stroke. But surely it also suggested the existence in the United States of a very widespread feeling that we've got something here—something working reasonably well and at any rate going full tilt—that defies all the old labels.

And I suspect that one reason why so many people feel this way is that here in the United States we have not been constructing a system as such, but tinkering with and repairing and rebuilding, piece by piece, an old system to make it run better, as I tried to suggest in the chapter on "The Revolt of the American Conscience"; and that accordingly we have arrived at a transformed product which might be likened to an automobile continually repaired, while running, by means of new parts taken from any old car which seemed to suit the immediate purpose of the repairers, with the result that in the end it is hard to say whether what we have is a Buick or a Cadillac or a Ford.

In the various chapters of this book I have tried to show how this patchwork process has taken place. In the nineteenth century we had in the United States a combination of federal and state and local governments—the federal component being small and very limited in its duties—which left business to operate pretty much as it pleased. But these governments permitted businessmen to organize corporations which were given special rights and privileges, and while these rights and privileges worked wonderfully in providing incentives for men to build up lively and inventive businesses, they had other unforeseen effects. They made the lone workman, whose income was determined by the Iron Law of Wages, pretty nearly helpless before his employer; they gave an enormous share of the fruits of the enterprise to this employer; and they also gave huge power to the men who controlled the supplies of money without which the employers found it difficult to operate. At the turn of the century America seemed in danger of becoming a land in which the millionaires had more and more and the rest had less and less, and where a few financiers had a strangle hold, not only on the country's economic apparatus, but on its political apparatus too.

This outraged the democratic spirit of the country, the national sense of fair play. So we went to work to change things—not by revolution but by a series of experimental revisions of the system. When it broke down badly in the Great Depression the repair work and reconstruction were pretty drastic, and some was foolish, but the same basic principle of unrevolutionary and experimental change prevailed. After some years of this there was considerable uncertainty whether the engine would ever run again without wheezing and knocking. But when World War II came along, we discovered that if Washington jammed the accelerator right down to the floor boards the engine began to run smoothly and fast. And when the war was over, and Washington released the accelerator, it still hummed. What had happened to bring about this astonishing result?

The answer, in brief, is that through a combination of patchwork revisions of the system—tax laws, minimum wage laws, subsidies and guarantees and regulations of various sorts, plus labor union pressures and new management attitudes—we had repealed the Iron Law of Wages. We had brought about a virtually automatic redistribution of income from the well-to-do to the less well-to-do. And this did not stall the machine but actually stepped up its power. Just as an individual business seemed to run best when it plowed part of its profits into improvements, so the business system as a whole seemed to run better if you plowed some of the national income into improvements in the income and status of the lower income groups, enabling them to buy more goods and thus to expand the market for everybody. We had discovered a new frontier to open up: the purchasing power of the poor.

That, it seems to me, is the essence of the Great American Discovery. And it has its corollary: that if you thus bring advantages to a great lot of previously underprivileged people, they will rise to their opportunities and, by and large, will become responsible citizens.

II

At present we have a very large and powerful central government. It continues to expand as if in response to some irresistible law of growth—not only because of the obligations which war and Cold War have imposed upon it, but because of our increasing interdependence as a more and more urbanized people with more and more complex institutions. The government regulates business in innumerable ways, as we saw in Chapter 16. It constantly interferes with the operations of the once almighty economic law of supply and demand, the law of the market place. It provides all sorts of subsidies and guarantees to groups who have convinced it, rightly or wrongly, that they need such help. And furthermore it acknowledges two great responsibilities, the recognition of which was forced upon it during the miserable years of the Great Depression. One of these is a responsibility for seeing that people in an economic jam are helped to their feet—if not by their relatives and friends, or by local relief, or by state relief, then by federal relief if necessary. And the other is a responsibility for seeing that the economic system as a whole does not break down.

The government therefore maintains certain control powers over the national economy *as a whole*; and in a time of emergency like that which has followed the onset of the Korean War, these powers are extended. But it does not try to run our individual businesses (with certain exceptions such as the atomic power industry, which for security purposes is an island of socialism in a sea of private management). For we recognize that our businesses are better run if they remain in private hands. The past dozen years or so have offered a triumphant demonstration of the validity of this belief. For they have seen privately managed American business not only do a brilliant job of huge-scale war production, but also foster a startling variety of advances in technology.

Nor, for that matter, does the federal government take over the power of our state and local governments, though it subsidizes them to do many things which they cannot adequately do unaided. So there is a wide distribution of governmental powers. Our road system, for instance, is part local, part state, and only in minor degree federal. Our university and college system is partly state run, partly independent. And our school system is mostly locally run (by local public authority), partly church run, partly independent.

Furthermore we have an extraordinarily wide and proliferating assortment of voluntary institutions, associations, and societies which in their manifold ways contribute to the public good. Not only universities, schools, churches, hospitals, museums, libraries, and social agencies in great variety, but also societies for the protection or promotion of practically everything: if you want to feed European children, or protect our wild ducks, or promote zoning systems, or agitate for more freedom for corporations, or extend church work, or make boys into Boy Scouts, or save the redwoods, you will find a private organization dedicated to this purpose, and sometimes there will be several of them. There are also the foundations, offspring of idealism and the estate tax. And an endless range of trade associations, professional associations, alumni and alumnae associations, service clubs, and lodges. As a people we are great joiners, campaigners, and voluntary group helpers and savers and reformers and improvers and promoters. Get together half a dozen like-minded Americans and pretty soon you'll have an association, an executive secretary, a national program, and a fund-raising campaign.

Nor is it easy to draw a sharp line between the voluntary organizations on the one hand and either business or the government on the other. When a good part of the money contributed in a Community Chest campaign comes from local corporations, and a mighty foundation draws its resources from an automobile company, and the private air lines fly over airways maintained by the federal government, and a university may be partly state-supported and partly privately supported (and in addition may be subsidized for certain research work by the federal government), the lines are blurred indeed. And as we saw in Chapter 16, there is constant consultation and collaboration between people who are working on the same problem in private business, in private public-service organizations, in the government, and in state and private institutions of learning.

Under such circumstances it is fair to say that the moral and intellectual strength of the United States is based in considerable degree upon private organizations which are as consecrated to the idea of public duty as governmental ones could be, and in part perform services almost indistinguishable from governmental ones, but provide at the same time vastly more diversity and flexibility of approach, and vastly more opportunity for the free play of individual talent and interest, than could be harnessed in any other way. And that the American system as a whole is such a mixture of different things, arrived at in such diverse, unsystematic, and even haphazard ways, that possibly its strength lies in the very fact that you can't put a label to it.

Over every proposal for a further change in the complicated design of the national economic machine there is hot argument. Will this measure undermine the incentive to work and save and invest and invent? Will it give tyrannical power to Washington? Does this group of people, or this industry, really need aid? Can the government afford it? Does it set a good or a bad precedent? People can get apoplectic over such issues—and no wonder, for the development of this new American system is highly experimental, and we don't know whether we can continue to make it work.

Take a look at a few of the uncertainties.

During the postwar years inflation, though never acute, has been almost uninterrupted, and in sum has been a serious menace to our economic health. We don't know whether we can maintain our fast pace without continuing inflation.

Even before the Korean war we had pretty nearly reached the limit of taxation—the limit beyond which the burden would become so intolerable that the incentive to produce would be weakened and tax evasion would become a monumental rather than a minor problem. We don't know whether we can reduce this load or increase our productivity fast enough to take care of it.

If the Soviets should change their policy so convincingly that we could ease up on military expenditures, we don't know whether we could step up domestic production fast enough to prevent a depression.

If total war should come, we don't know whether the federal debt would become so astronomical that the credit of the federal government would be shaken.

In any case, we don't know whether the government has taken on so many financial responsibilities, since it added to its own previous authority much of the authority once exercised by Wall Street, that there is not a danger of a new kind of panic and financial collapse at some time in the future—a panic resulting from the inability, not of private financiers, but of public financiers, to maintain the values they have undertaken to guarantee. We think we know a great deal more about economics than we did a generation ago, but we cannot be surer that we are living in a New Era than were the moguls of Wall Street who cherished that innocent faith in 1929.

And in addition, we don't know at exactly what point a policy of aid to disadvantaged men and women degenerates into a demoralizing policy of handouts to people who would rather accept federal bounties than extend themselves. Some are sure we have already crossed this line; others are sure we haven't.

So it is just as well that every time we tinker with this experimental system there should be energetic and protracted debate.

But the fury of our political campaigns, and the angry disputes over this or that congressional bill, detract our attention from a remarkable fact: that despite the purple language which is tossed about, very few Americans seriously propose any *really wholesale* change in our evolving American system. (And at that, our stormiest debates in recent years have not been over domestic policy but over foreign policy, or over the supposed influence of American Communists and their friends and alleged friends over foreign policy.) There is a large amount of antipathy to the administration in power in Washington. There are numerous people who would like to curb federal power, repeal various laws now on the books, pare down the bureaucracy, minimize relief. There are others who want the government to take on new labors and new powers, like that of running a great medical insurance program. Yet the vast majority of Americans agree that the government should continue to accept an overall responsibility for the satisfactory operation of the national economy; that it should continue to accept responsibility for relief when necessary; that it should supervise and regulate business to *some* extent; that it should subsidize and guarantee various groups to *some* extent —but that it should keep its intervention limited, and should let the great bulk of business remain under private management. The seething debate is over how much of this and how much of that we need, but the area of virtual agreement is very wide; and this includes letting private business remain in private hands.

For we believe we have demonstrated that business can be far more resourcefully and ingeniously run by private managers; and furthermore that these private managers can run most if not all of it with such consideration for the general public welfare that they can achieve for us all that government ownership would bring, plus the efficiency, flexibility, and adventurousness which government ownership would jeopardize—and without the danger of tyranny that government ownership might invite.

In short, there is subconscious agreement among the vast majority of Americans that the United States is not evolving *toward* socialism, but *past* socialism.

III

I say subconscious agreement because in our conscious thought most of us still seem to be the victims of an old idea that has become a delusion. This is the idea that there is in the world a sort of inevitable trend of progress toward socialism; that people who want the government to do more than it is doing are therefore liberal (if they are polite about it) or radical (if they are aggressive about it); and that people who want the management of business to remain in private hands are therefore conservative (if polite) or reactionary (if aggressive).

Historically there has been ample warrant for this picture of the political spectrum. During the past century or so the principal political changes have been in the direction of getting the government to do more and more for what was thought to be the common weal; and the people who didn't want the government to act, who wanted to dig their heels in and stop it from acting, were rightly known as conservatives. By contrast the people who went whole hog for government intervention, to the point of wanting the government to take over the ownership and operation of the principal private industries, in short the Socialists, were rightly known as radicals; and those who wanted it to take over virtually everything, by violent revolution if necessary, in short the Communists, were rightly known as extreme radicals. But now the United States has been demonstrating pretty convincingly that the system that works best of all, combining most of the genuine advantages of governmental responsibility and of private initiative, and avoiding the disadvantages of each, is one in which governmental intervention is limited and private industry and private associations have a great degree of freedom; and also that one of the mightiest advantages of this system is the way in which it diffuses very widely the decision-making power and the opportunities that go with it. In short, that the direction of progress is now different from what people had supposed it was.

Yet the delusion persists that the trend of the times is toward socialism—and perhaps even toward communism. Though our production, our wealth, our standard of living are the wonder of the world; though Britain under Socialist leadership had to come to us for financial aid; though, as Isabel Lundberg wrote in 1947, we are in a position to offer tangible goods and expert technological services to nations to whom the Russians, for all their loud talk of material benefits, could not offer so much as a shoelace; though our evolved system is potentially the most revolutionary force on earth, nevertheless so fixed in our minds is this delusion that when we face foreign problems we instinctively consider ourselves the natural allies of conservatism, and we tend to behave as if we wanted to stifle the natural hopes of mankind for a decenter way of life. Instinctively we set our faces against change. And preposterously we think of Soviet Russia —which has submerged the historic Communist aim of a better life for the masses of people in an aim of national aggrandizement through barbaric means—as if it and its allied zealots and dupes represented radicalism, represented a disposition of things toward which we ourselves might drift if we did not hold fast against change; as if Soviet Russia were something other than a despotic medievalism which was developed out of a revolutionary attempt to meet the problems of the nineteenth century—problems which we ourselves have long since surmounted.

It is time we rid ourselves of this notion about Russia. It is time we realize that when we battle against communism, we are battling against the past, not against the future. It is time, too, we rid ourselves of the notion that the direction of change at home is toward socialism or communism, and that therefore loyal Americans must stand pat. This notion is a stultifying force in our life. It causes well-meaning people to imagine that anyone with unorthodox ideas must be suspect of subversive intent. It tends to cramp men's imaginations into a timid conformity. It tends to constrict our generous impulses as a people. Combined with the fear of large-scale war, and especially of atomic war, it eats away at our bold confidence in ourselves and our destiny.

We would do better to put it out of our minds, and to realize that our sobering position of leadership in the world is founded upon the fact that we have not stood still. The story of the changes in the contours of American life that we have hammered out in the first half of this twentieth century, is a triumphant story, however harsh may have been some of our experiences in the interim and however obscure may be the shape of the future. We would do well to think of our accomplishment thus far as but the preface to what we may accomplish in the second half of the century if we can continue to invent, improve, and change—and can keep a good heart. The courageous nation, like the courageous man, is not unhappy at the thought of dangers beside the road ahead, but welcomes them as challenges to be faced and overwhelmed along an adventurous course.

Appendix

Sources and Obligations

This book grew out of an article entitled "The Big Change" which I wrote in the spring of 1950 for the Centennial Number of *Harper's Magazine,* published in October, 1950; which in turn drew upon the text of a talk I had given on "Social Changes of Our Time" before the Pennsylvania Historical Society on February 4, 1949, which was printed in *The Pennsylvania Magazine of History and Biography,* April, 1949. My Centennial article dealt with the changes in the United States between 1850 and 1950, with special attention to the distribution of wealth and opportunity; after it appeared, I decided to develop this theme in book form, but to concentrate upon the period between 1900 and 1950, which offered, it seemed to me, a more significant contrast than did the longer period.

While I was at work on the book I found that a number of other people were laboring in more or less the same vineyard. There was, for example, Lewis Galantière, who had written a fine article on "America Today" for the July, 1950, issue of *Foreign Affairs,* sketching the difference between the contemporary United States and European impressions of it. (This article was later printed in pamphlet form by the Overbrook Press, Stamford, Connecticut.) Mr. Galantière did much of the preliminary spadework for a Round Table Discussion on the Elements of a Free, Dynamic Society which was sponsored by the Advertising Council, Inc., and was held under the chairmanship of Paul G. Hoffman at the Waldorf-Astoria Hotel in New York on April 16, 1951. The various participants in that conference, especially Peter F. Drucker, who produced the principal paper for it, seemed to me to see the evolution of present-day America from points of view somewhat like mine. And so did Russell Davenport and the editors of *Fortune,* who in the February, 1951, issue of that magazine and then in a book called *U.S.A., The Permanent Revolution* (Prentice-Hall, 1951) played the changes on themes parallel to those of *The Big Change.* To all these people I am indebted for ideas which fitted so well with those I was putting on paper that I could not always be sure when I was appropriating what they had thought of first and when I was on my own.

I am indebted, too, to a number of colleagues at Harper & Brothers who have produced material for me, or suggested leads to follow, or have read and criticized my manuscript in early drafts, or have otherwise helped me: notably John Fischer, Eric Larrabee, Cass Canfield, Ordway Tead, John A. Kouwenhoven, Russell Lynes, Rose Daly, and Waldo W. Sellew. Others whose help I should particularly like to acknowledge—without involving them in responsibility for the results—are Donald K. David, Richardson Wood, John Bartlow Martin, William McNear Rand, Leo Wolman, Walter White, Robert L. Heilbroner, Carroll Wilson, and Wayne Andrews. I owe a bow to the staff of Facts, Inc., of New York, an organization which is a researcher's delight in checking information; to Theodore Bolton, the helpful librarian of the Century Association; and especially to Ralph A. Beals, Rollin Alger Sawyer, and numerous other members of the indefatigable staff of the New York Public Library. My thanks go also to my sister, Hildegarde Allen, who provided me with several useful sources on the 1900 period; my son, Oliver Ellsworth Allen, for aid at many points; and above all my wife, Agnes Rogers Allen, not only for general aid and comfort but for a great deal of material, a variety of suggestions, and illuminating page-by-page criticism.

This is an inadequately partial list of those to whom I am indebted; if I tried to make it complete it would be interminable.

In my previous books I have listed, chapter by chapter, the precise sources of facts which I thought serious scholars and other writers might question or for any reason want to track down. Since *The Big Change* is primarily a summary, arrangement, analysis, and interpretation of reasonably familiar data rather than a journey of historical exploration, and since I have indicated in the text the sources for some specific facts which might be subject to challenge, it seems unnecessary to do this here. But I should like to pay my respects to certain books and documents which I have found particularly helpful:

William Allen White's *Autobiography* (Macmillan, 1946) for its insights into politics at the turn of the century and later, and especially into the movement which I have called "The Revolt of the American Conscience."

The five volumes of Mark Sullivan's *Our Times* (Scribner) and especially the first three of them (published in 1926, 1927, and 1930 respectively) for varied sidelights on American life in the early years of the century.

Clyde Brion Davis's *The Age of Indiscretion* (Lippincott, 1950) for its brisk account of life in a Missouri town at the beginning of the century.

Oscar Handlin's *This Was America* (Harvard University Press, 1949) for its collection of foreigners' impressions of the American scene.

Robert Hunter's *Poverty* (Macmillan, 1904) for its conscientious study of life on "The Other Side of the Tracks."

Two books edited by Robert A. Woods, *The City Wilderness* (Houghton Mifflin, 1898) and *Americans in Process* (Houghton Mifflin, 1902), for their detailed and thoughtful examination of Boston slum life in those years.

A group of classics of economic and social analysis and measurement of the intermediate period: *Recent Economic Changes* (McGraw-Hill, 1929) and *Recent Social Trends* (McGraw-Hill, 1933); *Middletown* and *Middletown in Transition,* by Robert S. Lynd and Helen Merrell Lynd (Harcourt Brace, 1929 and 1937 respectively); and *America's Capacity to Consume,* by Maurice Leven, Harold G. Moulton, and Clark Warburton (Brookings Institution, 1934). And also the subsequent volume, *America's Needs and Resources,* by J. Frederick Dewhurst and associates (Twentieth Century Fund, 1947).

Gunnar Myrdal's *An American Dilemma* (Harper, 1944) for its searching discussion of the position and predicament of the Negro.

Van Wyck Brooks's *The Confident Years,* 1885-1915 (Dutton, 1952) for its fresh interpretation of trends in literary thought, including those after 1915.

Twentieth Century Unlimited, edited by Bruce Bliven (Lippincott, 1950), for its collection of studies of developments in various sectors of American life, especially the arts.

Low-Income Families and Economic Stability. Materials on the Problem of Low-Income Families. Assembled by the subcommittee on low-income families. Joint Committee on the Economic Report. 81st Congress, 1st session. I have drawn heavily on this document for my analysis of poverty at the mid-century at the beginning of Chapter 15.

And *Shares of Upper Income Groups in Income and Savings,* by Simon Kuznets. Occasional Paper 35 of the National Bureau of Economic Research, Inc. I have drawn on this document for my analysis of wealth's slice in the pie, in the same chapter.

I should also like to mention the reports of the President's Council of Economic Advisers for recent years; the successive British Productivity Reports, some of which are highly illuminating; successive volumes of the *World Almanac,* the figures in which often turn up interesting clues to what has been happening; and, finally, the 1949 edition of *The United States Since 1865,* by Louis M. Hacker and Benjamin B. Kendrick (Appleton-Century-Crofts, Inc.), which I have used for constant reference on the standard data of American history during the 1900-1950 period.

F. L. A.

Index

A & P stores, 115-16
Abrams, Frank Whittemore, 247
Accidents, industrial, 56
Adams, Henry, 115, 187-88, 196, 198
Addams, Jane, 100
Adirondack Mountains, 16, 32
Advertising, 117-18, 139, 224-25, 228
Advertising Council, 249-50
Agriculture, Department of, 129
Aiken, S. C., 16
Air-conditioning, 120
Albania, 160
Alger, Horatio, Jr., 63-65, 69-70, 80, 149
All-America team, 26
America First, 161
American Chemical Society, 243
American Dilemma, An, 181
American Federation of Labor, 53, 153
American Steel and Wire Company, 75
American Sugar Refining Company, 71
American Telephone and Telegraph Company, 70, 237, 247
American Tin Plate Company, 75, 76
American Tube Company, 75
Anderson, Maxwell, 138
Anderson, Sherwood, 138, 269
Antin, Mary, 60
Anti-Semitism, 266
Apperson automobile, 116
Archbold, John D., 71, 73, 87-88
Armory Show, *1913,* 134, 269
Armstrong, Edwin H., 119
Armstrong, Louis, 182, 276
Asheville, N. C., 29-30
Assembly line, 111, 188, 195
Astor, Mrs. William, 35, 40
Astor, William Waldorf, 34
Atlantic City, 16
Atlantic Pact, 174

Atom bomb, 165, 279
Atomic power, 174, 188-89, 196
Auden, W. H., 270-71
Audit Bureau of Circulations, 244
Austria, 160
Automobiles, 7, 33, 116-17, 190, 221
    closed car, 123
    maintenance, 123-24
    parkways, 124-25
    social effects, 125-30
    See also Ford, Henry
Automotive Safety Council, 128
Avery, Sewell, 250
Aviation, 118-19, 196-97, 244-45

Baedeker's guide, 14, 16
Baekeland, Leo H., 119-20
Baer, George F., 83-84
Baker, George Fisher, 64, 65, 103, 246
Baker, Ray Stannard, 128
Bankers, 78, 141, 149-50, 237-39
Bankhead, Tallulah, 227
Bar Harbor, Me., 16
Baseball, 24
Basketball, 25
Bataan, 165
Bathrooms, 20-21
Bauer, Hank, 209
Beaulieu, 34
Beaumont, Tex., 118
Beauty parlor, 135
Beech Creek Railway Co., 42
Beechwood, 35
Beiderbecke, Bix, 276
Belmont, Mrs. O. H. P., 101
Benedict, Ruth, 273
Benny, Jack, 224-25
Bentley, Irene, 35
"Berkshire Hills," 114-15
Berle, Milton, 268

Berlin, Irving, 134
Berlin airlift, 174
Berra, Yogi, 206
Bessemer process, 115
Beverly, Mass., 16
Bicycling, 25
Bierce, Ambrose, 5
Big Bull Market, 141, 148
Billboard magazine, 276
Biltmore, 29-30
Birth rate, 200-201, 203
Bliven, Bruce, 260-61
Blois, Château of, 29
Boardinghouses, 17
Bogart, Humphrey, 224
Bok, Edward, 100, 117
Bonus Army, 150
Boom, speculative, 141-42
Boston, Mass., 15, 45-48, 52, 55, 57
Bourget, Paul, 31, 35-36, 58
Bow, Clara, 135
Bowling, 25
Brain Trusts, 151-52, 155
Breakers, The, 29, 228
Briscoe automobile, 116
Bronx River, 124
Brook Club, 227
Brookings Institution, 144
Brooks, Van Wyck, 5-6, 269-70
Brown, Bobby, 206
Bryan, William Jennings, 23, 85, 89, 90
Bryson, Lyman, 274
Buffalo, N. Y., 21
Buick, David Dunbar, 116
Bulge, Battle of the, 165, 172-73
Bunche, Ralph, 182, 266
Burlington Railroad, 73-74
Burr, Anna Robeson, 31
Business expansion, 138-39
Busses, 125

Cadillac automobile, 123
Cahill, Marie, 35
Cahuenga Pass, Los Angeles, 125
Campanella, Roy, 183
Canby, Henry Seidel, 11, 13
Canham, Erwin D., 249
Cannon, Jimmy, 182
Cannon, Joe, 106
Carnegie, Andrew, 4, 27-28, 32-33, 64, 70, 115, 209, 246

Carnegie Corporation, 100, 248
Carnegie Steel Company, 70, 115
Carrier, Willis H., 120
Carthaginian culture, 259-60, 277
Casson, Herbert N., 76
Castellane, Count Boni de, 42
Cather, Willa, 138
Cedar Rapids, Iowa, 248-49
Cedarhurst, N. Y., 16
Century, The, 22, 91-92
Century Engineering Company, 248-49
Chandler automobile, 116
Chaperonage, 10-11
Chase, Stuart, 212
Chemical engineering, 194
Chewing tobacco, 21
Chiang Kai-shek, 175, 281
Chicago, Ill., 5, 15, 25, 52, 60
Child labor, 56
Chillicothe, Mo., 20, 23-24
China, 160, 176
Christian Science Monitor, 249
Chrysler Corporation, 246
Churchgoing, 136-37, 261-64
Churchill, Lord Randolph, 42
Churchill, Winston, 173, 272
Cigarettes, 21
Cigars, 21
CIO (Congress of Industrial Organizations), 153
Clark, Colin, 195
Clark, John Bates, 66
Clayton Act, 101, 153
Cleanliness, personal, 20-21
Cleveland, Anne, 266
Cleveland, Ohio, 33
Clews, Henry, 40, 73
Clift, Montgomery, 224
Clothing, men's, 230-31
    women's, 9-10, 134-35, 219-20, 231
    working class, 59-60
Coal strike, *1902,* 83-84
Cobb, Frank I., 96
Cocktail party, 135
Cod, Cape, 17
Coghlan, Ralph, 252
Colbert, Lester Lum, 246
Coleman, Jimmy, 209
Collins, Floyd, 133
Colony Club, 227
Colorado Springs, Colo., 16

Committee for Economic Development, 249
Committee to Defend America, 161
Commonwealth Ave., Boston, 45-48
Communication, mass, 22-23, 128
Communists, 150, 154, 159, 174, 180, 263, 280, 282, 292, 293
Commuters, 15-16
Competition, 74, 116
Conant, James B., 194
Conrad, Frank, 138
Conservation, 17-18
Control, government, 171-72, 239-40
Conventions, trade, 245-46
Coolidge, Calvin, 132, 140, 142-43, 171
Corbin, Louise, 42
Cordiner, Ralph J., 247
Corning Glass Co., 197, 252
Corporations, 68-69, 70-71, 168-69
Corporations, and bankers, 237-39
    directors, 235
    and government, 239-40
    management, 235-37, 250-52
    political nature, 252-53
    professionalism, 241-44
    and public, 240-41
    social nature, 253-55
    and stockholders, 235-37
    trade conventions, 245-46
    and unions, 255-58
Corsair III, 32
Cosmopolitan Magazine, 80
Costello, Frank, 265
Cottages, summer, 16-18
Cotton, 183-84
Craig, Cleo F., 247
Croly, Herbert, 31
Curtis, Cyrus, 22, 117
Curzon, Lord, 42
Cushing, Dr. Harvey, 203
Cuspidors, 21
Czechoslovakia, 160, 161
Czolgosz, Leon, 92

Dallas, Tex., 14
Damrosch, Walter, 275
Dancing, 136, 232
Davis, Clyde Brion, 20-21, 23-24
Davison, Harry, 101
D-Day, 165
Death rate, 202

Debs, Eugene V., 6, 89
Deficit spending, 154
De Forest, Dr. Lee, 119
Dell, Floyd, 269
Dempsey, Jack, 133
Denmark, 160
Department stores, 115
Depression, 158, 164, 165-66, 169, 171, 190, 201, 212, 232, 242, 252, 279, 280, 286-87
    Hoover administration, 146-47
    and Negroes, 179-80
    political consequences, 150-51
    psychological effects, 148-50
    stock prices, 147-48
    unemployment, 148
Desmond, Harry W., 31
DeVoto, Bernard, 272
Diesel, Rudolf, 120
Diesel engine, 120, 196
Diet, 1900, 20
Dill, James B., 75
DiMaggio, Joe, 206, 227
Dinners, wealthy class, 37-39
Divorce, 13, 135, 201
Dodd, Samuel C. T., 74
Doherty, R. F., 34
Dolliver, Senator Jonathan P., 103
Dos Passos, John, 138
Douglas, Lewis W., 248
Dreiser, Theodore, 5, 137, 138
Drinking, 135
Drucker, Peter F., 240, 252
Dunn, Keith, 248-49
Dunne, Finley Peter, 78, 95
Du Pont family, 116, 159
Durant, William C., 116

Eastern states, 25, 26
Eastman, Max, 269
Economics, classical, 65-68
    See also New Deal
Ederle, Gertrude, 133
Education, 46, 60, 222
    college, 65-66
    progressive, 137, 263-64
Egypt, 32, 176
Elections, 88-89
Electricity, 19, 115
Electric-utility industry, 191
Electronic machines, 193-94

Eliot, T. S., 138, 267, 270
Ellington, Duke, 182, 276
Ely, Richard T., 66
Emmett, Bay, 10
Engineering, 194, 242
England, *see* Great Britain
Entertaining, wealthy class, 34-39
Ethiopia, 158
Evening Telegraph, Philadelphia, 80

Factory system, 49-50
Fair Deal, 172
Fair employment laws, 182, 239
Farmers, 18-19, 20, 148, 150, 152, 169, 190-92, 195, 205, 211
Faulkner, William, 272
Federal Reserve Bank of New York, 248
Federal Reserve System, 143
Federal Trade Commission, 240
Ferguson, Bob, 10
Fessenden, Reginald A., 119
Fight for Freedom Committee, 161
Filling stations, 121, 124
Finland, 160
Fitzgerald, F. Scott, 269
Flagler house, Palm Beach, 30, 228
Flair magazine, 217
Fleming, Alexander, 189
Fleming, Sir John Ambrose, 119
Flexner, Abraham, 100
Football, 25-26
Foraker, Joseph B., 88
Ford, Henry, 101, 109, 114, 188, 195
   Model T, 110-11, 113, 116
   wages, 112-13
Ford, Henry, II, 246
Ford Motor Company, 110
Forestry, 30
Fork truck, 193
Fortune, 149, 197, 246, 248, 254
Foy, Eddie, 35
France, 160, 161
Franco, Francisco, 160
Franklin, Benjamin, 64, 65, 80
Franklin automobile, 116
Freud, Sigmund, 134, 137, 263
Frick, Henry C., 31

Galbraith, J. Kenneth, 154
Gallup polls, 159
Garages, 121, 124

Gas lighting, 19
Gates, Frederick T., 99, 100
General Education Board, 99
General Electric Company, 247
General Motors Corporation, 116, 215, 235, 246
Gerard, James W., 10-11
Germany, 158, 162, 165, 173
Giacosa, G., 57, 60
Gibson, Charles Dana, 40-41
Giddings, Franklin H., 61
Gifford, Walter S., 247
Goelet, May, 42
Goelet, Mrs. Ogden, 35
Goelet house, Newport, 30
Gold reserve, 82
Gold standard, 154
Golf, 25, 33
Gompers, Samuel, 53-54
Gould, Anna, 42
Gould, Jay, 72
Gould house, Lakewood, N. J., 30
Government control, 171-72, 239-40, 286-89
Grand Hotel, Rome, 32
Grand Trianon, 34
Grange, Red, 133
Granger, Farley, 224
Grant, Cary, 224
Grattan, C. Hartley, 251, 267-68, 271
Great Britain, 160, 161, 164, 292
Great Train Robbery, The, 119
Greece, 174, 259, 277
Gregg, Dr. Alan, 202
Guadalcanal, 165
Guggenheimer, Randolph, 37-39

Hadley, Arthur T., 80
Hall-Mills murder case, 132-33
Handy, W. C., 276
Hanna, Mark, 5-6, 85-86, 92
Harding, Warren G., 132
Harper's Magazine, 22, 91, 125, 211, 220, 251
Harriman, Edward H., 64, 65, 72, 73-74, 95, 246
Harris, Herbert, 54
Harrison, George Leslie, 248
Harvard University, 25, 204
   Graduate School of Business, 241
   School of Public Health, 203, 243
Hatteras, Cape, 165

Hayes, H. Gordon, 220-221
Haywood, William D., 102
Hearst, William Randolph, 87
Heilbroner, Robert L., 211
Heinz sign, 15
Hemingway, Ernest, 137, 138, 269
Henderson, Judge, 88
Henderson, Lawrence J., 202
Henry, O., 12
Henry Street Settlement, 100
Hepburn Act, 96
Herald, Boston, 80
Hering, Frank, 26
Highland Falls, N. Y., 32
Hill, George Washington, 250
Hiss, Alger, 282
Hitler, Adolf, 150, 158, 160-61, 162,
    173, 280, 281
Hoffman, Paul, 70, 113
Holderness, N. H., 123
Holding companies, 75-77, 152
Holman, Eugene, 247
Holmes, Oliver Wendell, 54
Hoover, Herbert, 143, 146-47, 152,
    155, 166, 171
Hoover, Ike, 82, 131, 132
Hoover Commission, 172
Hoovervilles, 148
Hope, Arthur J., 26
Hope, Bob, 249
Hopkins, Harry, 151
Horse-and-carriage life, 7-8, 15
Hotel Bristol, Paris, 32
Hotels, 21, 127
    resort, 17
Houses, middle class, 44-48
    wealthy class, 28-33, 228-29
Housing, working class, 57-58, 60
Houston, Tex., 14
Hull House, 100
Hunt, Richard Morris, 29
Hunter, Robert, 56, 59
Hyde, James Hazen, 34
Hyde Park, N. Y., 29, 228

Ice, 19-20
Idle Hour, 29
Immigration, 50-53
Income tax, graduated, 106, 215-16
Incomes, 27-28
    distribution, *1948,* 209-16
    middle class, 43-44, 45, 47

Indo-China, 176
Industrialism, 50-51
Inflation, 168, 173-74, **289**
Institutions, social, 23-24
Interchangeable parts, 111
International Ladies' Garment Workers
    Union, 56
International Workers of the World,
    102
Interstate Commerce Commission, 81
Iran, 176
Irish, 52, 158
Iron, 115
Iron Law of Wages, 49-50, 54, 61, 285-
    286
Islesboro, Me., 16
Isolationism, 158-60, 175-76
Italians, 52
Italy, 158, 244
Ivins Syndicate Building, 14

James, Henry, 270
Japan, 158, 161-62, 165, 173
Jazz, 182
Jekyll Island Club, 32
Jerome, Jennie, 42
Jews, 52, 227
Johnson, Tom L., 99
Johnson, Van, 227
Jones, Bobby, 133
Jones, "Golden Rule," 99
Josephs, Devereux C., 248
Journal of Commerce, New York, 83
Joyce, James, 138, 270

Kettering, Charles F., 123
Keynes, John Maynard, 150, 154
Kindergarten Chats, 29
King, Willford I., 101
Kinsey, Dr. Alfred, 136
Kittyhawk, N. C., 118
Knickerbocker Club, 227
Korea, 172, 174, 176, 282, 287, 289
Krohn, William O., 56
Ku Klux Klan, 179
Kuznets, Simon, **214**

Labor, child, 56
Labor Department, 101
Labor unions, *see* Unions
Lacrosse, 24
Ladies' Home Journal, 22, 101, **117**

La Follette, Robert, 99
Lakewood, N. J., 16, 30, 33
Landon, A. M., 152
Landowska, Wanda, 276
Lardner, Ring, 269
Larned, William A., 34
Lawrence strike, *1912*, 102
League of Nations, 131
Leeds, William B., 77
Lehr, Harry, 35
Leiter, Mary, 42
Leland, Henry M., 111
Lend-Lease Act, 162
Lenox, Mass., 16, 228
Leopold and Loeb trial, 133
Lewis, John L., 153, 240
Lewis, Sinclair, 137, 138, 269
Life, 218, 272
Lindbergh, Charles A., 133
Lindsay, Vachel, 269
Links Club, 227
Little Bull Market, 146
Lobbyists, 87
Locomobile automobile, 116
London, Eng., 32
Long, Huey, 150
Long Island, N. Y., 16, 29
Lorimer, George Horace, 117
Los Angeles, Calif., 14, 16
Louis, Joe, 182
Lowell, A. Lawrence, 259
Lucas, Anthony F., 118
Lundberg, Isabel, 292
Lynchings, 178, 185-186

McAllister, Ward, 40
MacArthur, Gen. Douglas, 173, 174, 283
McCall's, 42
McCarthy, Sen. Joe, 282
McClure, S. S., 91, 117
McClure's, 90, 98
McCormack, Cyrus, 111
Mackaye, Benton, 124, 125
McKeesport, Pa., 58-59
McKinley, William, 84-86, 90, 92, 95
McNamara brothers, 102
Magazines, 22, 117, 223-24, 244, 271-73
Mailer, Norman, 273
Manchester, Mass., 16
Manchuria, 158

Manufacturing Chemists' Association, 244
Marble House, 29
Marconi, Guglielmo, 119
Markham, Edwin, 61-62
Marlborough, Duke of, 42
Marriage, 13, 41-43, 201
Marshall Plan, 174, 175, 248
Martin, Bradley, 34
Marx, Karl, 50, 53, 280, 281, 282
Marxism, 114
May, Cape, 16
Medicine, 202-3
Mellon, Andrew, 143
Mencken, H. L., 137, 269
Merritt Parkway, 125
Metropolitan Life Insurance Co., 249
Metropolitan Tower, 115
Michigan, Lake, 17
Middle class, incomes, 43-44, 45, 47
    mode of living, 44-48
Middletown, 121
Midwest, 26, 158
Millay, Edna St. Vincent, 138
Millet, Jean François, 61
Millionaires, *see* Wealthy class
Mitchell, Charles E., 139
Mize, Johnny, 206
Mobile, Ala., 180
Model T, 110-11, 116
Monterey, Calif., 17
Moore, James H., 77
Moore, William H., 77
Morgan, John Pierpont, 3-4, 5-6, 31-32, 37, 65, 73-74, 78-79, 82, 95-96, 102-3, 143, 145, 149, 238, 239, 246
Morgan, J. P. & Company, 76, 115, 143, 145, 159
Morley, John, 98
Morris, Lloyd, 36, 159, 268
Morton, J. Sterling, 30
Motion pictures, 22, 119, 223-25
Mumford, Lewis, 124, 125
Muncie, Ind., 22
Munich conference, 160
Munsey, Frank A., 117
Music, 274-76
Mussolini, Benito, 158, 160, 173, 244
Mutual Life Insurance Co., 248
Myrdal, Gunnar, 181, 184, 185

Nahant, Mass., 16
Narragansett Pier, R. I., 16
National Bureau of Economic Research, 209, 214
National City Bank, 139
National Conference of Charities and Correction, 56
National Economic Review, 185
National Office Management Association, 230
National Recovery Act, 153
National Safety Council, 128
Negroes, 52, 130, 211-12, 265-66
    arts and sports, 182-83
    and depression, 179-80
    lynchings, 178, 185-86
    and North, 178-81
    population, 177-78, 182
    and South, 177-82
Nelson, Ozzie and Harriet, 225
Neutrality Acts, 160, 161
New Deal, 150, 166, 191
    and currency, 154-55
    and economics, 152-53
    government expansion, 171-72
    and labor, 153-54
New England, 52
New Jersey Holding-company Act, 69
New York Central Railroad Co., 42, 114
New York City, 3-4, 14, 28-29, 31-32, 33, 40, 52, 55, 57, 61, 226
New York World's Fair, *1939*, 156-57
Newport, R. I., 16, 25, 29, 30, 32, 34-37, 101, 228
Newsboys' Lodging House, N. Y., 63
Newspapers, 23, 132-33
Nichols, William I., 284-85
Normandy, 165
Norris-La Guardia Anti-injunction Act, *1932*, 153
North Haven, Me., 16
Northern Pacific Railroad, 114
Northern Securities Company, 95, 98
Norway, 160
Nye, Gerald P., 159
Nylon, 120, 196, 220

Oakdale, Long Island, 29
Ochre Court, 35, 228
Ogden, Robert C., 99

O'Hara, John, 217
Ohio, 52
Oil, 118
Oil lamps, 19
Okies, 170
Oldfield, Barney, 109
Olds, Irving S., 247
Olds, Ransom, 111
O'Neill, Eugene, 137, 138, 268
Only Yesterday, 156
Open-hearth process, 115
Operators, stock-market, 72-73
Oppenheimer, Dr. J. Robert, 243-44
Ormond Beach, Fla., 33
Orwell, George, 273
Otto gas engine, 110
Outing magazine, 26
Owen Magnetic automobile, 116
Oxford, Earl of, 42

Painting, 273-74
Palm Beach, Fla., 16, 30
Panic, *see* Depression
Paris, Fr., 32
Parking space, 127
Parkways, 124-25
Paterson strike, *1913*, 102
Patten, Simon N., 66
Pearl Harbor, 160, 162
Peck, Gregory, 224
Peerless automobile, 116
Penicillin, 189
Pennsylvania, 25, 52
Pennsylvania Railroad, 70, 114
Pennsylvania Turnpike, 125
Penrose, Boies, 71
Pension plan, 203
Perkins, Tharon, 243
Philadelphia, Pa., 52
Phipps house, Pittsburgh, 30
Phonograph, 275-76
Pickford, Mary, 135
Pierce Arrow automobile, 116
Pinchot, Gifford, 30
Pipe tobacco, 21
Pittsburgh, Pa., 76
Plastics, 119-20
Pocantico Hills, 33
Polanyi, Karl, 148
Poll tax, 182
Pope automobile, 116

Population, 14, 51, 199
  birth rate, 200-201, 203
  death rate, 202
  drift, 205-6
  Negroes, 177-78, 182
Populist party, 89, 97
Post, George B., 29
Progressive party, 107
Prohibition, 104, 131-32
Proletariat, see Working class
Promoter, 78, 116
Proust, Marcel, 138, 270
Psychoanalysis, 137
Pujo, Arsène, 103
Pulitzer, Joseph, 96
Pullman car, 18
Puritanism, 134

Race relations, see Negroes
Radar, 189
Radio, 119, 223, 275
Railroads, 8, 18, 20, 70, 72, 87, 114,
  117, 125, 127
Raschi, Vic, 206
Rationing, 168-69
Ravage, M. E., 57, 59
Rayon, 120
Reader's Digest, 224, 273, 284
Recent Social Changes, 199
Reconstruction Finance Corporation,
  146, 152, 238
Red Channels, 282
Reed, John, 269
Reed, Philip Dunham, 247
Reformers, 99-100
Refrigeration, 19-20
Reid, Daniel G., 77
Réjane, 34
Religious skepticism, 136-37
Republican party, 96, 147
Research, 242
Resorts, 16-17
Ricardo, David, 49
Riis, Jacob A., 55, 60-61
Rizzuto, Phil, 206
Roads, 121-25
Robinson, Jackie, 183
Rockefeller, John D., 33, 34, 64, 65,
  68, 71, 74, 99, 100, 101, 246
Rockefeller, William, 65, 71-72, 246
Rockefeller Foundation, 100

Rogers, Agnes, 228
Rogers, H. H., 65, 73, 246
Roman Catholics, 226, 261, 263
Rome, It., 32
Roosevelt, Eleanor, 10, 183
Roosevelt, Franklin D., 146-147, 150-
  151, 159, 160, 161, 173
  See also New Deal; World War II
Roosevelt, Theodore, 6, 83-84, 86, 95-
  96, 97-98, 99, 103-4, 107, 151
Rowing, 24
Roxburghe, Duke of, 42
Rural Electrification Administration, 191
Ruth, Babe, 133

Salerno, It., 165
Salesmen, 139-40
San Bernardino, Calif., 16
San Diego, Calif., 16
Sandburg, Carl, 269
Santa Barbara, Calif., 16
Saratoga Springs, N. Y., 16
Sarnoff, David, 119
Saturday Evening Post, 22, 31, 101,
  117, 272
Scanlon system, 257
Schwab, Charles, 115
Scopes trial, 133
Scribner's, 22, 91
Scripps-Booth automobile, 116
Seabreeze, 32
Sears Roebuck & Company, 127, 129
Securities and Exchange Commission,
  215, 240
Security affiliates, 141
Segregation, 182
  See also Negroes
Self-starter, 123
Senate, U. S., 87-88
Servants, 44, 45, 221-22
Sexual attitudes, 1900, 10-11, 13-14
  1920, 134-36
  1950, 231-33
Shaffer, Van Vechten, 249
Shepard, Mrs., 28
Sherman Antitrust Act, 1890, 75, 81, 95
Sherry's Restaurant, 34
Sibley, Congressman Joseph C., 87-88
Simmons, Brig. Gen. James S., 203
Since Yesterday, 156, 280-81
Sinclair, Upton, 5-6, 150

Singer Building, 115
Skibo Castle, Scotland, 32-33
Skyscrapers, 115
Slavs, 52
Slichter, Sumner H., 239
Sloane, Mrs., 28
Smith, Cecil, 274-75
Soccer, 24, 37
Social Democrats, 89
Social institutions, 23-24
Social Security, 153
Socialism, 89, 97, 104, 107, 155, 291-93
Society, see Wealthy class
Sonnenberg, Ben, 253
South End House, Boston, 53
Soviet Russia, 160, 172, 174-75, 279-81,
    289, 292-93
Spanish Civil War, 160
Speculation, 140-42
Spindletop, Tex., 118
Spitting, 21
Sports, organized, 24-26
Stalin, Joseph, 173
Standard Oil Company, 33, 71, 73, 87-
    88, 90, 101, 247, 251
Stately Homes in America, 31
Statler, Ellsworth M., 21
Steel, 115
Steffens, Lincoln, 98
Stein, Gertrude, 138, 269
Steunenberg, Frank R., 102
Stevens-Duryea automobile, 116
Stieglitz, Alfred, 269
Stillman, James, 65, 103, 246
Stock Exchange, 70, 72-73, 141, 145
Stockholders, 70-71, 235-37
Stork Club, 227
Stotesbury, E. T., 228
Street-lighting, 14-15
Strikes, 173, 255-57
Studebaker, Clement, 116
Stutz, Harry C., 116
Suburbs, 15-16, 126, 226
Subway, 15
Suffrage, woman, 104
Sullivan, Louis, 29
Sullivan, Mark, 84, 264
Summer cottages, 16-18
Sumner, William Graham, 67-68
Sun, New York, 83

Supreme Court, 181-82
Synthetics, 119-20, 196

Taft, William Howard, 97, 103-4, 106
Tannenbaum, Dr. Frank, 266-67
Tarawa, 165
Tarbell, Ida M., 90, 98
Tax, income, 106, 215-16
Taylor, Frederick Winslow, 111
Taylor, Myron, 154
Team management, 250-52
Telegraphy, 119
Telephones, 22
Television, 223
Tenements, 57-58, 60
Tennessee Valley Authority, 153
Tennis, 25
Terre Haute, Ind., 6
Texas, 14
This Week magazine, 284
Thomas, Norman, 89
Thomasville, Ga., 16
Thomson, Bobby, 283
Tillstrom, Burr, 268
Times, Los Angeles, 102
Times, New York, 3, 25, 35, 150
Tobacco, 21
Toscanini, Arturo, 275
Tourist homes and camps, 124, 126-27
Townsend Plan, 150
Track, 24
Tractor, 117, 125, 128
Trade conventions, 245-46
Trailers, 125
Transportation, public, 15
Trolley cars, 15, 114-15
Trucks, 117, 125, 193
Truman, Harry S., 173
Truman Doctrine, 174
Trusts, 74-75, 87-88
Turkey, 174
Turner, Frederick Jackson, 47
Tuxedo Park, N. Y., 16
Twenty-One Club, 227
Tyng, Ed, 239

Union Pacific Railroad, 114
Unions, 53-55, 101, 140, 150, 153-54,
    175, 239, 255-58, 270
United Mine Workers, 54, 83-84
United Nations, 173, 177

United States Express Company, 71
United States Steel Corporation, 4, 70, 76, 115, 154

Vanderbilt, Consuelo, 42
Vanderbilt, Cornelius, 29, 34, 228
Vanderbilt, Frederick W., 29, 228
Vanderbilt, George W., 29-30
Vanderbilt, William H., 28-29, 228
Vanderbilt, William K., 28, 29, 228
Vassar College, 204
Vay de Vaya und Luskod, Count, 58
Virden, Ill., 54
Virginia, 16
V-J Day, 173
Vorse, Mary Heaton, 257

Wages, 27, 44, 55, 112-13
  Iron Law of, 49-50, 54, 61, 285-86
Wagner Act, 153
Wald, Lillian D., 100
Waldorf-Astoria Hotel, 37-39, 227
Walker, Charles S., 66
Walker, John Brisben, 80
Wall Street Journal, 245
Wallace, Henry A., 281
Wallas, Graham, 278
War Labor Board, 169-70
Warburg, Paul M., 101
War Production Board, 247
Washington, D. C., 82
Watson, Forbes, 274
Watson-Watt, Robert, 189
Wealthy class, entertaining, 34-39
  houses, 28-33, 228-29
  incomes, 27-28
  Society, 39-43, 225-29, 264
Wells, H. G., 197
Welsbach burner, 19
West Coast, 14
Westchester County, 124-25
Western Federation of Miners, 97, 102
Westinghouse Company, 71
West Virginia, 16
Wetmore, Claude H., 98
Wheeler, Walter H., Jr., 267
White, Stanford, 34
White, Walter, 186
White, William Allen, 7, 84-85, 86-87, 107
White House, 82
White Mountains, 17

Whitehall Hotel, 228
Whitemarsh Hall, 228
Whitman, Walt, 278
Whitney, Eli, 111
Whitney, Richard, 145
Whyte, William H., Jr., 218
Widener house, Philadelphia, 30
Wild Rose, The, 35
Williams, Tennessee, 273
Willkie, Wendell, 161
Wills, Helen, 133
Wilson, Carroll, 197
Wilson, Charles Edward, 247
Wilson, Charles Erwin, 215, 246
Wilson, Leroy, 247
Wilson, Woodrow, 47, 100, 103-4, 121, 122
Winton, Alexander, 116
Wireless, 119
Women, clothing, 9-10, 134-35
  suffrage, 104
  working, 11-13
Woodling, Gene, 206
Woods, Robert A., 53, 55, 60, 61
Woolworth Building, 115
Working class, accidents, 56
  child labor, 56
  clothing, 59-60
  hours, 55-56
  housing, 57-58, 60
  wages, 55
Works Progress Administration, 151
World War I, 104, 118, 137, 159, 163, 165, 169, 180, 199, 204, 268, 278-79
World War II, 104, 118, 180, 184, 188, 204, 217, 222, 244, 270, 279, 286
  beginnings, 158, 160-61
  defense program, 161-62
  end, 172-73
  government expansion, 171-72
  morale, 163-64
  production, 165-67
  standard of living, 167-71
  U. S. entry into, 162-63
Wright, Wilbur and Orville, 118-19

Yale, 25
Young, Roy, 143

Zodiac Club, 37